Melbourne born and educated, Richard Champion de Crespigny AM got his first taste of a future flying career as a 14-year-old when his father took him on a tour of the Royal Australian Air Force (RAAF) Academy at Point Cook in Victoria.

In 1975, aged 17, he joined the RAAF. One year later, he started flying. During his 11 years flying transport, jet and helicopter aircraft with the RAAF, he was seconded as Aide-de-Camp to two Australian Governors-General – Sir Zelman Cowen and Sir Ninian Stephen. Richard remained with the RAAF until 1986 when he joined Qantas, flying Boeing 747, Airbus A330 and A380 jet aircraft.

In 2010 he was the Captain on board Qantas Flight QF32 when it suffered a catastrophic explosion. His multi-award-winning and bestselling book *QF32* is a blow-by-blow story of what went right when things went wrong in the air.

Richard still flies the Airbus A380. He delivers presentations on the elements of resilience (knowledge, training, experience, teamwork, decision-making, crisis management, post-traumatic stress and risk) to governments, government agencies and Fortune 500 companies.

In the 2016 Australia Day Honours, Richard was made a Member of the Order of Australia (AM) for his significant service to the aviation industry, both nationally and internationally, particularly to flight safety and to the community.

Richard and his wife, Coral, have two children, Alexander and Sophia.

For more information, please visit Fly-TheBook.com and QF32.com.

'I wish *Fly!* had been available as required reading back in my flight training days. Thoroughly researched, it takes a fascinating look at accidents and other crises – including Captain de Crespigny's own QF32 inflight explosion – and analyses them through the filter of cutting-edge research. From these, he gleans keen insight and valuable lessons for dealing with life's inevitable challenges. This book is essential reading for everyone, from fledgling aviator to grizzled airline captain, from medical student to heart surgeon, from nervous flyer to corporate CEO – basically, anyone who wishes to take command of their own ship called "life".'

Eric Auxier, A321 International Captain for American Airlines, *Airways* magazine columnist, and author of *The Last Bush Pilots*, *There I Wuz!* and *Code Name: Dodger*

'*Fly!* is a remarkably accessible and important book. Richard de Crespigny's extensive research reveals important insights into the science of how we learn, make optimal decisions and deal with stress. *Fly!* goes beyond what we teach people in schools. Life skills like focus, perspective, leadership and resilience are essential to building human potential and key to improving patient safety and quality in health care. We need to get these important messages out. *Fly!* is a must read for every healthcare provider or manager who wants to succeed in the twenty-first century.'

Paul Barach MD, MPH, Maj (Ret.), Clinical Professor, Wayne State University School of Medicine, USA

'*Fly!* is the compelling follow-up to the bestselling *QF32* and the book every leader needs to read. Authentic leaders build deep foundations at every level, and Richard's insights come from an impeccable intellect and real-world experience, where human lives and iconic brands are at stake. In an age where we've lost trust in many people and institutions claiming to serve us, Richard shows us what genuine leadership and resilience is, how to foster it in ourselves, others and in teams, and how to rebuild trust for a better world. Read it and give a copy to anyone you believe has the potential to make a real difference.'

Tony Hughes, bestselling author and international
sales leadership keynote speaker

'From flight deck to everyday life, *Fly!* details the hard-won lessons on dealing with crises, both large and small. Richard de Crespigny faced the ultimate test of his resilience in the form of QF32 – one of the most amazing episodes of teamwork and skill in aviation safety.'

Tim Robinson, Editor in Chief of *Aerospace*, the flagship
magazine of the Royal Aeronautical Society

'*Fly!* brings together the science and real-life reality of all the factors that will shape your journey through the stressful minefield that is life today, wrapping it in a warm, caring and easy to understand narrative. For a 17-year-old this book is your life bible. For a 71-year-old it is not too late to get back on course. *Fly!* is a must read.'

Geoffrey Thomas, Australia's most awarded
aviation journalist and author

'To all those who believe in "heroes" Captain Richard de Crespigny has a confession to make: he is not one. Everything he did the day Qantas Flight 32 suffered a near-catastrophic uncontained engine failure after taking off from Singapore's Changi Airport, was not the result of heroics. On the contrary it was training, preparation and experience that allowed him to land safely and save the day for 469 people. In *Fly!* Captain de Crespigny explores the science of success and reveals techniques we all can use to enhance our performance and be ready for anything.'

Christine Negroni, author of *The Crash Detectives:
Investigating the World's Most Mysterious Air Disasters*

RICHARD DE CRESPIGNY

FLY!

LIFE LESSONS FROM
THE COCKPIT OF QF32

VIKING
an imprint of
PENGUIN BOOKS

VIKING

UK | USA | Canada | Ireland | Australia
India | New Zealand | South Africa | China

Penguin Books is part of the Penguin Random House group of companies
whose addresses can be found at global.penguinrandomhouse.com.

Penguin
Random House
Australia

First published by Viking Australia in 2018

 A catalogue record for this
book is available from the
National Library of Australia

ISBN 978 0 67007 873 8

Cover image © Nick Cubbin, courtesy of Newspix
Cover design by Louisa Maggio © Penguin Random House Pty Ltd
Typeset in Minion Pro by Midland Typesetters, Australia
Printed in Australia by Griffin Press, an accredited ISO AS/NZS 14001:2004
Environmental Management System printer

*To Coral (my wingman) and
Alexander and Sophia (our co-pilots) –
together FLYing through life.*

Contents

CHAPTER 1

Sharing the Lessons of Resilience

Thursday, 4 November 2010 started like any other day. I woke that morning in my Singapore hotel refreshed and ready for the task ahead: to fly an A380, then the world's biggest and most advanced commercial passenger airliner, from Changi Airport back home to Sydney. There would be 469 souls aboard our aircraft, the *Nancy-Bird Walton* – 440 passengers and 29 crew. The weather was ideal, and it promised to be an easy trip.

What ensued was anything but easy. I found myself facing the ultimate test of my resilience: a situation that had the potential to become one of the world's worst aviation disasters. It was a crisis that would draw on every strength I had developed as an individual, as a pilot and as a leader. Along with the incredible teamwork by all those caught up in the incident, the knowledge I had developed and honed over a lifetime meant we were able to avoid our crisis turning into a catastrophe. Instead it became a case study of 'what went right'.

This book is a guide to the underlying capabilities and techniques that ensured we survived the unthinkable that day: the teamwork, leadership, problem-solving, risk-assessment and deep understanding of how the human brain works that enabled everyone involved to perform at their best.

My aim is to show you how to develop and sharpen these strengths for yourself, building the kind of resilience that will enable you to deal with whatever life throws at you. And not just to survive, but to thrive.

I had been flying for three and a half decades when I boarded Flight QF32. First with the Royal Australian Air Force, to which I had eagerly signed up at 17, then with Australia's national carrier, Qantas, which I joined 11 years later. I loved my job and regarded it as a privilege to make my living doing something so challenging and satisfying, accompanied by skilled and dedicated colleagues at the top of their game. I feel exactly the same pride today.

The take-off was perfect. I pushed the thrust levers forward from their idle position. The four Rolls-Royce Trent 900 engines roared to life as 14 litres of jet fuel and 120 tonnes of air poured into them every second. My heart rate rose, not from fear, but from anticipation. As all pilots must be, I was prepared for the worst but hoping for the best.

The 464 tonne aircraft surged down the runway. We launched into the air at 350 km/h then the 22 wheels retracted. It was 9.57 am and everything was running exactly to plan. We actioned the routine 'After Takeoff' checklist. The Electronic Centralised Aircraft Monitoring (ECAM) system gathers data from 250,000 sensors and parameters to manage 1320 checklists. For this checklist, ECAM confirmed that all systems had successfully transitioned from take-off mode to the configurations needed for climbing, then cruising.

You never drop your guard in charge of an incredibly complex piece of machinery with four million parts, in which hundreds of people are sitting atop 108 tonnes of jet fuel. As we passed 6000 feet it really was looking like a picture-book day. We climbed up through 7400 feet and at 10.01 I was about to turn off the seatbelt sign when we heard a relatively small boom, followed one second later by a huge BOOM! which was like nothing I'd ever heard before.

Alarms rang out through the cockpit as the master warning system sprang to life. It turned out that inside engine 2, a short connecting pipe that delivers lubricating and cooling oil into the centre of the engine had not been manufactured to the correct specifications. This 'stub pipe' had fractured, allowing oil to leak out into the engine, causing a fire.

An engine fire is always potentially dangerous in the air. But it is far from unknown and the aircraft has built-in systems to deal with it, notably a cockpit-activated extinguisher inside the engines themselves. Similarly, engine failure is an anticipated problem, with well-rehearsed procedures in place if it occurs. The A380 is designed to fly on its remaining three engines if one fails. But while neither fire nor engine failure is catastrophic, what happened next was.

Leaking engine oil created a fire front that burnt through seals, then advanced up against the intermediate turbine disc. As the over-heated disc weakened, it wasn't long before the 126 turbine blades, generating 51,000 horsepower, wrenched the disc free from the shaft holding it in place. This unpowered the compressor, causing the engine to backfire. That was the first, smaller boom.

The engine was failing from the outside in, but for an unknown reason, the inner (high pressure) turbine and compressor kept oper-ating. The engine's computers detected a thrust loss, and so did what they were programmed to do – increase the fuel flow. That's when things went from bad to worse.

The increased fuel flow generated higher gas flows that spun up the now disconnected 160 kg turbine disc until it burst like a super-nova. Hundreds of pieces of shrapnel blasted through the engine, travelling at more than 2.6 times the speed of sound. That was the second huge BOOM!

The usual engine failures, the ones we train so carefully to deal with, are 'contained failures', in other words something goes wrong, and the engine can no longer work but there is no external damage. The damaged parts remain contained inside the engine housing. What we faced on QF32 was an uncontained engine failure, and it represented danger on an entirely different scale.

Of the aircraft's 22 different systems, 21 were damaged. In all, 650 wires and network cables were severed. Less than 50 per cent of our electrics and hydraulics were operational. We had less than half our roll controls, but worse, the aircraft was out of its balance limits in three areas because computers, pumps and pipes used to redistribute fuel through the eleven fuel tanks in the wings and tail were not working. The landing gear could only be lowered using an emergency gravity option and none of the three remaining engines were operating normally. Fuel and hydraulic fluid leaked from the badly damaged left wing.

ECAM was designed to help pilots. It prioritises actions based on which system's failure presents the most immediate danger. In four years of flying A380s I'd never seen more than two or three failed systems during a flight. But on QF32 there was so much damage to both the systems needed to fly safely and the sensors which reported problems that ECAM became ECAM Armageddon. We faced what felt like an overwhelming barrage of urgent checklists, some replaced so quickly by the next one that we didn't have time to take them in.

The procedures I had learned to manage crises were not working. Twelve minutes after the engine exploded, the mounting and cascading failures overloaded my mind. I figured there had to be another way out of this mess. Sometimes we have to create our own novel solutions.

The Australian Transport Safety Bureau (ATSB) spent 966 days investigating exactly what happened – the largest investigation in its history. The ATSB analysed our workflow and said we actioned 100 ECAM checklists in the air and another 20 on the ground. While this was a record, they could never measure the stress and distractions created by the loud and piercing warning bells that forewarned us every time of a deteriorating situation. The result was that the cockpit was one of the most stressful environments it's possible to imagine.

And yet, we all worked together and drew on all our resources to find a way to save the lives of those aboard. We spent two hours in the air assessing the damage and developing plans to maximise our chances of landing safely back at Changi. We had no option but to come in too fast (with brakes malfunctioning), too heavy (because we were loaded with excess fuel we could not jettison), with a broken wing, little roll control, no autopilot or auto-thrust. And we calculated, because of these problems, that we would stop just 139 metres short of the end of the four-kilometre-long runway.

If I landed hard the tail and landing gear would break off the fuselage, sending us sliding down the runway in a sea of sparks and leaking jet fuel. Because of our lack of brakes, if I didn't pull up soon enough, we would overrun the runway with disastrous consequences – beyond it was a paddock, an access road and then sand dunes and ocean.

Just before commencing the landing I followed my air force training and conducted what are called control checks – manual tests of various crucial controls – as a dress rehearsal. This is not something that would normally ever be done in an aircraft with passengers aboard, but we were a long way from normal.

Shockingly, as we descended below 1000 feet the flight warning computers blared out 'SPEED! SPEED!', something I had only ever heard before in a simulator exercise. More shockingly, just before touchdown we got an even worse warning, one no pilot ever wants to hear, 'STALL! STALL!'. Despite these warnings, the flight control checks I completed minutes earlier gave me the confidence and courage to deal with these very disturbing alarms and persist with landing at this most critical stage.

We finally came to a stop 3900 metres along the runway at 11.46 am. Eight fire trucks immediately surrounded our smoking and leaking hull. We had landed safely but the emergency was far from over.

The warning bells and ECAM checklists kept coming at the same time the control tower instructed us to shut down our three remaining engines and radio the fire controller. When we followed their instructions, things only got worse. Our two remaining electrical generators failed, taking out most remaining systems. More computers failed, cockpit and cabin lights went off, emergency lights illuminated, and bells and alarms started sounding throughout the cabin. Evacuation messages began flashing up on the screens in front of passengers. Despite this, our extraordinary cabin crew managed to maintain control and keep passengers calm.

In the cockpit we were fully occupied managing the enormous risk of fire. Our brakes were white-hot, off the scale at over 995 degrees Celsius, and highly flammable aviation fuel was flooding down near them. But there was no fire, not yet. Evacuations down emergency slides are difficult and dangerous procedures, with injuries almost inevitable. So I made the complex decision that our passengers and crew were safer inside the aircraft than out of it.

At this point the Changi fire controller told us to shut down engine 1. We looked at our display to double-check, and told him we had already done so. He then gave us the unwelcome news that this engine was still running. We operated three more emergency switches to try to kill that engine, but nothing worked. There was nothing we could do to stop it, so instead the fire crews concentrated on hosing water on the brakes and covering the fuel with foam.

As the brakes cooled so did the commensurate chance of fire. But engine 1 was still running uncontrollably when I decided conditions were safe enough to finally begin disembarking passengers down stairs on the opposite side of the aircraft and onto buses 52 minutes after we had come to a stop. Three and a half hours after we had landed, the fire fighters pumped foam into engine 1, finally stopping it but destroying it in the process.

Almost two hours after stopping on the runway, the last of the passengers were safely on their way to the terminal. Ten minutes later, I set off for the terminal myself, intent on the task of debriefing everyone who had been on board.

The crisis, which had unfolded in the aircraft over a total of four hours, was over but it would have long-lasting repercussions for many, including myself. As well as the effects on individuals, there was a significant impact on the organisations involved. The repairs to the *Nancy-Bird Walton* cost more than $130 million over a period of almost 18 months, making it perhaps the longest and most expensive repair in aviation history. Many people suffered post-traumatic stress.

In aviation, improbable failures are those that are calculated to occur once in one billion flying hours (numerically that is 10 to the power of 9) or expressed another way, once in 114,000 years of continuous flight. They're highly unlikely, but they are still planned and trained for, with the ECAM system engineered to provide solutions for even these oh-so-rare occurrences.

What happened with QF32 was so much more improbable than that. In fact, by my calculations, which the Airbus and Boeing experts agreed with, the chance of such an event happening again is one in ten to the power of 14.7, or almost one million times less probable than their most improbable but planned-for possibilities. It was a genuine 'Black Swan event'; unforeseen, improbable and with massive consequences.

From a cold and calculated risk perspective, aircraft are not designed, and crew and passengers are not expected, to survive such a crisis. However, great things happen when preparation meets opportunity and the QF32 incident gives us a rare opportunity to trace resilience back to its component parts.

We responded to those unthinkable and unprecedented events by drawing on our deep reserves of knowledge and learned and practised skills in the areas of leadership, teamwork, risk assessment and decision-making. We understood human behaviour and crisis management and, as I'll explain later, I used specific techniques (such as inverting the logic) to create novel solutions.

These elements that turned what could have been a terrible tragedy into a textbook success, can be adapted to an endless array of other situations, at work and at home. They are skills and techniques that can be learned and applied by anyone who wants to flourish in this rapidly changing, often turbulent world, where opportunity and danger are intertwined.

The only certainty in life is uncertainty. We journey through order and chaos, coupled tightly like yin and yang. Order is stable and secure, but without change and adaptation everything eventually dies. Equilibrium is the precursor to death. Chaos is challenging but it is necessary for progress and growth. Survival depends upon being confident enough to embrace risk, adapt and change. Resilience gives you this confidence.

By deliberately building your personal and corporate resilience you will become confident enough to anticipate, respond to and recover from any challenge. Resilient people have the best chance of surviving when the unthinkable occurs, but they're also the ones who thrive in the normal everyday challenges of life and work.

This book is for those who understand we can't control the future, but we can control how we respond to what life throws at us. It's for those who want to learn how to master their minds, fail well, and recover from adversity so they can triumph when it matters most.

When you harness the elements of resilience, you will have the confidence and mental flexibility to expect the unexpected, and the adaptive performance to triumph when it matters most. You will become the best you can be.

So, let's *Fly*!

CHAPTER 2

Mastering Your Mind, Maximising Your Performance

QF32's success was partly due to the ability of the pilots and cabin crew to master their minds. We kept calm, mentally agile and performed well under stress.

To perform at your best in any situation, to be resilient and let yourself *Fly!*, you must also master your mind. This is more than passing a written test or doing a few easy exercises. It's building the skills that allow you to remain calm, confident, courageous and creative in any situation, including when others are panicking.

Mastering your mind means knowing how to optimise memory, train yourself in expert skills and create habits. It's about preserving your free mental space and situation awareness (what has happened, what is happening and what should happen) so you can delegate and lead.

It also means controlling your fears, giving you the power to remain calm, rational and in control instead of succumbing to emotional and illogical dread.

The alternative is to remain at the mercy of the primitive startle response: fight, flight or freeze. These instincts helped us long ago, but they are poorly suited for modern life.

The first step to mastering the mind is understanding how it works.

Your own personal super-supercomputer

The average person knows little more about how their brain works than they know about the processor in their mobile phone. That doesn't prevent them using either, but the more we understand about how the brain works, the more effectively we can use it to make faster and better decisions.

The neuroscience of the human mind is similar to the computer programs and kinematic flight control laws in modern aircraft. Both receive inputs, store and process data, then drive outputs to achieve the desired result. While the scales of these two systems are different, both use feedback loops to observe, try, learn and adjust.

The Airbus A380 has more than 500 computers and 530 km of wiring, conveying inputs from 250,000 sensors and parameters, and driving 51 flight control surfaces. This information would overwhelm any human, so Airbus engineers designed ECAM warning systems and simplified 'chunked down' views that pilots can understand. If the A380 is impressive, the human mind is amazing.

The human brain has about 90 billion neurons interconnected by more than 100 trillion synapses connected by about 150,000 km of nerve fibres. It receives inputs from more than four million sensory fibres and drives outputs to control hormones and 650 skeletal muscles. It does 100 peta (10^{15}) operations per second using 1/10 millionth the energy of an equivalent supercomputer.

The brain is energy-hungry. Typically weighing about 1.3 kg in an adult male, under two per cent of the total body weight, it consumes 20 per cent of the body's energy at rest. Eighty per cent of the brain's energy consumption is used to power neural activity.

The brain is also elusive. It's the only part of our body that has no senses, so you can't see, touch, smell or taste with it or service it. And there's no diagnostics, process or performance monitor to explain how it works.

Like the A380's flight warning computers, our mind 'chunks' (aggregates) complex information down into simpler forms and presents us with simplified body and mental models. It also has a warning system (amygdala) and fills sensory gaps. The chunking creates bias, the filling creates illusions, and our mental model is a tiny tunnel-visioned view of our vast sensory world. It takes a lot of effort to keep the body and mental models updated, and sometimes they can be wrong.

Fast and slow minds

Psychologists use the terms 'fast mind' and 'slow mind' to describe different parts of the brain in action. If you haven't heard these terms before you might think that slow mind doesn't sound very appealing; you might guess that outstanding achievers must be powered by a fast mind, while others are being held back by a slow mind.

The truth is that each and every one of us has a fast mind and a slow mind, and we need both to survive. Together, they feed our senses and build our body model, mental model and situation awareness.

Your fast mind is the automatic, almost instantaneous connection between brain and sensory input – sight, sound, smell, touch and taste. It has 'co-processors' to speed vision and hearing and to coordinate movement. It's also your mental 'autopilot', making extremely familiar connections 'without thinking' and performing tasks you've done so many times that you could (and you often can) do them 'in your sleep'.

The fast mind is optimised for defence and survival. When you involuntarily jump at a loud noise, that's a reflex in your fast mind at work. When you read the word cucumber, your fast mind instantly links (associates) it with the colour green. If your phone starts to fall from your hand, you don't stop to consider what you should do about it, you 'instinctively' try to grab it. That instinct is your fast mind at work.

The slow mind is optimised for consciousness, thought and rationality. Your fast mind gives you the instant answer to a cucumber's colour, but you need the slow mind to deal with more complicated questions such as, 'What is the Italian word for cucumber?' or, 'Is a cucumber a fruit or a vegetable?' Hearing footsteps in your house in the middle of the night and being simultaneously flooded with fear is your fast mind alerting you to potential threats; remembering that you have a house guest and being flooded with relief is your slow mind doing research and then restoring calm.

When it comes to the mind, fast and slow are relative terms, as the footsteps example (above) shows. The brain takes a few milliseconds to raise the alarm and trigger the hormone-driven fear response. It takes about a second to consciously search through possible explanations for the creak of a floorboard and decide if it's a friend or foe.

Fast mind and body language

Your fast mind processes signals before your slow mind realises they exist. Body language is a classic example. Most people can identify a stranger's emotional state simply by looking briefly at a picture of them. You don't have to know anything about their personality or circumstances – their stance, movements and facial expressions are enough to give you a clear impression of their mood. This happens in a fraction of the time it took you to read this sentence.

The fast mind's decoding of body language adds information which is separate to, and possibly different from, what is said. We have all heard a person say 'Yes' while at the same time noticing the subconscious side movement of their head transmits 'No'.

Let's imagine you have a brief and relatively neutral encounter with one of your child's new teachers: a simple introduction, handshake, generic good wishes for the year ahead and you both move on. Yet you walk away with a more positive impression of that teacher than you do of any of the others you meet. It's hard to put your finger on why or explain it in words; you 'just have a good feeling' about them. The opposite happens when you meet your company's new regional manager. Again, it's an initial brief encounter, and on the surface it all goes smoothly, yet your 'gut instinct' is unfavourable.

While your slow mind was listening to what was said in each situation, your fast mind decoded the finest details of the speaker's body language and tone and made an instant judgement. Given enough time with the teacher or the manager, your slow mind will confirm or modulate this judgement, storing away experiences that justify or challenge your first impression. But until that happens, your instant impression from your fast mind stands.

How important is body language really?

There is a lot of misinformation and misunderstanding about body language. You will often hear it claimed that 93 per cent of all the information we absorb when we communicate with someone else is non-verbal: 55 per cent comes from body language, 38 per cent from tone of voice, and only seven per cent from the actual words spoken.

The source for this often-quoted 'fact' is work done in the 1960s by Albert Mehrabian, now UCLA Professor Emeritus of Psychology. Mehrabian and his colleagues conducted two small studies. In the first, the word 'maybe' was said in different tones while 17 participants looked at photos of facial expressions. In the second, a single speaker said nine different words in a tone that contrasted with the word's meaning (harsh words in gentle tones, etc) while 30 people listened. In each case, participants said how they thought the speaker felt.

Mehrabian came up with the 55/38/7 formula based on this very limited research, but he noted that it only applied when people talked specifically about feelings or attitudes, that is, likes and dislikes. He repeatedly tried to correct what he described as the subsequent misuse of his work but had little success.

Whatever the actual percentage breakdown turns out to be, it is true that our body language is an open window exposing the deepest parts of our mind.

Mirroring and feedback

Mirroring is a foundation of human communication and empathy. As a part of active communications, we replicate behaviours we observe in others. Have you noticed that people you converse with influence your feelings and emotions? A smiling person will help you feel good. A whining and whingeing person tends to pull your spirits down. Even the cry of a distant baby in distress tears at our hearts.

There are two reasons for this. First, humans are mostly social creatures who mirror behaviour in others. When we communicate with another person our 650 skeletal muscles subconsciously adjust to mirror the other person's stature. For example, when someone smiles at us we smile back. The second reason has to do with a feedback process I call 'pumping senses'. When we move our body, sensors at the moved locations feed information up to our brains that, in a reverse process, induce feelings.

Imagine we are conversing with another person. When they express an emotion, their brain sends signals subconsciously that cause them to project a certain posture or body language. When we move our muscles to mirror the other person's posture, nerves at our peripheries send signals back to our brain that induce the same emotion in our mind.

Imagine a happy baby who smiles at us. We feel happy in return mostly when we move to mirror the baby's smile. Likewise, when an angry person challenges us with a threatening posture, our act of mimicking their posture 'pumps' anger and aggression in us.

When you understand this mirroring and 'pumping', you are in a better position to control your mind. Mirroring is an important ingredient of empathy. In his book *NeuroLogic*, neurologist Eliezer Sternberg notes that paralysing a person's facial muscles with Botox inhibits their ability to mirror other people's body language and detect their emotions. The concept of priming/pumping senses is disputed, but I find these techniques successfully help people who have a fear of flying (more on this later).

I analyse body language and communication in later chapters. By educating yourself on body language you can move past 'gut feelings' and learn to break down the reasons you feel a person is trustworthy or not (the position of their arms, the direction their palms faced, the way their eyes moved as they spoke, and so on).

Most importantly, you can learn to ensure that your own body language is sending the correct signals to others. You are being continually judged, as much as you subconsciously judge others. Stand up straight with your head high (confident), look people in the eye (engaged), smile (happy and approachable), don't cross your arms (dismissive) or clench fists (stressed). Be careful – your feet subconsciously point where your body wants to go.

The autopilot fast mind and multi-tasking slow mind

As well as reacting to sensory information and making snap responses, the fast mind is also the brain's much relied upon autopilot.

If you're an experienced driver it's your fast mind that's in charge when you scan the road ahead, and glance at your speedometer while gently braking as you approach an easy curve on an empty sunlit highway. Even though numerous activities are taking place (foot pressure on brake, eyes moving, refocusing, checking for obstacles, registering speed, and assessing the degree you'll need to turn the steering wheel) they are such familiar, well-practised actions that you can do them with very little or no conscious effort. You can even engage in conversations or sing along to well-known songs at the same time.

But if you're relatively new to the road, what's going on in your mind and body will be very different. You have no subconscious auto-pilot or habitual behaviours for this situation. A new driver needs to actively concentrate in order to do all the things required. Their blood pressure and heart rate will be higher. They won't be able to take in the song or participate in conversation without losing their all-important focus on the road. That's because the slow mind cannot multi-task.

Influential Nobel Prize-winning psychologist Daniel Kahneman writes about this in his book *Thinking Fast and Slow*. He explains that the phrase 'paying attention' contains a lot of truth, because the slow mind has limited resources to spread around. It focuses its resources on one task at the expense of another – it can't do both without something falling through the cracks.

This inability to multi-task was cleverly demonstrated by American psychologists Christopher Chabris and Daniel Simons. They devised a selective attention experiment in which they filmed six people in a tight circle throwing two basketballs back and forth. Half wore white shirts and half black, and they moved continuously, weaving in and out as they passed the balls.

Study participants were told to count the number of passes made by those in the white shirts. Sounds simple enough. Although the people with the balls are ducking and turning, they're not running, and there are only three people to keep track of – those in white.

It turns out to be a lot harder than you might think. You can't just count any movement of the ball; you also have to consciously ignore the passes thrown by players in black. While the fast mind is automatically 'seeing', the slow mind's resources are maxed-out trying to analyse or 'read'. Overall, the brain is tracking movement, making quick judgements, discarding extraneous senses and data and keeping count as the number of relevant passes increases.

Spoiler alert: The study findings are coming up. If you can, take the test yourself by searching 'Selective Attention Test – Daniel Simons' on YouTube before reading on.

Partway through the film, a person wearing a gorilla suit enters the screen from the right, steps into the middle of the busy group, looks directly at camera, thumps its chest, then strolls off-screen to the left. The amazing part is that half the people who watch the film and attempt the task without knowing what to expect, say they do not see the gorilla. Told about it afterwards, they initially refuse to believe it existed. 'Come on,' they say, 'how could anyone miss something like that!'

As Kahneman puts it, this little experiment, which has become known as 'the Invisible Gorilla', shows us many important things about the way our minds work: not only are we 'blind to the obvious, we are also blind to our blindness'.

Pilots are very aware of the dangers of distractions. Losing situation awareness is very dangerous because you don't know you've lost it, and when you realise you have, it's far too late.

Pilots are taught to recognise the warning signs of losing free mental space and situation awareness. The symptoms include:

- fixating on one task, missing and so not responding to what others say (for example air traffic controllers)
- not anticipating, so being behind and surprised by events
- making errors
- a bad gut feeling
- singing or talking to yourself (due to increased stress)
- going quiet (due to increasing confusion and overload).

As a consequence, pilots make a point of limiting distractions. We talk only about operational matters below 20,000 feet of altitude. We don't play music or read newspapers on the flight deck. From the start of the take-off until the landing gear is up, or from gear down until leaving the runway after landing, no contact is permitted from the cabin to the cockpit.

Life-saving lesson # 1: Humans cannot safely drive and text. Even you.

It's easy to expose the limitations and frailty of our slow mind. Have you ever tried to solve a mathematical problem such as 63×27 while driving through tricky traffic? Unless you have an exceptional facility with numbers, it's dangerous. You can *try* to drive well and multiply at the same time, but you won't succeed. Something's got to give, even if just for a moment or two. When you're behind the wheel, that's a lapse you can't afford.

Here is a simple truth that might save your life or that of someone you love, or someone who will encounter you on the road: humans cannot safely drive and text at the same time. While you're thinking about your message and typing it out, your slow mind is effectively blind and deaf, unable to monitor outputs from your fast mind and the risks around you. It's not a matter of opinion. It's clear-cut neuroscience. Attention is an exception handler. You are only made aware of things that deviate from your mind's predictions. Your cognitive skills and situation awareness for the primary task collapse when your mind is distracted.

To make the rule more general: distractions from the task at hand cause us to make errors. In high-risk situations: distractions can cause us to make errors that lead to death.

Practice puts you in control

'Practice makes perfect', the old saying goes. I prefer 'Practice makes habits and intuition'. However you want to express it, it's clear that practice is more than just a powerful tool. In fact, practice is a must.

Even the most complex skills become automatic when they're practised sufficiently. Crawling, walking and running are the first coordinated movements we progressively train and store in the brain's cerebellum. Driving cars and flying an aircraft are others. With practice, skills that initially required every tiny bit of your slow mind's capacity become so familiar that they are stored as habits in the fast mind, processes that can be actioned subconsciously on demand, freeing up the slow mind to deal with other tasks or solve unexpected problems.

A pilot's skill level is often measured in terms of the number of flying hours they have undertaken. But for every hour in the air there are many more spent in purposeful, structured practice on the ground. Some of this work takes place at a desk, reading manuals and memorising emergency checklists until they become as familiar as the alphabet. Some takes place in simulators, where skills are put to the most extreme tests. And believe it or not, some takes place in bed.

Captain Chesley Sullenberger III, better known as 'Sully', is a good example of a pilot who never rested on his laurels during his 42 years of flying. Sully was catapulted to international fame in January 2009 thanks to the 'Miracle on the Hudson' in which he and co-pilot Jeff Skiles safely landed their Airbus A320 on the freezing Hudson River after multiple bird strikes destroyed both engines. Sully and Jeff saved the lives of all on board. (Clint Eastwood subsequently directed the film *Sully*, telling the story of the incident and its occasionally fictionalised aftermath.)

The successful outcome was no accident. Sully studied human factors and safety to supplement his aviation knowledge and had Sidney Dekker's book *Just Culture: Balancing Safety and Account-ability* in the cockpit on that fateful day.

Following the incident, Sully did an interview with *Newsweek* in which he said, 'It was a day like literally 10,000 other days – until it wasn't . . . Even though this was an unanticipated event for which we have never specifically trained, I was confident that I could quickly synthesize a lifetime of training and experience, adapt it in a new way to solve a problem I had never seen before and get it right the first time, and so that's what I did.'

The National Transport Safety Bureau investigators who conducted the inquiry into the incident agreed, telling Sully that even though this was an unprecedented event, 'You trained for those four minutes every day of your career.'

Training for the startle effect

When the proverbial hits the fan, the brain pulls down the shutters to block distractive senses and chunks massive information down into smaller understandable sizes. Our mental model shrinks as focus is narrowed to the essential senses, at the expense of pain and all other input. Adrenaline and cortisol reprioritises and turbocharges the body for survival. High-priority habits and survival instincts take precedence over cognitive skills, processes and finesse that reside in the slow mind. This is the startle effect.

In the mind's war-room, trained habits and instinctive reactions provide the first line of defence. This is the perfect response if you're an early human confronting a lion, but it's counterproductive in any situation where you have to stay calm and think your way out.

We can reduce our predisposition to stress and panic. The key is to put in enough practice beforehand to train and desensitise the fast mind (habits and instincts) so it remains our autopilot, handling the immediate responses during stressful or threatening situations. The slow mind is then free to assess the situation and monitor the results of actions.

The way to make people resilient is to replicate the startle factor in training. To move beyond the startle response, we must be exposed to the things we are afraid of until we learn to feel uncomfortable while still retaining control. We must develop the confidence, courage and skills to endure and then solve any problem. We must learn to expect the unexpected, keep calm whatever happens then set clear priorities and make decisions to survive Black Swan events.

If you can do this, you will be able to perform at your best in any situation of high stress, including a salary review meeting, speaking in public, or when you feel white-knuckle fear on a flight.

Startle effect on QF32

When the engine exploded on QF32, our knowledge, training, experience and purposeful practice gave everyone on the flight deck the tools to deal with the emergency without being startled into panic. We all kept our composure because we habitually knew what we had to do. There were many situations where we had to make

Sully Sullenberger on unanticipated threats

Even though Sully reacted so well when put to the test, he still sees room for improvement in the way people in high-risk occupations such as aviation are trained:

'In some ways, I might have been better prepared for Flight 1549 earlier in my career – while still a fighter pilot, perhaps. In that part of my career, I had more frequent equipment failures that I dealt with on a regular basis, and we were always operating closer to the limits in nearly every way.

'But airline flying is different. While by no means complacent, I had been flying well within the boundaries for many years in an environment where I was – fortunately, of course – not challenged in any significant way. When so much goes right for so long, and our training is so scripted with no surprises, one does not get any recent practice at handling sudden, unexpected, dire situations, and those require different skills, and there is a huge practice effect.

'We need to find ways to replicate the startle factor in training. The challenge is that without actual jeopardy, it's just not the same. But we need to try to duplicate what pilots may experience in the real world. The performance of even the very best pilots is affected in predictable ways by the stress of threatening situations. We should train pilots to be able to handle the unanticipated and be able to set clear priorities in situations they have never seen. We should have a well-internalized paradigm that allows us to solve any problem. There can't be a checklist for everything, and automation can only do what has been foreseen and for which it has been programmed.'

decisions without all the facts, but thanks to our training we were confident and not scared.

A friend asked me, 'What do you think happened in your mind when you heard the engine explode?' He probably meant, 'What was your thought process?' In which case, my nerdish answer might have surprised him:

> *My brain instantly became fully alert. First, my amygdala triggered the startle reflex. It interpreted the sounds as a threat and signalled the brain to activate my sympathetic nervous system, which would have caused adrenaline to pour into my bloodstream to prepare my body to fight, freeze or to flee.*
>
> *Shortly afterwards, my slow mind, sitting atop my brain on a slower network, received similar signals of the problems and linked the sounds of the explosions and vibrations and sirens to known events. These were patterns etched into the grey matter by past experiences and deliberate practice in aircraft simulators.*
>
> *Amid the initial chaos, the slower cortex would then have sent a modulating response back to my fast amygdala saying 'Hey, it's okay. Turn off the panic alarm. I've heard, seen and felt this before. I've trained for this; I know what's happened and I know what to do!'*

My slow mind reasoned that our lives were not threatened and throttled back the fast mind's startle effect. None of the other pilots panicked either. Although we were each on high alert, we were able to control our response and 'sit on our hands and initially do nothing' (also known as 'arousal modulation'). Nothing, that is, except follow the first commandment of aviation: 'aviate' – fly the aeroplane and stay alive.

The Deliberate Practice I had put in and the good habits and knowledge I had acquired were put to excellent use. They guided me to ignore the blare of the warning horns, the many big red lights and the ECAM warnings until I did what was required to guarantee safe flight. We began working our way through the ECAM engine failure checklists only after this point was achieved. That was around 20 seconds after the initial explosion. Twenty seconds may not sound like much, but in many other events (such as the fatal

Concorde crash in France in July 2000), it has made the difference between life and death.

Armchair simulation produces real results

Many pilots use a technique called 'armchair flying' to practise their skills and convert them into habits and intuition. This involves simulating a particular flight sequence by sitting down with eyes closed, then 'pumping' mental sounds and imagery in coordination with physical movements.

Armchair flying is not like daydreaming or fantasising about a situation. It can realistically simulate complex emergency procedures that must be recalled and actioned quickly and perfectly in stressful situations, including aborted take-offs and landings, engine failures and collision avoidance.

The process builds what is known as proprioceptive (or muscle) memory. The scenario takes place in the mind, complete with recalled imaginary sights and sounds, but the body mimics the real movements required. Feet move, hands reach for switches, and eyes, still closed, see a vision of the instrument panels as the sequence unfolds at the same pace it would in the aircraft.

Sitting in an actual armchair closely mimics the body's posture in a cockpit, but I don't limit my practice to that. Before my quarterly simulator tests, I also practise engine failures at night lying in bed, eyes closed, moving my arms and legs exactly as I would in the aircraft. My wife, Coral, found this behaviour mighty odd at first, but now accepts it as one consequence of being married to a pilot with unusual study techniques.

Elite athletes also make use of this simulated practice. In *Neuro-Logic*, Sternberg tells the story of British javelin champion Stephen Backley, who won a bronze medal at the 1992 Barcelona Olympic Games. Backley was all set for the 1996 Atlanta Olympics when he suffered a debilitating ankle injury in the crucial lead-up to the

Games. He was told to use crutches for six weeks, during which time he was not to do any physical training. This would normally be a recipe for disaster at such a vital point in an athlete's preparation. However, instead of giving in to frustration, Backley began what Sternberg describes as 'a gruelling workout in his mind'.

Sitting, with eyes closed, Backley imagined in great detail every moment of a throw, from the initial grip of the javelin to his muscles tensing in preparation all the way through to the release followed by the sensation of watching the javelin's arc and landing. During his compulsory time out of his physical routine, Backley completed 1000 of these intense mental simulations. He returned to the field better than ever, winning the silver medal in Atlanta.

Sternberg explains that these extremely detailed mental simulations matched and reinforced familiar and pre-existing actions in the mind. In other words, detailed armchair practice activates the same processes and senses in the brain as doing the action for real would. Practising a sequence over and over in a simulation strengthens the same neural pathways that were created when you first learned to perform the sequence, controlling both your thought processes and the muscles needed to respond to your brain's commands.

You don't have to be an elite performer to benefit. Any regular golfer or tennis player can improve by supplementing their real-life practice swings or serves with simulations, as long as they have the mental discipline to do it in full detail, synchronised with the choreography for the actual event.

But what about more open-ended, unbounded situations – ones that don't involve checklists or a single sequence of actions? Simulations can help here too, and they can be applied to many different aspects of life.

Police and military organisations around the world have adopted this approach in their 'Killing Houses' (mock dwellings purpose-built for hostage-rescue training). Specialist teams practise in these facilities over and over, learning from their mistakes.

Thankfully, the scenarios in which the rest of us can learn from simulations don't involve flying bullets. But we can all also benefit from practising responses to situations we hope never occur. Practise doing donuts in your car on safe, icy skid-pans under supervision in order to build protections when you inadvertently encounter ice on a road. Run regular fire drills at home with the family to practise escaping the building. Learn CPR skills then regularly refresh them so you don't freeze in panic when you need to spring into action.

Deliberate Practice, Purposeful Practice and the 10,000-hour theory

The term 'Deliberate Practice' (DP) sprang from a 1993 academic paper written by psychologists Anders Ericsson, Ralf Krampe and Clemens Tesch-Römer called 'The Role of Deliberate Practice in the Acquisition of Expert Performance'. The paper reported on two studies they had run with student musicians of different skill levels, who had all started playing around age five.

The researchers asked the musicians to retrospectively estimate how many hours each week they had engaged in what they dubbed 'Deliberate Practice'. They found that players at 'best level' reported having accumulated an average of more than 10,000 hours by the age of 20. Those at 'good level' reported an average of less than 8000 hours. And those at the lowest level of achievement reported an average of less than 5000 hours.

The conclusion they reached from this was that 'many characteristics once believed to reflect innate talent are actually the result of intense practice extended for a minimum of 10 years'. Or, as a different co-authored paper by Ericsson in 2007 put it, 'Consistently and overwhelmingly, the evidence showed that *experts are always made, not born*' *and* achieving genuine expertise in a field would take 'at least a decade'.

Bestselling author Malcolm Gladwell reported on Ericsson's research in his 2008 book *Outliers: The Story of Success*. Gladwell called one of his chapters 'The 10,000-Hour Rule'. He wrote, 'Researchers have settled on what they believe is the magic number for true expertise: ten-thousand hours.' The idea that by doing anything for 10,000 hours, from pitching a baseball to performing surgery, you would master it, took off in a big way.

Ericsson did not agree. In a 2012 paper he noted that many of the best musicians in his study had accumulated 'substantially fewer' than 10,000 hours of practice. The difference between high performers and others wasn't just about the time spent practising; it was about the type of practice. 'The quality of the practice was important,' he insisted, not the quantity. The expert violinists in his original paper spent up to half their time practising alone. They also practised things that were hard. And they had expert coaches who could guide their progress. This is what Ericsson and his co-authors meant by 'Deliberate Practice'.

Deliberate Practice

In his 2007 paper Ericsson noted, 'When most people practice, they focus on the things they already know how to do. Deliberate practice is different. It entails considerable, specific, and sustained efforts to do something you *can't* do well – or even at all . . . You will need a well-informed person not only to guide you through deliberate practice but also to help you learn how to coach yourself.' Ericsson warns that Deliberate Practice 'requires struggle, sacrifice, and honest, often painful self-assessment. There are no shortcuts.'

You can still benefit from practice without a coach – Ericsson calls this 'purposeful practice'. It involves targeting something specific you want to improve and then finding a specific training activity that will get you there. If you want to improve your backhand in tennis, Purposeful Practice means focusing on this alone, not playing a game in which you attempt a few backhand shots. Practice is best when you learn to measure your performance and coach yourself.

Repetition is not Deliberate Practice (DP). The experience gained from flying the same one-hour flight a thousand times does not equate to the experience gained flying 1000 hours over many routes. The dedication to continuous hard learning is what elevates the effectiveness of DP above the arrested state produced by easy, playful practice.

Mozart, NASA astronauts and Tiger Woods all achieved what they did as a result of DP. DP trumps age, desire, passion, intelligence, money, seniority and genes (except in sports where height and body size confer advantages). Geoff Colvin provides an excellent overview of this in his book *Talent is Overrated*.

The DP I undertake paid dividends during the QF32 incident. Pilots train to acquire minimum skills. Acquiring skills gives us confidence. But I have always wanted more. I regularly fly manually without the use of the autopilot and auto-thrust systems. It's hard and sometimes frustrating work, but it keeps my skills intact and boosts my confidence. Good manual skills are necessary when the automatic systems fail, as they sometimes do. I always push myself to the maximum limits (or beyond) when practising in the aircraft simulator.

The A380's crosswind limit is 40 knots for landing. Simulator exercises normally require us to land with 20-knot crosswinds. That's not good enough for me. I ask for 40-knot crosswinds. If I do a poor landing and fail, I ask for help and repeat the approach until I am successful, confident and comfortable. This establishes my ability to land at the maximum limits.

Then I ask the instructor to repeat the sequence with a higher degree of difficulty, without key equipment (such as instrument landing system receivers, visual approach slope guidance and flight directors). Then I do it yet again, but this time introducing turbulence and turning off the auto-thrust computers. The instructor and I debrief every landing. Deliberate Practice like this is challenging, exhausting and sometimes humiliating, but it works.

From training comes confidence. Confidence is like a muscle. You have to exercise to create it, then work to keep it strong. My confidence always peaks after these simulator sessions – I feel as confident as Arnold Schwarzenegger when I drive home. Going the extra mile gives me the courage to know that I can manage the aircraft to its limits or beyond them in extreme circumstances. It means that when I have to do so, I will keep my sense of calm and protect my spare mental capacity to maintain my situation awareness and deal with other problems. My confidence slowly ebbs over time until the next training session.

There is a degree of vulnerability when aiming higher, thereby increasing the risk of failure. Even with more than 40 years of flying, I still make mistakes. But for me, the need for safety and heightened confidence outweighs any fears I have of failure. Failure is my motivator to try again.

There comes a point in DP where you can repeatedly exceed the higher standards and deliver excellence on demand; when you clear the bar with little effort. This is when you gain the confidence to face higher risks, to be 'bulletproof and not gun-shy'.

In the DP mindset, 'good enough' is never good enough. Complacency is abhorred and the temptation to become overconfident and stop practising is resisted. That's hard to do because DP is not fun or inherently enjoyable. It's effortful and tough on the ego. The 'reward' for reaching the skill level you are currently striving towards is a new, harder level. The driver to persist is the knowledge that complacency grows when you stop trying to improve yourself, and competence falls away, setting the stage for avoidable mistakes and a drift to failure.

You must remain vigilant, as I found after the QF32 incident. I was very busy, with many demands on my time, and I let these distractions interfere with my duties. I turned up for a simulator training exercise having not memorised two of the required checklists word-perfectly. I was correctly scolded and vowed never to embarrass myself this way again.

Stress-Proof Deliberate Practice

I have developed my own modified version of the Deliberate Practice that Ericsson described. I call mine Stress-Proof Deliberate Practice and it has four stages.

The first phase is knowledge-building. This is where you learn the minimum foundation skills. If you're an aspiring pilot, you're still on the ground learning about engines, aerodynamics and airspace. If you're a first-year medical student, you're still in the anatomy lab. If you're an apprentice electrician, you're in the classroom learning to read regulations, schematics and understand safety procedures.

The second phase is when you begin to apply these skills. It's a hybrid apprenticeship of doing and learning. Novices are closely monitored.

The third phase starts when you have graduated with sufficient skills to be proficient. Pilots are ready to fly solo with their first passengers, doctors are ready to make their own assessments of patients, electricians are ready to work unsupervised. Your skills will continue to improve with additional experience. Phase three finishes with you being comfortable and confident with the standard operations of your job (the known knowns).

The good news is you are experienced. The bad news is your skills will plateau or decline if not maintained. Skills stagnate in any environment where there is no novelty or change. There is no incentive to learn, create or experiment in this environment and things not repeated are forgotten, starting a drift to failure.

To survive into the future, we must resist complacency. The skills that got us here will not get us there. We must commit to a lifetime of study, learning and experimentation: Deliberate Practice.

The fourth phase creates experts, eminence and resilience. People committed to continuous improvement undertake research to extend their knowledge and practise the hardest things until they have the well-earned confidence and skill to handle events that others dread. They expect, and are not afraid of, the unexpected. Their Deliberate Practice feeds a growing tree from which hang the fruits of knowledge.

Doing Deliberate Practice

To get the most out of DP, start by synchronising it with your circadian rhythms. Wake up at approximately the same time each day. Start your practice shortly thereafter.

Ration the time you spend on DP. For most people, two hours of such practice five days a week (about 500 hours per year) will see them achieve their expert level in 10 years. Few people can do more than this. Many musicians practise for five hours a day, although world-class Russian pianist Konstantin Shamray tells me that only half of that would actually be Deliberate Practice.

When undertaking your own DP, take small progressive steps. Attempt a task repeatedly and master it before moving on to the next. You need a wise coach to guide you. You must brief, train, debrief then repeat until the required level is achieved. You must welcome all feedback, good or bad. In the process you will learn how to coach yourself.

Many people will coach and guide your DP if you ask. If you can't afford teachers and instructors, ask for help from your managers, mentors and experts in your field. Over my 45-year career, each of these types of people has helped me enhance my aviation, presentation and media skills.

Developing expertise also requires struggle, sacrifice and honest often painful self-assessment. Leading tennis coach Ben Sternberg, who describes his sport as 'chess on legs', provides Deliberate Practice coaching by giving feedback after each play so technique can be adjusted and improved.

In their 2007 paper, Ericsson and his colleagues wrote that most expert teachers and scientists set aside a couple of hours in the morning to undertake mentally demanding tasks such as writing about new ideas, adding, 'While this may seem like a relatively small investment, it is two hours a day more than most executives and managers devote to building their skills, since the majority of their time is consumed by meetings and day-to-day concerns.' Think about what you could accomplish if you devoted two hours a day to Deliberate Practice.

Fangio: 'I was aware of something different'

Each time you master a skill, it moves from the slow conscious mind to the fast automatic mind. DP enhances ability and confidence, reduces the startle effect and panic, and improves mental agility and performance. Conscious effort becomes habit. Trained thoughts become intuition. Habits and intuition free the slow mind from the mundane, increasing free mental space and allowing it to maximise its situation awareness and sensitivity to anomalies.

Argentinian racing car driver Juan Manuel Fangio showed this in action. Fangio was one of the greatest drivers of all time. He won five Formula One World Championship titles, a record that stood for almost half a century. At 38, Fangio had been racing for 16 years but was in his first year of World Championship events when he started in the 1950 Monaco Grand Prix on the narrow streets of Monte Carlo.

The race came to grief during the first lap at the Tabac corner. Nino Farina, in second place behind Fangio, was attempting to manoeuvre at over 100 mph through the corner when he skidded on a wave of harbour water that flooded the track. Farina spun and crashed, blocking the track just beyond the sight of all drivers behind him. Eight of them subsequently crashed in a huge pile-up.

Fangio was unaware of the crash behind. Yet on the second lap as he approached Tabac corner he braked heavily, stopping short of the wreckage that had been out of sight when he hit the brake. It seemed nothing short of remarkable. Did Fangio have a sixth sense?

He modestly said later, 'I was lucky.' But the truth was that his 'luck' was the result of DP giving him the ability to increase his free mental space and situation awareness. As he explained, 'There had been a similar accident in 1936 and I happened to see a photograph of it the day before the race. As I came out of the chicane, I was aware of something different with the crowd – a different colour. I was leading, but they were not watching me. They were looking down the road. Instead of their faces, I was seeing the backs of their heads. So, something at Tabac was more interesting than the leader, and then I remembered the photograph and braked as hard as I could.'

Stress-Proof Deliberate Practice

Stress-Proof Deliberate Practice (SPDP) is my version of Deliberate Practice delivered at a controlled rate to manage and limit excessive stress. SPDP enables a personalised training path for every individual. Sequences are trained and repeated until a level of excellence is achieved at the minimum stress level. Cognitive load is measured as a proxy for stress:

Step 1 – Select the method to measure the student's stress levels. Proxies for stress include pupil size, heart rate and sweat. The range of low-cost wearable sensors is increasing.

Step 2 – The student selects the maximum/minimum level of stress they are aiming to achieve during/at the end of training respectively.

Step 3 – Personalise the training for the needs of the role and student. Focus on skills that need attention and reduce training for mastered skills.

Step 4 – Adjust the rate of learning to keep stress between the two thresholds. Introduce harder tasks only after the student has proved proficient at easier tasks at the minimum (comfortable) level of stress.

SPDP builds well-earned confidence, expertise, courage and resilience.

Conquer your stress – fear of flying

Learn how to control your reaction to stress. Whether it's a fear of places, activities or people, there are things you can do to block, distract or reduce its effects and resume a calm life. I have had success helping people reduce their fear of flying.

Many people, as many as one in six according to some studies, have a fear of flying (or aviophobia). Remember this if you have a fear of flying and are convinced you're the only one suffering. I encounter nervous passengers on almost every flight.

Fear of flying can have devastating effects. About seven per cent of Britons and Americans are so afraid of flying that they avoid air travel. Sufferers miss friends and family events, weddings, holidays and business opportunities.

Fear of flying can include the specific fears of:

- in-flight turbulence
- having no control
- the aircraft falling into 'air pockets'
- the aircraft breaking up in flight and crashing
- not being able to escape
- having a panic episode on board.

But no matter where the focus lies, fear of flying is not rational. It is not justified by objective facts.

- In-flight turbulence is a nuisance but will not harm you if you fasten your seatbelt.
- There is no such thing as an air pocket. Turbulence is caused when aircraft fly through air that is changing speed and direction.

It's akin to the rougher bits when you paddle a canoe through currents crossing a fast-flowing river. Except you're not going to get tipped out.

- Aircraft are stronger than humans. Aircraft are certified to ultimate stress of –1.5 G (1.5 times your weight inverted), +3.8 G (upwards) and 15 G longitudinally (in a sudden stop). You could not hold on or stand under these conditions.

Fear of flying is illogical. Why do most people who have a fear of flying not have a fear of travelling in cars, despite the much higher risk of death? Journalist David Learmount, who focuses on safety issues, said in 2018, 'You would need to fly in five million flights before expecting to be in a fatal flight.' In fact, while in many countries you have a one per cent (one in one hundred) chance of dying in a car accident, you have only a 0.000014 per cent (or one in 7.36 million) chance of dying in an aircraft accident.

But logic is irrelevant, because for most people fear of flying has an emotional origin that feeds back and amplifies itself. It is normally an irrational fear or dread that originates in the primitive fast and emotional mind. Fear is reinforced by positive feedback from the slow mind.

Don't believe everything you think! Confirmation bias (see page 130) occurs when the mind's frontal lobes unite with the limbic system to provide a unified response to a perceived threat. Our highest stress builds when we allow confirmation in our slow mind to reinforce our emotional fears. Collusion begins when the monitoring stops. When this happens, our sensations, thoughts and resulting 'truths' become distorted. This creates a feedback loop that amplifies fears into terror, dread and panic.

Canadian psychology professor Jordan Peterson writes about this in his book *12 Rules for Life*. Fear increases stress, causing physiological changes such as increased heart and breathing rates, which in turn leads to hyperventilation. Hyperventilation can trigger physiological changes that people identify as a heart attack. This conscious fear creates more stress that, when we become aware of it, leads to growing fear, which in turn causes the initial symptoms to worsen. This feedback loop strengthens until both our fast and slow minds become locked in a state of panic.

The solution for this kind of dread is not the insistent presentation of more facts – they just won't make an impact on the panicky fast mind. Instead, we need to train both the fast and slow minds together through expectation and experience. Before flight, I prepare my passengers if the take-off (or landing) will be rough. I say, 'Good news, I am expecting a lot of crosswind when we take off today. But don't worry. Even if we get bounced around a bit, you are always safe. It's also a great opportunity to watch the A380's patented "Dance of the Ailerons". The A380 has the most advanced flight controls of any aircraft, and these are what give the aircraft its signature smooth ride.'

Fear of flight is fear of the unexpected and unknown. When I warn of turbulence, I arm the slow mind to expect turbulence, and inhibit fear in the fast mind when the turbulence later occurs. Giving a reason for the turbulence prevents confirmation bias feeding back and elevating fear. Finally, the reference to the 'Dance of the Ailerons' usefully distracts the mind.

Helping people manage their fears

I ask my cabin crew to alert me to passengers who admit having a strong fear of flying. When I have an augmented crew of pilots, I follow a procedure that has proved effective in helping these passengers. Once the aircraft is in cruise mode with pilots in all control seats, I leave the flight deck to visit the cabin. I introduce myself to passengers the crew have discreetly identified. I talk to them, I answer their concerns (including who's flying the aircraft if I'm out here with them) and try to instil in their minds a sense of calm.

Then I take them with me when I conduct my 90-minute-long tour through the cabin. I talk about the A380, its strength and capabilities.

I tell them truthfully that even if it were possible for turbulence to tip us upside-down, which it's not, the aircraft would still be within its acceleration limits.

We talk to other passengers in a way that helps allay the fear of flight. These conversations create verbal overshadowing that helps to reset fears. Nothing is off limits. We talk about: aircraft certification requirements and strength; air pressure; the atmosphere; clouds; depressurisation; distractions; ditching; door openings; engine failures; hijacks; jet streams; mechanics; nervousness; noise; physics of flight; thunderstorms; turbulence and windshear. That's all technical stuff – but the real value is in the psychology and neuroscience. I also discuss the ability each of us has to be mindful, control our emotions and remain calm.

We discuss two key features of our fast emotional mind.

First, I explain that you can control your emotions. Your slow logical mind can calm your fast emotional mind in critical situations. For example, regardless of the anger you might feel for a person, if they are holding a weapon your slow mind will inhibit your emotional mind from making the situation worse.

Second, I explain how we 'pump' our senses. The kinetics of human movement is similar to the bi-directional kinetics in fly-by-wire aircraft. The brain sends signals to cause our extremities to move, and monitors feedback from sensors to detect when they are in the correct position. The communications between our emotions and body position are also bi-directional.

If the body's response to fear is to clench the fists then the simple act of clenching our fists can 'pump' our senses and increase fear. Everything is fine when we are relaxed. But when fear takes control and our sensitivities rise, 'positive' feedback can drive our senses into overload.

The key to 'pumping' senses is to recognise the body language of fear, and then take positions to 'pump' the senses to induce calm. Hopefully the aircraft experiences light turbulence during our tour.

As we walk around the aircraft, I help the fearful passengers recognise the body language when they become afraid: when they tense up, stoop, cross their arms, clench their fists or move in an under-confident manner.

I help them recognise that these movements are a consequence of their feelings and, if not reversed, will feed back to the brain and so escalate their fears. I then demonstrate a posture that 'pumps' their senses and takes back control. You can do lots of things to reduce stress when you are seated. Lifting your arms off the armrest and legs off the floor settles movement. Talking and doing 17 or 19 times tables distracts the mind.

The passengers return to their seats feeling as relaxed and in control as if they were at home. If they're not rushing to catch a connecting flight, I give them a private tour of the cockpit after landing and finish with photos of them smiling in the pilot's seat wearing my hat with their fingers in a classic stress-reduction posture – stretched out like a fan.

I've managed to update their knowledge, beliefs, awareness and predictions. I've also given them the tools to recognise their own signs of stress and recognise when they are 'pumping' their own fear senses, and I've shown them how to 'pump' their senses to induce calm instead. They've learned to train the slow mind to control the fast. By doing so, they have taken charge and conquered their fear of flight. You can do the same thing.

Irma Sullivan: 'I look forward to flying'

My standout example of how even the most fearful passenger can reprogram their response and master their mind is Mrs Irma Sullivan.

Irma lives in England and was a passenger on my flight from Dubai to London on 28 October 2013. The European weather conditions that day became known as the St Jude storm, aka Cyclone Christian, when Force 12 winds slammed the continent's north-west. We were alerted that all the usual alternative airfields in western Europe were closed to diversions. I called a meteorological officer in Sydney and spoke to him for 15 minutes. After this intensive discussion I decided it was safe to continue, but I loaded the A380 with more excess fuel for contingencies than I had ever carried before.

It would have been challenging for any passenger to keep calm if they knew the forecast, but none more than Irma. She had already decided this would be her last flight ever. Her beloved children lived back in Australia and despite the reassurances of her husband, a former air traffic controller and air safety investigator, her fear of flying had become so great that she told them she could not visit them again.

Irma's husband, who was working in Oman, had alerted Qantas to her condition and asked us to look after her. I went to meet her before we departed, and she got straight to the point, asking why we were flying to London when at least one other airline had cancelled all flights to the UK because of the storms.

We discussed the factors in my decision to continue and Irma said that her husband had also assured her it was safe to fly despite the weather. Once we were underway, I walked her through the procedures described above, and I could see her relax as I did so. By the end of the hour she was in a completely different frame of mind.

After she returned home, Irma's husband sent a note to Customer Care in which he wrote, '. . . when she spoke to me after the flight, she was calm and happy – much to my surprise . . .' She explained to him that the time taken to address her fears and the fact that she'd never been made to feel silly for being fearful had made all the difference.

Helping Irma was a very special experience for me, knowing as I did that helping her lose her fears meant she could continue to visit her family. In December 2017, I was thrilled to come across her on another of my flights. She was happily travelling back and forth regularly to visit her family in Australia and had remembered my procedures for 'pumping' her senses. When I asked her permission to include her story in this book she wrote a very kind note in which she said, in part, 'I never thought I would write these words – I look forward to flying on your aircraft again.'

Bottom line

To take control and perform at your best in any situation, you need to understand and master your mind.

Anything you can do 'without thinking' or 'in your sleep' is being taken care of by the fast mind. The slow mind can't multi-task, but you can increase free mental space and increase situation awareness by moving repeatable processes to the fast mind and storing them there, where they become habits and intuition. The way to do this is by practising something until it becomes automatic.

You need to free up the slow mind so that if there is any change from standard conditions – a broken down car stopped on the road ahead, an equipment failure or a medical emergency – your unburdened slow mind can deal with the novel problems.

When you practise the skills needed to drive a car, fly an aircraft or serve a tennis ball, you strengthen neural pathways to the point where the required actions can become habits performed by the fast mind. Repetition builds habits. Experience builds intuition. Together, they free the slow mind to be aware, think and predict, and to be available to perform the most sophisticated tasks.

Roger Federer's moves are habits in the fast mind, freeing his slow mind to observe the other player's body language and intuitively adjust the game plan. While Konstantin Shamray's fast mind moves his hands across the piano keyboard, his slow mind is looking bars ahead. You do the same thing, if not to the same level. When you ski down a slope or drive a car, you look up and ahead to plan your path, leaving your fast mind to take care of the movement of your limbs.

Generally, believe your gut feelings. 'Gut feelings' or intuition are the fast mind responding to subconscious signals such as body language. But the oldest parts of our brain have few connections to the newer language centres, which is why gut feelings and intuition cannot be expressed easily with words.

Body language is important. Just as you subconsciously judge others, they also subconsciously judge you. Educating yourself about body language isn't just an interesting exercise; it lets you see deep into the minds of others. When you understand how your behaviour 'pumps' not just your emotions, but also the emotions of those around you, you can ensure you make the best possible impression.

Purposeful Practice and Deliberate Practice both improve specific performance. Deliberate Practice requires feedback and a coach. Research has shown that it is an extremely effective way to achieve mastery of any chosen area, for those who are prepared to commit the time and effort. It is a demanding, time-consuming and ongoing process, in which each skill gained is a stepping stone to the next hard task. But it works, and those who push themselves in this way gain unbeatable confidence and courage.

Even those who choose not to engage in Deliberate Practice will benefit from applying Purposeful Practice to help face challenges in work and life.

Stress-Proof Deliberate Practice is my method to build expertise with an attitude of well-earned confidence (not overconfidence) and courage (not recklessness) even in the most challenging situations. When you can bring these three qualities together, then you rise to a state of feeling bulletproof, not gun-shy.

And when you understand your mind, you can take charge and conquer even the most seemingly insurmountable fears.

Mastering Your Mind: Checklist

Understand the fast and slow minds
The fast mind is automatic:
If your response is fast, instinctive and can't necessarily be explained in words, it's the fast mind at work.

The slow mind is rational:
The slow mind offers considered thoughts, consciousness, prediction and creative solutions to novel situations.

The slow mind can't multi-task:
Increase free mental space by practising key skills until they become habits in the fast mind. Avoid distractions during critical events.

Practice makes habits, intuition and expertise:
To improve and maintain your performance in any area, you need to expend time and effort.

Not all practice is equal:
Purposeful Practice works in a way fun practice doesn't.

Deliberate Practice is structured effortful work doing the hard things beyond your comfort zone, with the addition of feedback. Those who want to attain true mastery commit to long-term Deliberate Practice.

Stress-Proof Deliberate Practice is Deliberate Practice modulated to build confidence and courage and optimise stress.

Mastering your mind puts you in control:
Use neuroscience-informed techniques such as 'pumping' your senses to build confidence and reduce fears.

CHAPTER 3

Surviving Crisis Situations: You CAN Make It Through

We're all going to experience a crisis of some form, at some point. For airline pilots or nuclear power plant safety managers, a crisis might be a catastrophic equipment failure that puts hundreds of lives at risk. For communities, it might be natural disasters that devastate thousands. For corporations, it might be crippling financial loss or reputational damage. For families, it might be a frightening medical diagnosis, a job loss or a car crash.

The tactics needed to survive and respond to crises vary significantly depending on the situation. The QF32 incident unfolded over four hours packed full of continuous risk assessment and decision-making. A car crash is over in seconds, with no weighing of options. A cancer diagnosis can trigger agonising years full of difficult choices. And yet there are underlying principles that will help you get through any crisis.

Here are the strategies I learned over 40-plus years of flying which helped me and everyone else aboard QF32 walk away safely:

- stay alive ('Aviate, Navigate, Communicate')
- create time

- accept your reality
- mitigate threats
- assess your options
- reassess priorities
- don't rush
- think for yourself and resist stampedes
- forget perfection
- try inverting the logic
- communicate
- remember, there's no such thing as an 'unimaginable' crisis.

Stay alive

'Aviate, Navigate, Communicate' is the pilot's mantra to prioritise the initial actions in a crisis.

Aviate means staying alive. Regain control, establish your correct role in the team and together focus on achieving a safe state.

- When both engines failed on Sully Sullenberger's Flight 1549, *aviate* meant lowering the nose to stop the wings 'stalling' then flying at the minimum drag speed to maximise endurance.
- For Sully's passengers *aviate* meant fitting life jackets then adopting the brace position.
- For soldiers, *aviate* means keeping your head down and not getting shot.

Navigate and *Communicate* are used only when a safe state has been achieved:

- *Navigate* means planning then moving to a safe location, clear of threats. *Navigate* during QF32 meant climbing safely above the Indonesian mountains. For the people in the Twin Towers at the start of 9/11, *navigate* meant immediately evacuating down the stairs.

- *Communicate* your situation and initial decisions only when the first two aspects have been achieved. During QF32, I made the first communication with air traffic control one minute after the engine exploded.

Create time

Slow down to regain mindfulness. On QF32, we positioned and circled for 70 minutes close to Singapore airport while we assessed damage, fixed some systems, mitigated others that failed, then worked out how we would land.

Some in the international pilot community criticised this approach, saying they would have landed immediately. But I had educated myself on historical accidents that could have been avoided if pilots had taken the time to understand the problems and plan a safe return. No way was I going to rush complex procedures and endanger lives. As every good pilot will tell you, fuel gives you time, time gives you options.

Your first priority is to create time. Often in life when a crisis hits, you feel like you're out of time. This is rarely true.

Create time by finding a safe environment and stopping things getting worse. It doesn't matter whether the crisis is a family accident, a digital security breach, a medical diagnosis, a legal dispute or a production disaster – the aim in all cases is to remove distractions, maximise your free mental space and give you time to think.

Stop what you are doing. If you're in a safe building, find a quiet space. If you're on the road, pull over. Cancel appointments. Delegate your duties. Throw out the anchor. Enter a 'holding pattern'.

Sometimes, time is out of your hands. In the case of something sudden and catastrophic, like an oncoming car veering towards you or a building crane crashing down without warning, you don't have time to think. Things may seem to switch to slow motion, but in reality, it's all happening so quickly that you can only react instinctively, relying on your fast mind to control the steering or jump out of the way before you know what you're doing. You will then need to use physical panic-reduction techniques to get your mind back into gear.

But these are the exceptions. In the majority of crisis situations, you will almost always find you have more time than you think you do.

My then 20-year-old son Alexander got a good lesson in creating time when he was alone in our speedboat. What should have been a straightforward zip across busy Sydney Harbour turned into an emergency when partway through the trip the engine suddenly failed and refused to start again. Investigating, Alex discovered the engine bay was flooding with salt water. To make matters worse, in the windy conditions he was getting rapidly swept towards nearby rocks. He called me, raced through a brief explanation of what had happened then said, 'Quick, I have little time. How do I get the engine going?' I said, 'Alex, calm down, breathe. Throw out the anchor, then call me back.'

Anchoring was the obvious step and something he would have thought of himself if he had remained calm. But the very real and imminent danger posed by the rocks had sent his fast mind into panic mode, robbing him of his ability to think rationally. He called back ten minutes later, anchored and calm, having found and fixed the leaking hose that was causing the problem.

Find your calm

To make the most of available time you must remain calm and mindful, and that means controlling stress. This in turn means inhibiting the amygdala, and with it the startle effect and frenzied panic that sends your stress sky high.

Heart rate is a proxy for stress. At your resting pulse rate you are calm, rational; you feel you have 'all the time in the world'. As your stress rises, the pulse rate also rises, and this is when things start to change.

The following description relates to your maximum heart rate (in beats per minute, roughly calculated as about 220 minus your age).

- In the range of 65 to 85 per cent of the maximum heart rate (for example, 115 to 145 beats per minute for a 45-year-old) the effects of stress are beneficial. Your awareness of sounds and time may warp, but you're in the optimal state of arousal, just 'keyed up' enough to perform at your best. This is the state an experienced, confident actor is in before they step out on stage.
- Above 85 per cent, detrimental effects start. Rising adrenaline levels cause the muscles to get stronger and contract faster, producing increasing tremors that interfere with fine movements.
- Physical and cognitive skills break down above 100 per cent. Rising adrenaline and cortisol levels reduce the forebrain's ability to inhibit panic. Fight, flight or freeze might be your only options. Pain is blocked. You lose the ability to think or speak coherently. Your bowels 'turn to water'. You'll have trouble controlling your hand tremors enough to dial the emergency number on your phone.

Your body and mental models configure for survival. Muscle protections are inhibited, giving your muscles full authority and strength to lift a fallen tree off someone, but at the risk of the muscles pulling themselves to self-destruction. As focus increases, your mental model zooms in on the essential things at the expense of all others. You become effectively deaf – that's why cabin attendants scream their evacuation commands. When sight is affected, it's called 'tunnel vision' – that's why we suffer 'blind panic'.

It's initially difficult to control this primitive-brain response, but it can be done.

Breathing affects our ability to handle stress. Often in situations of high tension we hold our breath without even realising. This only makes things worse. I've investigated an accident where two military scuba divers panicked, held their breath during an emergency ascent and died. Hyperventilating, or over-breathing, is dysfunctional because you could unknowingly lower your blood's carbon dioxide level to the point where your cerebral blood vessels constrict, causing you to pass out. Breathing into a paper bag recycles the CO_2, reducing this effect.

Breathing is a key to regaining calm. To bring your heart rate down and reduce the feeling of panic, breathe in for four seconds, hold for four seconds, then breathe out for four seconds. Then repeat.

Now get the rest of your body involved.

Build your courage – the 'Wonder Woman pose'

The 'Wonder Woman pose' builds courage. Stand up straight, head high, shoulders back, feet shoulder-width apart, hips forward with your hands on them, eyes focused ahead. This is a position of confidence, power and authority. You might feel ridiculous, but what you're doing is positioning your limbs in a way that 'pumps' your senses and causes the release of serotonin.

Serotonin is a status chemical, reinforcing relationships between caregiver and receiver. High serotonin levels increase feelings of pride, dominance, recognition and status. It increases sociability, making people feel euphoric, talkative and wanting to hug. People with higher serotonin are likely to be leaders. It's good to feel like the king!

In his book *12 Rules for Life*, Canadian psychology professor Jordan Peterson writes that low serotonin levels mean lower confidence, less happiness, more pain and anxiety, more illness and a shorter lifespan. Higher serotonin levels reverse these states. The good news is people in groups synchronise their serotonin levels. People with lower confidence, pride and social status join teams to get the benefits that come with higher serotonin levels. They offer trust and loyalty to the leader in return. Peterson writes, 'the importance of this cannot be overstated'.

Taking the power posture increases your dominance, responsive-ness, strength and confidence, and that in turn reduces your feeling of fear and replaces it with increasing courage, which is what you need to start working your way through the crisis unfolding around you.

Try the Wonder Woman pose the next time you feel stressed before a job interview, when answering a difficult phone call, or facing a bully. My wife, Coral, has an additional trick when dealing with angry or aggressive callers on the phone. In this pose she lifts her eyebrows to inhibit anger.

If you can't stand, consciously uncross your arms and legs, sit straighter and make yourself drop your shoulders as you exhale. Release your grip. If your hands are balled into fists, uncurl them. Extend your fingers in a fan shape. All these actions reduce tension.

Remember to keep monitoring yourself. If you find you've reverted to a state of physical tension, run through the process again. Do it as many times as you need to. By de-escalating your response to stress, you're giving yourself the most valuable tool you can have in any crisis: time to think.

When panic escalates, the fast brain often responds: *Do some-thing! Anything!,* yet you are in the worst possible state to make any decisions, let alone the really important ones. That's what NASA's Gene Kranz was getting at with his first rule of flight control: 'If you don't know what to do, don't do anything!' Pilots say, 'Sit on your hands.' If you can ignore that internal compulsion long enough to get back down to a rational state of mind, you give yourself an infinitely better chance of coming out the other side in good shape.

Accept your reality

When you find yourself mid-crisis, it's perfectly natural to want to deny reality or wish it away. A parent whose child is diagnosed with cancer and someone being swept down a swollen river will each think, 'This can't be happening. Please let me wake from this terrible nightmare.'

Mostly people find a way to get past this very human response, and the faster the crisis is unfolding, the faster that happens. The person in the river might have those thoughts one second and the next be scanning the water ahead for an escape route. The parent of a very sick child might feel they've dealt with that feeling, only to have it return during the months of treatment.

But occasionally the refusal to accept reality is so strong it causes the brain and body to go into lockdown. In this dangerous state people freeze, turn inwards and become unable to help themselves or those around them. All their mental effort is focused on denying reality, leaving none to plan a survival strategy.

If you feel this start to happen, fight back. Acknowledge the shock and distress and fear you are experiencing. Admit to yourself that your world has been shaken up. By accepting this reality, you free up your slow mind's capacity.

Save your emotional energy – worry only about the things you can change. Regret is a waste of energy. Focus on the enemy in front. The three most useless things to pilots are the runway behind them, airspace above and a second ago.

Mitigate threats

Even as a crisis is still unfolding, before you have found a safe path out, look for ways to mitigate threats.

- If you've had a car crash, find a way to warn approaching traffic and get yourself and those with you off the road out of the way of further harm.
- If you're a pilot flying into deteriorating weather, plan your last point of diversion to an alternative airport, hours before reaching that point.

- If you're stuck on the side of a mountain with no help in sight, figure out your shelter plan while you still have energy and light.
- If you're in an unfolding natural disaster, don't wait to lose power and water before you prepare torches and fill the bath.
- If you're about to embark on medical treatment that might affect your memory, set up an automatic payment system to ensure important payments including health insurance premiums stay up to date.

The more threats you can identify, manage and mitigate, the more you can focus on getting through the central crisis. Distractions, fatigue and miscommunication are threats in any stressful situation. Acknowledge these and, if you can, put in place systems to prevent, fix or mitigate them. If you have a group around you, agree to monitor each other's fatigue and performance. Speak up if you have an issue.

Use checklists

Checklists mitigate many problems that lead to 'human error'. Boeing introduced checklists in 1935 after its first B-17 'Flying Fortress' crashed during its initial demonstration when the pilots tried to take off with locked flight controls.

Of the 1235 checklists in the Airbus A380, 22 are 'Do-Confirm', and 1213 are 'Read-Do'.

- 'Do-Confirm' checklists confirm that essential Standard Operating Procedures (SOPs) have already been completed.
- 'Read-Do' checklists add an extra layer of safety in dynamic or non-normal situations. The aim is to slow down, protect your team's shared mental model and make no errors. One person reads aloud the item to be actioned, then actions it, before moving on – all the time ideally being monitored by another person. My First Officer, Matt Hicks, actioned about 120 'Read-Do' checklists on QF32.

It's critical with all checklists that actions are not skipped. If an action can't be completed, the process must be halted until it can be.

Team actions can be accomplished in series or parallel.

- In parallel means two or more people doing multiple things at the same time. A final checklist picks up any mistakes.
- Serially means that the people come together to deal with one item at a time. This ensures the right outcome for critical or irreversible actions.

During QF32, Matt focused on actioning the ECAM checklists while I flew the aircraft. But before I made any radio contact with air traffic control, I said, 'Stop ECAM.' Matt stopped the checklist and monitored my call, keeping our shared mental model intact. At the end of the call I said, 'Continue ECAM,' the command for Matt to resume his checklist. The same happened in reverse when Matt needed my full attention to monitor critical and irreversible actions such as pulling fire switches or disconnecting hydraulic pumps.

You can adapt the checklist process to many crisis situations.

Assess your options

As well as feeling that you have no time in a crisis situation, it's common to feel you have no real options. Again, this is rarely true. Those you do have may be staring you in the face waiting to be recognised, or they might be last-ditch, high-risk brainwaves. If you can free up your capacity to think things through, you'll almost always find there are more options than you initially realised.

Gather information from multiple sources. Depending on the nature of the crisis, this could be anything from the location of functioning exits to the reputation of different surgeons. Share observations and ideas with other experts and friends.

Take nothing for granted. Don't assume or presume. Check your sources and double-check if you can. If the information is too much to take in, chunk it down: break it into smaller pieces that you can grasp.

Reassess priorities

If after all of this you still feel you have no options, then reassess your priorities. Would switching them around open up more poss-ibilities? Recognise your own decision-making biases (you'll find more on this in Chapter 6) and check that you're not discarding options because they don't fit your expectations.

In an ongoing crisis, keep checking to see if your options and priorities should change.

During the QF32 crisis:

- We reviewed our fuel and endurance every five minutes in the air. We decided whether to change our priorities to remain in the holding pattern and continue with our checklists or give up the checklists and just land.
- When on the ground, the decision not to evacuate down the slides was continually re-evaluated. We received updates from the crew and rescue services, enabling us to assess and balance the risk of fire versus the risks of a passenger evacuation.

Don't rush

Famed RAAF pilot Brian Lugg is a great example of someone who kept cool in a crisis and found options when others assumed there were none. In 1985, Brian was part of the Australian Contingent to Multinational Force and Observers, a peacekeeping mission in the Sinai Desert.

Flying back to the El Gorah base in Egypt after a routine obser-vation trip to the Israel-Egypt border, Brian's Iroquois helicopter suffered what could have been a catastrophic failure when the controls to the tail rotor suddenly stopped working. He and his co-pilot were ferrying four military observers, flying at an altitude of about 5000 feet on what was supposed to be a routine flight. The black objects sticking out of the sand reminded them of the risks from 21 million landmines left behind by various armies over the years.

Tail rotors fail in many ways. Some are recoverable by pilots who have been trained the hard way for such eventualities, some aren't. But helicopter pilots live in dread of them. My friend Squadron Leader Derek Knights died in a terrible accident as a result of a tail rotor failure a few years before Brian's incident. When Brian Lugg told the American observers the tail rotor had failed, they believed they were going to die. Not immediately – provided the helicopter maintained a high speed, the tail fin would keep directional control. But you can't stay in the air forever, and even for a pilot who has trained for it, landing with failed tail rotors is extraordinarily difficult and fraught with dangers, likely to end in a fiery crash.

Lugg had a huge decision to make. While he had trained for such a landing in theory, he had hoped he would never need to do it for real. He was about 30 minutes from El Gorah, darkness was approaching and the runway had no lights. He wanted to get the craft down, but he knew that all aboard would probably perish if he rushed an unpre-pared approach. So he decided to create time.

First, he radioed the instructors at the base, filling them in on his situation and asking for their ideas. He mitigated threats by circling for an hour to burn fuel, which reduced the aircraft's weight and lowered the chance of a crash sparking a fireball. It also gave people on the ground time to position their cars to illuminate the base's old runway with their headlights. Finally, he planned his approach and briefed his passengers. Only then did he start his final move.

To get this landing right, Brian needed to fly a long, low and fast approach. It had to be fast to ensure directional control (the tail fin needed to provide lift to counter the engine's torque). But even at the right speed, the fin only produces enough lift when the cabin is yawed (angled) 30 to 60 degrees to the direction of travel. The best way to understand this is by imagining what it would be like to drive a car at 70 miles per hour, looking out the side window, in a continuous 45-degree slide – oh and six feet off the ground at night.

Brian's 'running landing' was perfect. He approached at the right speed, at the right height above the black desert, with the helicopter cocked 45 degrees into the wind. Then, when everything was stable, lit by the cars' headlights he shut down the engine, straightened the fuselage then settled the helicopter onto the ground. Sparks sprayed from the skids as the machine slid to a safe stop.

Creating time was the key to Brian's resilience. His cool-headedness made him legendary and the observers 'shouted the bar' at El Gorah for weeks afterwards.

Think for yourself and resist stampedes

As well as the steps above, there is one more thing you must do in order to emerge from a crisis.

You must fight the herd instinct and resist the urge to stampede. When people are gathered and a crisis happens, groupthink and the herd instinct are always a risk. We react differently in a group than we would on our own. Panicking and lost for ideas, people instinctively follow the assumed safety of the herd. The bigger the threat, the more we feel safe in numbers.

Stampeding herds of humans are not resilient. Individuals in a stampeding herd abandon common sense and ignore safety instructions. People at the back of a crowd in an emergency will sometimes rush away from their nearest exit, simply because the herd is moving in that direction.

There is no shortage of examples from aviation of the danger caused by herd behaviour. BA Flight 2276, taking off from Las Vegas for London's Gatwick in September 2015, is at the mild end. Engine 1 exploded as the plane accelerated along the runway for take-off. The pilots stopped the aircraft. The high-pressure compressor had blown itself out of the engine and ruptured the inner fuel tank. Fire engulfed the left wing and the pilots ordered an evacuation. Panic spread through the passengers. 'I saw the flames and thought, "That thing is full of petrol and it's going to blow", said one afterwards.

Too few people had paid attention to the pre-flight safety announcement. I can say this confidently because it's the case on most flights. The passengers, many screaming, ignored the crew's evacuation instructions to 'Slide and just keep on running'. Some stood blocking the aisles. Against direct instructions, many took their cabin baggage from overhead lockers, barged with it to the exits, and jumped onto the slides holding bulky and breakable items including computers, bottles of duty-free liquor and strollers. No-one died, but in all, 20 people were injured – in the circumstances it's amazing this number wasn't higher.

As noted previously, not all crises are life-or-death emergencies, and not all herd behaviour involves physical stampeding. Sometimes the panic is just as real but the individuals are scattered far and wide. Stock exchange collapses are a good example. What can begin as a few skittish sellers quickly becomes an unstoppable wave of desperation, with terrible consequences.

To avoid your own stock-related crises, do your own research and trust yourself. Even well-respected financial commentators are prone to misreading the market. Alan Kohler is one such reputable observer of the markets, a financial journalist for more than four decades who provides investment advice to a receptive audience.

On the evening of Friday 16 December 2011, Kohler told a television audience in Australia that he was sure a market fall was imminent, saying, 'I believe the conditions are in place for another major panic sell-off on the share market . . . on Monday I will be significantly reducing my already reduced exposure to equities, to possibly zero.' One of the many thousands taking notice of this alert was my father-in-law Roy Ford, then rapidly approaching 100 years of age.

Roy is a former air force pilot and farmer, moulded by the Great Depression of the 1930s. A traditionalist who was very successfully living off the proceeds of long-term low-risk investments in companies whose businesses he understood well, he watched this pronouncement with great interest. Roy had seen the signs of panic many times before. His intuition told him this wasn't a sign to rush to sell, but probably a signal for an opportunity to buy.

Secure in his own deep knowledge and experience, Roy shared the view espoused by another successful investor, Warren Buffett: 'Be fearful when others are greedy. Be greedy when others are fearful.' Having resisted a panicky herd response, Roy could comfortably watch as, over the following days, weeks and months, the market continued to rise. (Alan Kohler wrote later, 'I thought a violent sell-off was coming . . . but ended up looking silly because it didn't happen.')

Forget perfection

Standing back waiting for the 'perfect' plan is just as big a risk in its own way as rushing into action before you understand the situation. When time is critical don't be paralysed into indecision. Scott Howe, British commando turned business executive, says delaying in the hope that you can gather all the relevant information is counterproductive.

As Howe explained in an interview for the Australian Institute of Company Directors, 'You don't have to wait until you have 100 per cent of the information you need to attack the enemy. We get 80 per cent of the information we need, make a decision, then go for it. In business, people procrastinate because they are trying to gather all the possible information. By doing that they stifle the decision-making process.' Or as General George Patton put it, 'A good battle plan that you enact today can be better than a perfect one tomorrow.'

Aim for the sweet spot between too little information and too much. If you have enough of the picture to be able to come up with options and the likely (though not complete) risk each entails, you are ready to act.

Try inverting the logic

If you've gone through all the steps above and you still can't come up with options, or the options you've tried aren't working, try inverting the logic. Inverting the logic can mean many things.

- Don't worry about what you've lost, focus on what you have. Gratitude is a powerfully liberating mind set.
- Be creative, ignore the rules, conjure opposites.
- Keep it simple, reject the complex. Work from the bottom up, not the top down.

During the QF32 incident, I reached the point where I was feeling overloaded with information about the seemingly endless systems failures the aircraft had suffered. The alarming ECAM lists just kept coming, at times delivering contradictory information. When we followed their instructions, we were sometimes left even more confused. ECAM was supposed to be our master source of information, yet I was rapidly losing confidence in it. But if we didn't have it, what did we have? My First Officer, Matt Hicks, was doing an extraordinary job of managing ECAM, but it must have been equally and overwhelmingly stressful for him too.

At that moment, I was struck by an epiphany. I remembered how Gene Kranz had reacted when an oxygen tank exploded on board Apollo 13, setting off an increasingly catastrophic chain reaction. As the problems escalated in space, back at Mission Control in Houston, Kranz observed his engineers becoming increasingly confused by the stream of error messages. He said, 'Hold it, gentlemen, hold it! I don't care what went wrong; I need to know what is still working on that aircraft.' By tipping the problem on its head, the NASA engineers were suddenly able to see that it didn't matter why the tank had exploded, it mattered how they could use what they had left to rig up something that would keep the astronauts safe.

On Flight QF32, I suddenly realised that instead of trying to make sense of nonsensical readings, a sea of red lights and endless lists of failures, I needed to flip my perceptions on their head. It was clear to me: we needed to go back to basics and focus on what we had, not what we'd lost. Okay, so the fuel tanks, pumps, jettison, transfer and computer systems, vital parts of the A380's operation, were about 80 per cent failed. Well, what did we have, then? We had gravity, which would allow fuel to drip from three small tanks down into each engine below . . . and so on. Inverting the logic freed us up to find simple solutions instead of trying to climb up a mountain of complicated problems.

QF30 – another oxygen explosion

We responded to unexpected, unthinkable and unprecedented failures by working with what we had, rather than lamenting what we'd lost, just as fellow Qantas pilot John Bartels had done almost two years earlier. The Boeing 747 that Bartels was captaining suffered an oxygen cylinder explosion near the Philippines. The explosion ripped massive holes in the fuselage, cut wiring and caused the cabin to depressurise.

John and his crew were confronted with an avalanche of spurious and distracting warnings and caution messages, significantly increasing their workload. Bartels responded by working from the bottom up, not the top down, and was able to land safely in Manila. His story wasn't in my conscious mind while we were still in the air, but it was there in my subconscious as another resource to draw on.

An hour after QF32 stopped on the runway in Singapore, it came to me that in inverting the logic, I had responded, as I remarked, 'just like John Bartels'. For him, and NASA's Gene Kranz and me, reversing the logic during a crisis had proved key to our resilience.

Four months after the QF32 incident, we held a party to thank everyone who had contributed to our successful outcome. John Bartels was on the guest list.

Communicate

With so much going on during a time of crisis, it's crucial that you don't forget to communicate.

If you're in a leadership position, quickly acknowledge the situation and reveal what you are doing about it. This reassures people that you are alive, in control, aware of the problems and working on them. On QF32, I understood how important it was that the passengers hear from the cockpit as soon as possible. I was still fully occupied following the first rule of aviation – fly the aircraft – so I delegated the task to fellow captain Dave Evans, on the flight deck as Check Captain, asking him to include the critical words, 'You are safe.' Dave's announcement was textbook reassurance, but he was well trained in responding to emergencies.

If you need to address people during a crisis and don't have that kind of experience, here are some useful tips that will help. Fear makes you hold your breath. When you do speak, you might be short of breath, with a fast, mumbled, high-pitched, wobbly voice. You will broadcast your panic and induce it in others if you speak in this state.

- STOP!, breathe, relax.
- Take time to think about what you need to say, and how you want to say it.
- Then take a few seconds to consciously slow your breathing, slow your tempo and lower your pitch. These activities 'pump' your senses and induce calm.

- Only then, when you have found your sense of calm and control, is it time to broadcast your intentions to others. Speak more slowly than you think you need to. Adrenaline speeds up speech to the point of gabbling, and people in crisis find it hard to understand what's being said to them. Slowing your speech will help on both fronts.

Give a longer, follow-up communication after you have stabilised the situation and formulated a plan. Put yourself in the shoes of your audience. Think what their concerns are likely to be in the circumstances. Then tell them everything they need to know at that time.

Spell out everything. Don't assume other people can fill in the gaps; they may not be thinking along the same lines as you at all.

Use NITS

I use the NITS acronym when structuring a crisis brief:

N – state the **nature** of the problem
I – state your **intentions** for dealing with it
T – estimate the **time** it will take
S – clearly explain any **special requirements**.

NITS was a valuable tool during the QF32 crisis and I used it many times, including after we had landed but were keeping everyone aboard. It went like this:

N: 'Ladies and Gentlemen, we have a complex and dangerous environment outside the aircraft. There are fuel leaks, hot brakes, an engine still running and many other dangers. Fire services are protecting us. You are safer inside this aircraft than outside.'

I: 'This is why we are not evacuating down the slides. We will stay seated and await stairs, but can change our minds if the situation deteriorates.'

T: 'Stairs and buses will arrive in about 30 minutes. We will then disembark you slowly, carefully and methodically down the stairs into the buses.'

S: 'I require you to stay seated and keep the aisles clear unless you need to go to the bathroom. Talk to the roaming pilots or your crew member if you have any concerns. I will update you every ten minutes.'

If you are in this situation, remember many people will record and upload your announcement to social media – you have only one opportunity to get this right.

Don't forget the second victims outside the eye of the hurricane

If you find yourself fully occupied navigating through and recovering from a crisis, spare thoughts for those close to you who are also experiencing it vicariously. If you are finding things hard, so will your close family and friends.

Here is my wife Coral's perspective of her QF32 crisis:

'I arrived home. As I inserted the key into the front door I could hear the phone ringing. It was Alan Rowlandson from Qantas calling.

'He introduced himself and our conversation went something like this:

' *"Oh, hi, Alan. You must be 'Rowly'. Rich talks about you all the time. He thinks you're great . . ."*

' *"Yes, yes, Coral. That's me. I need to tell you that Richard has landed safely in Singapore."*

'This immediately sent shivers down my spine – it's not standard procedure for Qantas to call me every time Richard lands safely!

' *"Okay . . ."*

' *"Coral, there was an inflight engine explosion on Richard's flight, but you need to know he's okay and he's safe. Don't believe anything you hear otherwise."*

' *"I understand what you're telling me. I know you have many other people to notify so I'll get off the phone. I'm okay and I understand."*

Rowly's timing was deliberate. He didn't believe the first reports that QF32 had landed safely. He rang Coral only after ringing the air traffic controllers in the control tower at Singapore Airport and getting their first-hand visual confirmation that we were alive.

Rowly later told me, 'In 1982 I was serving overseas, night-flying in one of three Buccaneer fighters at RAF Base Lossiemouth. My friend John Jolly was in another. Our wives were together at John's house, which overlooked the airfield. They witnessed an aircraft crash and a huge explosion and realised there was a 66 per cent chance that John or I was involved.

'The rudder on John's aircraft failed on finals, causing the aircraft to spiral into the ground. I went into an orbit over the fireball and was relieved to hear the sound of an emergency beacon, which meant at least one of the two crew had survived.

'What is important about this story is that the wives heard no news for over 90 minutes and had to suffer the anguish of not knowing if we were okay, even though they had seen the fireball. Being dark, they did not see any parachutes.

'I will always remember the pain the ladies suffered because of the lack of communications, even though formal procedures were in place. It is better to let people know what you do and you don't know quickly after an event like this, rather than let them hear it through the media.'

'I steeled myself and ran for the TV, flicking through to a news channel, where the screen was filled with the news an A380 had crashed. I sat on the couch and burst into tears. "Don't be silly," I said to myself. "Rowly said Rich is okay. Rich is okay. They wouldn't tell me he's okay if it wasn't true. Be strong!"

'The flood of emotion was overwhelming. Our children Alex and Sophia were both at university. I knew I had to tell them before they heard the news some other way. I couldn't call them as I was a blubbering mess, so I texted them and my best friend, Julie Ford. The text said: "QF32 has just returned to Singapore safely after a mid-air explosion. Dad was the captain. He's safe. Mum xo."

'Alex immediately called me, asking what was going on. I tried to find the words but couldn't talk for crying. Alex asked if I wanted him to come home and if his dad really was fine. I reassured him, telling him to stay at university and that I'd be okay.

'I also had to let Rich's adored father and [step]mother know. "Pull yourself together, stop crying, be strong," I told myself. Peter and Mariea took the news well but I'm sure they were feeling as stunned as I was. After the phone call, I collapsed back onto the couch and just watched the re-enactments on TV over and over. I couldn't stop my tears.

'Knowing Rich had his hands full, I didn't want to take up precious time so I just texted him: "Holy Cow, that was close . . ." I knew he would be extremely busy and distracted, and the last thing he needed was an emotionally demanding wife. I didn't need attention; I just needed to know he was safe. There would be time for me later.

'I knew Rich would contact me when he could. When he was ready. When there was time. When he had done everything he had to do for the passengers and crew. When it was quiet. When he needed me.'

I am lost for words every time I read Coral's story. 'When he needed me', repeats in my mind. The engine exploded at 10.01 am Singapore time and I did not talk to Coral until midnight, 14 hours later! It was not that I did not want to call earlier; it's just that I instinctively prioritised the wellbeing of the crew and passengers. I wish I had learned earlier about protecting the secondary victims, just as you are learning about it now. When I did finally ring we spoke for more than two hours.

I am proud of the culture of safety at Qantas, the teamwork on the flight deck, and what our crew managed to achieve for the safety of 440 passengers. I was proud that we debriefed all involved so thoroughly. I am proud of Coral, 'the wind beneath my wings'. But I am ashamed that I did not call her until midnight.

There's no such thing as an 'unimaginable' crisis

The terrorist attacks of 9/11 were Black Swan events – unexpected and improbable with significant outcomes. For all the horrors the world had witnessed, it had not seen anything like this before. The methods used and the scale of the destruction made it deeply shocking to billions around the globe. Most people wouldn't hesitate to say that until it happened, they would never have thought such a thing possible. If he was still alive to tell his own story, Rick Rescorla would say otherwise.

Like so many other people, I remember exactly where I was when I heard about 9/11. I was tens of thousands of feet in the sky, as First Officer at the controls of a Boeing 747 Jumbo flying from Hong Kong to Sydney.

The Jumbo's cockpit is beautiful at night. If systems are working normally, their lights stay extinguished for that phase of flight. All was dark and quiet except for the dim glow of green, blue and magenta displays and the low 'whoosh' of supersonic air over the roof. The windows framed a panorama of brilliant stars. This is the best time to be a pilot and I was enjoying every moment of it, when the radio came to life.

'QF28, this is QF26 on 123.45.'

'Go ahead,' I said.

'Have you spoken to Operations Control? Have you heard the news?'

'What news?'

'We have word that there has been an attack in the USA. The Twin Towers have collapsed. All USA airspace has been closed. Aircraft in the USA have been instructed to land ASAP.'

After a pause to absorb what I had heard I asked, 'Is this an exercise?'

'No.'

Pilots expect the unexpected, but I was not prepared for this.

Our radios are not encrypted. I knew that meant that in theory anyone within our 240-km line of sight could be tricking us, for some reason, with false transmissions.

I said, 'Thanks, I'll call operations', feeling very sceptical, as was the Second Officer. My disbelief turned to shock when the Flight Operations Centre in Sydney confirmed the news.

'Okay, we are one hour flying time from Darwin. Do you want us to divert to Darwin?'

'No,' came the answer, 'continue to Sydney and we'll keep you informed via the data link and SATCOM.'

The airways went quiet again. We realised there were flights in the air right now, heading for the US and just hours from landing. What would happen to them? And how far did this thing spread? Were terrorists on board our aircraft?

I decided to not wake the Captain, who needed rest before our descent into Sydney. We also decided to hold off telling the cabin crew, on the grounds that the information would unsettle them and the passengers would pick up on this. It proved a good decision. I later learned that my next-door neighbour had been on an overnight United flight from Los Angeles to Sydney. The pilots on that flight woke the passengers to tell them the news and, unsurprisingly, they became very distressed as a result.

Ninety minutes from Sydney, Flight Operations sent us a text message describing what had happened, which we were to read to the passengers before they disembarked. We had more than 100 Chinese passengers on board and wanted to make sure the message was relayed to them in their own language, so we asked for a cabin attendant who spoke fluent Mandarin and Cantonese to come to the flight deck.

The arrival early that morning was unlike any other. Pilots and air traffic controllers were stressed. There was an eerie quiet – no idle or extraneous chatter over the airways. Everyone was brief, but even so pilots made mistakes reading back instructions.

After shutting down the engines at the terminal, the Captain instructed everyone to remain seated. It took him about two minutes to read the message describing how two aircraft had flown into New York's World Trade Center and one into the Pentagon, while another had ploughed into a field. He made it without breaking down, but our cabin-crew translator broke down twice getting through it.

I will never forget the atmosphere as we entered the public arrivals hall. Families and friends held arriving passengers tight while behind them a wall of TVs showed the Twin Towers collapsing over and over. Most people were quiet, many were crying. The word 'unimaginable' was used often in the days afterwards.

But Rick Rescorla had imagined crisis on this scale, and the preparations he put in place saved more than 2700 lives.

Rick Rescorla – imagining the unimaginable

Rescorla was the head of security at Morgan Stanley Dean Witter at the World Trade Center. Born in England, he had served in the British Army before moving to the US to join its army and fight in Vietnam. The military honours he earned there included the Silver Star and the Purple Heart. Having become a US citizen, Rescorla gained university degrees in law and English and became a lecturer in criminal law and an author before moving into corporate security, where he used his excellent risk management skills and discipline to plan for every contingency.

As early as 1990, Rescorla had recognised the fact that the towers' status as New York's tallest structures made them a target, and had identified trucks loaded with explosives being driven into the World Trade Center garage as a specific threat. His warnings about this to New York's Port Authority, which owned the complex, were ignored. Three years later, in 1993, a terrorist drove a truck full of explosives into the garage. It exploded, but failed in its objective of bringing down the towers.

Rescorla then identified another threat, the possibility of a plane full of explosives or chemical weapons being flown into the iconic buildings. He recommended that Morgan Stanley move out of the World Trade Center, but it still had several years to go on its lease, which did not expire until 2006. Unable to eliminate the threat, Rescorla mitigated it by conducting periodic practice evacuations of all the company's employees using a buddy system.

Rescorla was in the South Tower at 8.46 am on 9/11/2001 when the first aircraft struck the North Tower. A Port Authority official made a public address urging everyone in the South Tower to remain at their desks. But Rescorla recognised the folly in staying inside a burning tower complex and immediately commanded all 2700 Morgan Stanley staff who were housed on floors 44 to 74 of the tower to evacuate down the stairs, and ordered 1000 more in another building within the complex to evacuate as well.

Nineteen minutes later, the second aircraft hit the South Tower. The calm, controlled evacuation was still underway, and Rescorla shifted it to an alternative stairwell. He stood on the stairs, booming commands and singing folk songs from his youth to calm the staff evacuated below him. He called his wife between songs saying, 'Stop crying. I have to get these people out safely. If something should happen to me, I want you to know I've never been happier. You made my life.'

Only seven of the 2700 Morgan Stanley staff died in the attack. This included Rick Rescorla and two of his security officers who were last seen on the 10th floor of the stairwell just before the tower collapsed, making one last check that everyone was out.

All those other lives were saved because Rick Rescorla was able to imagine what others considered unimaginable, to prepare for it in detail and put his plans into action during the crisis itself.

Increase your resilience

You can greatly increase your own chance of surviving and recovering from crisis by doing the same sort of thinking about your own life and taking some very simple steps to mitigate the threats you identify. The risk officer in Australia's largest bank told me the organisation now spreads its headquarters across many locations, never in a prominent landmark or skyscraper, and never above a train station.

Stretch your mind to imagine the 'unimaginable', then plan to survive it.

- Everyone should learn CPR skills and regularly brush up on them.
- No matter how competent a driver you are, if you get behind the wheel you should anticipate the possibility of a car crash and plan for it. Know where you are at all times. Carry a first aid kit, fire extinguisher and reflective or flashing warning triangles.
- Anticipate the possibility of a fire. Check and change the batteries in your smoke alarms on the same day every year. Know your escape routes (taking into account things such as deadlocked doors) at home, clubs and cinemas.
- If you're hiking, anticipate getting injured, lost or stuck outside overnight. Your survival kit should include items for protection, location (EPIRB, a spare phone battery and matches), water and food in that order.

Bottom line

At some stage, we all face crises of varying kinds. Even when the circumstances that have caused the crisis are out of your control, the actions you take can make a significant difference in how well you survive.

Crises are becoming more frequent. In the past decade, the number of headlines featuring a Top 100 US company and the word 'crisis' is up 80 per cent on the decade before that.

Whether the crisis is public or private, immediate or unfolding over months, there are strategies that will help you find your best options to deal with the situation. They will help you tap into your own resilience and strengthen your ability to deal with adversity.

Deep in crisis mode, it's easy to feel overwhelmed. It's common to feel you have no options and no time. You actually have more of both than you realise. It's just a matter of knowing how to create time and free up your mind. The QF32 crisis isn't something I would have chosen to experience. I'd have been perfectly happy with a smooth, steady, predictable flight that day. But even so, I was sure that by calling upon decades of experience and the support of my teams on the aircraft and the teams supporting us on the ground, I would be able to come up with potential solutions. They mightn't all work. Maybe none of them would, but I'd keep on trying things and never give up.

You can't control what life throws at you, but you can control how you respond. Millions of people around the world deal with crises every day. They might not be in the cockpit of an A380 but they are dealing with something that is pushing them to their limits, and finding a way through. Prepared and resilient, you can too.

Surviving a Crisis: Checklist

You have more time than you think:
Create time if possible. Resist the panic response. Breathe, keep calm and free up mental space.

Accept your reality:
Don't waste energy pretending the crisis isn't happening. Accept your reality, look ahead and fight the enemy in front.

Manage threats:
Even as a crisis is still unfolding, stop it getting worse by identifying threats and then avoiding, addressing or mitigating them.

Invert the logic:
If you're overwhelmed by what's going wrong, turn the problem on its head. Go simple, be creative and work with what you have, not what you've lost.

Don't freeze looking for perfection:
There is no 'perfect' plan. It's true you shouldn't leap in blindly, but nor should you stand back until it's too late.

Communicate:
You can never communicate enough. When you think you've communicated enough, double it. If you're leading, deliver a NITS brief.

Imagine the unimaginable:
Preparing for 'the unimaginable' won't stop it happening, but it will greatly increase your chances of surviving it.

Remember you're not the only one affected:
Spare time for those who care for you; they're going through it too.

CHAPTER 4

Managing a Crisis: How Not to Trash Your Brand

Beyond the challenge of actually surviving a crisis situation is the challenge of managing the perceptions and opinions around it. The bigger and more public the crisis, the trickier this challenge is and the higher the cost of getting it wrong.

That's true for individuals as well as organisations. We all know that a company's brand can be damaged by a crisis, but so can personal 'brands' – the reputation each of us carries based on our capability, credibility, achievements, vision, values, compassion and care. Corporate or personal, your brand is the measure people use when judging you.

Reputations that have taken years to build can be smashed in days if crisis situations are mishandled. If this happens, it's no use kidding yourself it will all blow over. Memories live forever on the internet. None of us can hide past mistakes or indiscretions from social media and search engines. We all need to know what to do and even more importantly what *not* to do when it comes to managing a crisis and limiting damage to our brand.

Crises *will* happen, so how will you handle them?

Crises come in all different forms and sizes, from heart-racing near misses that remain private, to the kind of unfolding nightmares that end careers and send companies to the wall.

Never waste a crisis because it can be the catalyst for positive change. Once we accept that crises will happen, the challenge is to manage these situations successfully, then change attitudes and systems to prevent a reoccurrence. Let's say, for instance, you're a junior publicist who intends to email sensitive financial information to your boss, but you accidentally select the wrong recipient name. If you send it to the company receptionist, realise your mistake and have the unopened email immediately deleted, the 'crisis' is over as soon as it began; the only management it requires is changing your work practices to ensure it can't happen again. If, however, you accidentally send it to a journalist who publishes it, the consequences for you and your organisation are very different.

When it comes to corporate crises, it's usually the potential personal impact that determines how people respond and how their view of the brand is affected. For example, if the convenience store franchise you favour for its handy location was revealed to have been systematically underpaying and overworking employees for years, would you drive kilometres out of your way to use a different store? Or, to use another example, what would you require from an airline that has just suffered an accident before you decide to fly with that airline again? Would you regain trust and return once the problems were declared fixed?

Death is the ultimate personal impact. There are no higher corporate stakes than those arising from a deadly or potentially fatal crisis. It's impossible to overstate how much was riding on the handling of our QF32 incident. In the end everyone walked away safe and sound, but the crisis management team on the ground had no way of knowing if that would be the outcome while the crisis was still unfolding. And the threat for reputational damage remained well after the physical danger had passed. These threats faced the iconic brands of Airbus, Qantas, Rolls-Royce and all the individual leaders and employees interviewed.

Thanks to the excellence of its preparation, systems and people, Qantas emerged with an even stronger brand reputation than it had before the incident, a remarkable outcome. As in any situation, there were many things that could be done better next time and lessons to be learned. I'm proud to state, however, that you'd go a long way to find a better example of corporate crisis management than QF32 – both in the air and on the ground.

What not to do

Unfortunately, you don't have to go so far to find examples of badly managed crises. The recent history of Malaysian Airlines and BP's Deepwater Horizon disasters spring to mind.

Malaysia Airlines had a good safety record before 537 lives were lost on two planes over a four-month period in 2014. The disappearance of MH370 and then the shooting down of MH17 caused sadness and alarm across the world. But adding to this distress was the frustration and anger felt by the families of those aboard, particularly in the case of MH370. People were vocal about feeling that they were being kept in the dark, and when they were updated it was sometimes in remarkably insensitive ways. A prime example is the airline's choice to use a text message to inform relatives that all hope was gone of finding those on board.

My friend Christine Negroni is an American aviation reporter who travelled to Kuala Lumpur after the accident. Christine told me during the crisis, 'It's chaos here. I'm trying to report the facts, but no officials are talking to the families or media.'

The Malaysian Airlines brand suffered significant damage. In 2015, the Malaysian Government nationalised the company. One year later,

Fuad Sharuji, the head of crisis management, said during an interview that while the company had made 'a few mistakes here and there', he felt that 'on the whole, we handled those two crises extremely well'. While acknowledging it was an extraordinarily difficult situation to face, many observers disagreed.

The fatal and catastrophic explosion and sinking of BP's Deep-water Horizon offshore oil rig in 2010 (which you can read more about in Chapter 6) was an avoidable accident, which better safety and check systems could have prevented. The way BP dealt with it is a textbook example of what not to do before and during a crisis.

Days after the explosion, BP executives not only failed to apologise, they refused to accept responsibility, insisting the fault lay with contractors. Their response when investigations revealed oil was continuing to gush into the Gulf of Mexico was to continually underestimate the possible flow rates. (It took three months to cap the flow and another two months to seal the well.) The man who came to symbolise BP's dire PR performance was its British-born CEO, Tony Hayward.

Hayward was a disaster for the brand, despite the fact that he was far from new to the oil exploration business and its risks. He has a PhD in geology and started his 28-year career with BP as a rig geologist. Despite this, his response to the ongoing incident came across as so uncaring and inadequate that he was for a while, as *The Guardian* put it, 'the most hated man in America'. Among Hayward's memorably awful moments was his decision to take a day off to enjoy a relaxing sailing trip in the midst of the crisis and his comment, 'There's no-one who wants this thing over more than I do. You know, I'd like my life back.'

The lessons of QF32 – getting it right

Even under normal circumstances airlines are a high-stakes, high-cost business. Worldwide, 3.8 billion passengers flew in 2016. It's not uncommon for airlines to insure each flight for up to $2.5 billion (this is an industry figure, not a Qantas figure). Like all insurance, those policies are taken out in the hope they will never be needed, although plenty of passengers find they have need to call on their own personal travel insurance because of a problem that occurs during a flight.

A medical emergency is the most common reason commercial flights divert. In fact, passengers require medical attention from fellow passengers who happen to be doctors on about 35 per cent of my A380 flights. Our onboard medical kits, including defibrillators, and satellite communications to dedicated medical services on the ground provide effective support in most cases.

Diversions also occur in the event of poor weather at the destination airport or if the aircraft suffers the loss of a critical system such as engines, fuel, hydraulics, electrics or pressurisation. Every grounded or diverted A380 incurs up to half a million dollars of lost revenue each day (again, this is an industry figure and not Qantas-specific). But while aircraft diversions might not be the norm, they are not crises. What happened on QF32 was different and everyone involved knew that immediately.

So, what did Qantas do right that the organisations above got wrong?

The first factor was that Qantas had an excellent Crisis Management Centre in place long before it was needed for QF32. As part of my quest to learn as much as possible about every part of my job, I had made a point of visiting the Qantas Crisis Management Centre. If you work in an organisation large enough to have a similar set-up, I urge you to do the same. In fact, I would say it should be mandatory for anyone in any management or team-leader role.

During my visit I learned the conditions under which the centre would be activated, who would attend and what their roles and tasks would be. I hoped to never need its services, but if something did go wrong I was confident the teams had planned for every contingency.

This knowledge proved invaluable and gave me comfort high in the skies over Singapore just one month after that visit. Even though both of our aircraft's satellite communications systems had failed, I trusted the Crisis Management team to do their job as much as they trusted me to step up and do mine.

Like all good crisis response systems, Qantas's has three strands: procedures, facilities and people. Roz Wheatley was in charge – her formal title was Manager Emergency Response. Roz initiated crisis management procedures 13 minutes after the QF32 engine explosion and activated the Crisis Management Centre (CMC).

The CMC is split into four tiers, layered like an onion:

1 Crisis Executive, where company executives meet to oversee the crisis from the highest level and to maintain corporate governance and business continuity.
2 The Crisis Management Team comprises managers in a dedicated Think Tank Room with walls covered with monitors where invited parties are given the responsibility and authority to manage the crisis.
3 Three Crisis Management Team Support Rooms to provide operational, technical and other support. These crisis rooms were still in session five days after QF32.
4 Local Response Teams quickly brought together on the ground in appropriate locations, in this case Singapore's Changi Airport.

In every organisation, the ultimate responsibility always falls on the people at the top. As Richard Branson noted from personal experience, 'The test of a company's leadership, and of a CEO in particular, usually comes during a crisis.' The separation of the Crisis Management Team and the Crisis Executive not only allows each group to work in the most efficient manner possible, it prevents the groupthink that can take hold when everyone is in the same room listening to the same arguments.

Even though not every procedure enacted for QF32 is applicable in non-aviation crises, the company's overall approach has much to teach anyone about very effective handling of extreme and stressful situations.

Golden Hour? What Golden Hour?

One of the biggest challenges the Crisis Management Centre faced was managing QF32 news through traditional media and social media. This is a common problem during public crises.

The term 'Golden Hour' used to be standard in PR and crisis management training. It's borrowed from medicine where it refers to the treatment given to a person in the first 60 minutes following a traumatic injury. The decisions made in this period have a major impact on the patient's chances of survival and recovery. For corporate PR people responding to an incident, the Golden Hour was the period they had to take control and set the tone of the media coverage, which would shape public perceptions and protect the brand.

The standard operating procedure is: gather the facts internally and agree on how much information would be released and how much would be held back and who would deliver it; contact the media; establish yourself as the trusted source; define the story; anticipate media needs and requests from on-air interviewees to technical data; and shut down false leads, unhelpful rumours and speculative theories.

The worst possible outcome is the story getting away from you. When it comes to traditional media, it's a truism that if there is a hole in the story being reported about you or your organisation, someone else will fill that hole if you don't. If someone else fills it, the story has moved out of your control and there's no getting it back.

By November 2010, with Twitter four and a half years old and its users posting more than 65 million tweets a day, the Golden Hour had already gone the way of the dodo, although few communications experts understood that. After the QF32 incident, everyone did.

On the Indonesian island of Batam, just south of Singapore, more than 400 parts and shrapnel fell, crashing onto cars, buildings and through a school's roof. Among the pieces sent flying by the explosion in engine 2 was the rear cowling, 126 turbine blades and three chunks of the 160-kg turbine disc travelling at 2.6 times the speed of sound. Miraculously, no-one was hurt.

The locals who looked up saw what they thought was a Qantas plane on fire. In the air, we were still trying to understand exactly what had happened but many people on the ground thought the plane had crashed. The first tweet to that effect went out just minutes after the engine explosion. An avalanche of tweets and retweets followed. Reputable media organisations including Reuters began reporting the story, some saying the plane had exploded, others slightly more cautious. One Asian transport safety bureau called a press conference to announce that QF32 had crashed, based only on a tweet.

Twitter had a profound effect. Thirteen minutes after the engine exploded, the Qantas share price dropped five per cent. Due to the speed of these events and the fact that both cockpit satellite telephone systems had failed, the stock price and the social media flurry were the first warning signs for CEO Alan Joyce and the then Group Executive of Government Relations and Corporate Affairs Olivia Wirth. Olivia said later, 'We first found out about the QF32 incident when our share price fell, and news of the incident had gone nuts on Twitter. That's not a good way to find out about a disaster.'

Social media is the new reality. The Golden Hour is gone. Today, when an incident happens, every person with a smartphone becomes a reporter. Twitter, Facebook, Snapchat and other social media spread news worldwide in seconds, creating opportunities for trolls to create fear, doubt and uncertainty.

Open disclosure – 'I am telling you the truth'

By the end of the day's trade on the Australian stock market, when the real story was known and the passengers were safe, Qantas shares had recovered all the losses and even gained a little. Many teams contributed to the incident's successful outcome. The first seven were: pilots, cabin crew, air traffic control, police, firefighters, Qantas ground staff and the Qantas Crisis Management Centre.

But even after we were back on the ground, the company's reputation was still at risk. With media ready, waiting and keen to savage the brand, that reputation was protected by the eighth team, a group no-one could argue with – the QF32 passengers. That didn't happen by chance.

I knew our communication with the passengers was crucial. While the incident was unfolding in the air I told my fellow pilots, 'Everything we say will be on YouTube within half an hour of our landing.' Once the emergency was over and I had finished searching the aircraft to make sure all the passengers were safely in the terminal, I was determined to visit them and speak directly, truthfully and from the heart. I was going to provide something that I regard essential in crisis management: full and open disclosure.

Too few people understand the importance of this approach and, unfortunately, sometimes for pilots it's not even an option. People outside the aviation industry are astonished when they hear that my friend, an Airbus A330 captain, was apprehended on the tarmac after making an emergency landing in Osaka, Japan, in 2005, denying him the ability to care for his passengers.

Three years later, after an unavoidable crash landing at London Heathrow, Captain Peter Burkill of British Airways Flight BA38 was whisked away by police and taken straight into lengthy investigation sessions (you can find out more of Peter Burkill's story in Chapter 9). Both pilots were prohibited from protecting their crew and passengers, a terrible error that I was adamant would not be forced on me.

I was determined not to be arrested. I approached a Singapore Police Officer at the bottom of the aircraft stairs and said in a deep, clear, confident and firm voice, 'Take me to the passengers at the terminal – NOW.' It was an order, not a request. I was set on seeing my passengers even if it meant refusing police orders. Fortunately, my tone and manner did the trick and the officer took me in his car on the 15-minute ride to the passengers at the terminal.

Even though we'd arrived in Singapore as an unplanned emergency, passengers had been separated into groups following the usual protocol. I went first to the main lounge where the 354 Economy and Premium Economy passengers were waiting.

Tension was low when I arrived. We had deplaned everyone on the healthy side of the plane, so no-one had seen the full extent of the damage. Initially the prevalent feeling in the room focused on the inconvenience of interrupted travel plans. Passengers wanted to know what had happened and how soon they could resume their journey.

But as time passed I watched those attitudes slowly change. Airport lounge TVs were all tuned to CNN's continual breaking news of our flight, including the initial reports that we had crashed and those aboard had perished. The chorus of mobile phone ring tones increased as distressed observers called to confirm their loved ones were alive.

The passengers' mood was shifting. Some became confused and emotional when they understood the incident was worse than they had initially thought. Unless I took steps to help them, they would feel uninformed and powerless when they left my care. And I was also worried that the media, rather than celebrating our safe outcome, would spin the story into a damaging frenzy that would create panic. Left unchecked, this was a spiralling crisis.

The only way to stop it was to take control, build trust and calm everyone down. I took about 15 seconds to gather my thoughts. I had to be seen to be the calm leader because calm, like panic, is contagious. I had to be truthful and open. Most importantly, I had to care. I pressed my hat firmly onto my head and keyed the public-address microphone.

I spent 45 minutes addressing the passengers. For the first 15 minutes I explained what had happened, why, what would happen next and what they needed to do. I told them why we stayed in the air for one and three-quarter hours before landing. I explained why passengers were safer at that point inside the aircraft than evacuating down the emergency slides. I let them know that jet engines only fail about once in every 300,000 hours of flight, so everyone should feel happy that, having experienced this failure, they were statistically unlikely to ever experience another engine failure. Then I fielded group questions for 15 minutes.

I prepared the passengers to handle the media. I told them to expect to be approached by the media outside the terminal. I said, 'I am telling you the truth. You know more about this flight than anyone else. Be confident meeting the press outside. Correct their rumours and tell them the truth. Don't let the press suggest that we were on fire – we were not. Don't let the press suggest the crew were scared, because we weren't. We were busy, but we were never scared.' Then I did something that surprised everyone.

Personal guarantee

I gave the passengers my personal guarantee. Even though the passengers felt reassured and confident and safe, I knew that as days and weeks passed, they would feel increasingly uneasy, maybe even bewildered and angry as authorities released further information which would raise more media speculation. If that happened I wanted my passengers to have a remedy at hand.

I made an announcement through the public-address system, selecting words not from any company procedure or manual, but straight from my heart, 'When you fly Qantas, you're flying with a premium airline and you have every right to expect more. So here is my personal guarantee. If you think Qantas is not looking after you, or if you think Qantas doesn't *care*, then call me on this number and I will look after you.' I recited my mobile number several times.

Others had more questions, which I was happy to answer over the next 15 minutes. Finally, when I stood alone in the centre of the lounge with no-one approaching me, I knew my job was done and I could go on to debrief the crew, thanking and congratulating them on the superb job they had done. I asked two pilots to debrief the 62 Business Class passengers, while I delivered another 45-minute debrief including full disclosure and my personal guarantee to everyone in the First Class lounge.

Personal motivation and brand protection align

I was conscious of the effect my actions would have and I saw them as an important step in protecting my company's brand, but that's not why I undertook them. I did so because I was driven by the empathy and responsibility I felt for every person.

Each person has a WHY, the locus of values and motivations that fuels them.

My WHY is, '*The parent or partner of every passenger on my aircraft has the right to expect their loved one to come home safely. It's my responsibility to deliver that person home. It's more than just landing safely. I'll get them a taxi or personally drive them to their front door.*'

My WHY drives how I think, act and communicate. My actions can all be explained by my WHYs. I could not have acted in any other way.

Most people just didn't get it. Friends said, 'You were mad giving out your phone number! You must have been swamped by media and angry passengers.' I wasn't, not then nor on two other less dramatic occasions when I have given my phone details to all my passengers. In all, those occasions accounted for about 1500 people and the result was not a single call of complaint, just three messages asking for assistance with various things, which I was happy to provide.

There is no downside in giving a personal guarantee. The personal guarantee is a gesture of compassion, empathy and care. It transmits honesty, modesty and humility and exposes vulnerability. It makes victims feel safe, respected, confident and in control. It melts anger and conspiracy. In return, those making the guarantee receive support, commitment and trust. If it's done in a corporate context and you care for your customers, they will care for your company, which will in turn reward its shareholders.

My full and open disclosure and the personal guarantee I provided as the leader at the coalface protected the company's brand more than any action other than bringing the plane safely to ground.

This two-pronged approach satisfied people's logical and emotional fears. First, if you find yourself in a similar crisis situation, deliver the facts in order to take control. I knew the facts of what had happened. Sharing them shut down the spread of rumours.

Second, emotions drive our perceptions more than facts do during a crisis. Generally, people don't remember what you said; they remember how you made them feel. By being transparent and expressing genuine compassion and care, you make people feel safe, calm, respected, informed, confident and in control. Honesty, modesty and humility melt feelings of anger or fears of conspiracy. In their place is support, commitment and trust, the ingredients for teamwork.

When the media shoved microphones in front of the QF32 passengers asking, 'Did you think you were going to die?' the response was consistent: 'No, the captain and crew were fantastic; they kept us fully informed at all times.' Hard as some of the less scrupulous journalists tried, they could not find a single passenger who was critical of our performance. On the contrary, those 440 people returned to all corners of the globe elevated to the best brand and public relations agents Qantas management could have ever hoped for.

Clamming up only makes things worse

One of the most common reasons for not providing full disclosure is that it exposes you or your company to a legal minefield. It's certainly true that you need to be mindful of the legal consequences when disclosing information. You also need to be mindful of the rights to privacy of those affected. Be confident you will deliver the best support by respecting these concerns while standing in the shoes of the people impacted and your company.

Ratan Tata, former chairman of Tata Group, India's most valuable brand, understands the value of disclosure. He said, 'The most telling thing is there are leaders who deal with the crisis and there are others who cover up the crisis. If you have a crisis, you should deal with it in the correct way so that you can hold your head high and say you made a difference. Not that you swept it under the carpet and lived with it, knowing that it is either dying or decaying.'

The Australian Transport Safety Bureau (ATSB) set new standards for open, fast and public disclosure by releasing facts about QF32 as they became available. The ATSB disclosed facts early to proactively correct misinformation, shut down conspiracies, open up communications and support all stakeholders. The US National Transportation Safety Board (NTSB) was initially critical of the ATSB, stating information should have been held back until the 30-day preliminary report. The NTSB has wisely reversed this position and now follows the path set by the ATSB.

You cannot occupy a neutral position between disclosure and concealment. 'No comment' is not neutral. Whether it's a PR person or a CEO saying it, 'No comment' projects defensiveness, weak attitudes and a lack of empathy. It creates a void that allows fear, misinformation and uncertainty to grow.

Take the sage advice of Brian Duff, who was Director of Public Affairs for NASA during the Apollo 13 crisis: 'When things are going well, tell the media everything they want to know. When things are going badly, tell them even more.'

Crisis management requires leaders, not freezers

In Chapter 2 we looked at the startle effect and how dangerous it can be for those during a precarious situation. But you don't have to be on the spot to succumb; workers, managers and company directors in boardrooms far from the immediate peril can also become startled in a crisis.

John Connolly, esteemed public relations consultant and an expert in restoring corporate reputation, says, 'I have seen chief executives freeze during crises. Some want to leave to go to a scheduled but unimportant appointment or to take their kids to sport. Some directors freeze, others want to immediately micro-manage or worry what the crisis will do to their reputations rather than what the company needs to do.'

During a crisis, leaders should lead, not do. They need to free up mental space to protect their situation awareness. They need to:

- prioritise and focus only on the critical parameters
- filter out (load-shed) lower priorities, then
- trust, defer and delegate to expertise.

Support people should monitor and support their immediate leaders. When it is warranted, they need to interject, raise concerns, challenge the leader's actions and offer remedies. Every expert should be prepared to call STOP! or even take over if necessary.

No matter the size of the crisis, you must always ensure someone is 'flying the aeroplane'. If everyone is fully focused on watching the crisis you might not have a viable brand left when it's over. Task someone with ensuring business continuity, keeping the business running with the aim of returning to normal operations as soon as possible.

Presence matters, and so do perceptions. I agree with the view that showing up is 80 per cent of life. Leaders MUST get to the scene of life-and-death or large-scale crises as quickly as possible. They must exhibit genuine empathy and compassion for the victims and their families, take responsibility, offer condolences, provide accurate information, assign a point of contact, offer resources and assistance, steer media contact, and protect their company's brand.

Richard Branson exemplifies a leader who turns up and communicates during crises. For instance, when a woman died as a result of a Virgin train crash at Cumbria in the UK in 2007, Branson, who was in Switzerland, reacted immediately. Photos of the crash scene spread through the country, threatening the company. Branson battled snowstorms to make his way to the scene, where he calmly took control, spoke to the media and defended the train driver. His leadership during the crisis sets the highest standards for crisis management and disaster recovery.

Unfortunately, there are many examples of leaders who have left themselves open to criticism by the slowness or tone of their response. British Prime Minister Theresa May provided one such example in 2017 when she made her first visit to the site of the dreadful Grenfell Tower fire in London in which 72 people died. She met with emergency responders but no survivors or locals. As a result, she was accused of being afraid to meet the victims and being reluctant to take responsibility or provide real support. When she returned the following day she was booed and jeered by angry protestors.

Sorry doesn't have to be the hardest word

Apologies can be an extremely important part of managing a crisis but only when they are honest and handled properly, which is all too rarely. The mealy-mouthed going-through-the-motions apology is far too familiar, especially from public figures who have been caught out doing or saying something in private that shows them in a nasty light. Instead of actually apologising for the action, these apologies usually run along the lines of 'sorry to anyone who was offended'.

Too often apologies are overlooked or actively avoided. This might be out of a fear of incurring legal liability or from a defensive need to feel powerful and project invulnerability. Sometimes people in leadership positions lack the empathy to understand how much difference a genuine apology can make – after all, it's just words. But those words, if they come from the heart, mean so much to a person whose life has been disrupted, maybe irrevocably altered, by a crisis not of their own making.

Follow through with your promises. If you say, 'I take full responsibility for this crisis', then mean it and do it because inaction will kill your brand.

Never let ego get in the way of a frank and sincere apology.

Medical professionals have historically been among those least likely to acknowledge and apologise for their errors and mistakes. This intransigence makes an already bad situation much worse for those affected. I know this from personal experience, as does my friend Peter.

Two years ago, Peter presented to a hospital for what he expected to be routine day surgery. Both of his eyes were to receive laser treatment to correct his vision, so he would no longer have to rely on glasses. There's nothing experimental about laser surgery, doctors around the world have been doing it for decades, and Peter had made a point of going to one of the most reputable ophthalmologists around. But when the time came to remove his bandages, Peter's eyes weren't fixed; in fact, he was effectively blind, unable to see properly out of either eye.

With no idea of what had gone wrong, Peter returned to the surgery for a post-surgery check-up. The first clue that this might not be a run-of-the-mill hitch was that, instead of conducting the exam himself, the doctor palmed Peter off to be tested by the receptionist. Finally, the doctor revealed that the procedure had not gone as planned . . . and offered Peter a 50 per cent discount on the additional surgery needed to correct both eyes.

It took a great deal of digging by investigators and medical licensing authorities to expose the truth. It turned out the doctor had installed a new state-of-the-art machine in the surgery. Believing himself to be experienced enough, the overconfident specialist had not bothered to take the time to learn how to use his new equipment. Peter was the first to be exposed to the new machine.

The vision correction needed was different for each of Peter's eyes. The doctor's first error was to apply the laser settings needed for the left eye to the right eye. This type of error is called 'Wrong Side Surgery'. On realising his error, the doctor left the operating theatre for 20 minutes. Things should have been stopped at that point, with the doctor disclosing the error complete with apologies, promises to report, investigate, remedy the problem and prevent it from happening again. This is how things happen in aviation. But Peter's luck went from bad to worse.

The doctor's second error was to return to the surgery and, without speaking to Peter, who was fully conscious throughout, inexplicably proceed to apply the right-eye laser setting to the left eye. Peter had now become the innocent victim of reckless Double Wrong Side Surgery and was left 80 per cent blind.

Peter felt aggrieved, ignored, scared, vulnerable, powerless and angry. These feelings were exacerbated by the attitude of the doctor, who failed to report the incident to the medical authorities, avoided taking full responsibility and offered insincere apologies. My anaesthetist friend Paul Barach and I steered Peter to the medical authorities who then acted to help prevent a reoccurrence.

Peter's story should be food for thought for the medical industry. Paul estimates 2100 Wrong Side Surgeries occur every year in the United States.

But it doesn't have to be this way, and 'Susan' is living proof.

Susan (as we shall call her) is the doctor in charge of the emergency ward in a London hospital. Not many doctors can endure the high-stress work environment of emergency wards, where random crises comprise a normal shift. But Susan is different. She loves her job and excels at it because she provides every element of great crisis management, including full and open disclosure, apologies and personal guarantees. Everyone has accidents and makes mistakes – it's the way Susan manages those situations that puts her at the top of her profession.

Susan presents to the patients' loved ones after mistakes are made in her ward. She gives frank explanations of what happened, apologises and takes responsibility, then promises to rectify the problem to prevent reoccurrences. Her disclosure works. She has never had a malpractice claim made against her. (There are some unscrupulous operators who might take this as a challenge, hence the pseudonym.)

Full disclosure has been linked in one report to a 27 per cent fall in Australian public hospital medical indemnity claims. Michael Smith, Clinical Director of the Australian Commission on Safety and Quality, said, 'People will sue because they think something is being hidden from them. They want the truth.'

Bottom line

A crisis can be an opportunity, even if it's not one you would have chosen. The hallmarks of crisis management are stamped and embedded in your company or personal brand.

Exceptional crisis management sees you emerge with a brand that is even stronger than before, which is what happened as a result of the QF32 incident. An outcome like this doesn't happen by chance. The seven coordinated teams that dealt with the QF32 crisis comprised more than 1000 knowledgeable and competent people who functioned admirably in their roles, followed procedures and enacted prepared contingencies.

I started playing my part long before I even boarded the plane by consciously preparing for, researching and understanding critical elements of crisis management in order to help turn a potential blow into a victory for the brand.

Trust is fragile. It takes a long time to build yet can be destroyed by a single event. When a crisis unfolds, everyone connected to that brand – corporate or individual – plays a vital part in enhancing, protecting or destroying its reputation. Open disclosure is a must. It displays your honesty, humility, strength and commitment to maintain your values and regain control. This rebuilds trust and protects your brand.

It is futile to think you can prevent coverage of an unfolding crisis in either traditional media or social media. However, you can influence the tone of coverage and limit misinformation by providing the full facts as you know them. Don't feed media desire for fear and drama.

Accept that no matter how much effort you make, you won't always get the desired result. I tried to maintain a smile whenever I was in front of the media, knowing that cameras were continually rolling. Nonetheless, some reporters hung around until they snapped photos of me frowning, because it suited their chosen narrative better.

When it comes to social media, follow the lessons learned by large organisations and ensure you participate in the conversation and monitor it.

Be positive, take ownership, work with and acknowledge your teams and their efforts. Your mood is contagious, so develop the skills that will enable you to remain confident, mindful and calm when you most need to be.

Managing a Crisis: Checklist

Be prepared:
Conduct a vulnerability audit – canvass every conceivable crisis that might hit your brand and plan for each one in minute detail. Where appropriate, include hierarchies of roles, tasks, procedures, people and facilities.

Move fast:
You have only minutes to respond to a crisis. The Golden Hour is dead.

Stay calm:
Instil calm by your example. Calm, like panic, is contagious.

Don't hide:
Be visible, available, responsive and responsible. CEOs need to get on site ASAP if it is a physical event.

Participate:
Don't leave social media to run wild. Embrace it as a critical communication channel.

Practise open disclosure:
Explain the facts; be transparent; answer questions; support and empower those affected.

Apologise:
And mean it. Express regret, explain what went wrong and, when it's your fault, acknowledge responsibility and offer care. Request forgiveness.

Provide your personal guarantee:
Give your contact details as the single 24-hour point of contact to victims and families.

CHAPTER 5

You're Going to Fail:
Failing Well and Just Culture

To do and err is human, but to do nothing is disastrous

No-one wants to fail. Failures extract a cost, delay success and hurt the ego. But failures are part of human survival and evolution.

You will fail many times in your life. So will every other person on the planet. Both human history as a whole and our individual lives are a series of failures and successes. Some failures will be huge and public; some will be so tiny they're barely noticeable. I've enjoyed many successes over the course of my life and career, and almost as many failures. I've learned much from both.

Errors are opportunities to improve. Evolution is proof of the positive results that can come from mistakes (in this case, errors in DNA reproduction). When we learn to own our mistakes and fail well we can go on to succeed.

But hang on, you might be thinking, how does that fit with the culture of High Reliability Organisations (HROs) in which failure is considered to be simply out of the question? Didn't NASA's Gene Kranz, the gold standard for effective leadership, call his memoir *Failure Is Not an Option*? How can failing be both a good thing when it's also something to be avoided at all costs?

The explanation lies in the fact that what Gene Kranz was describing, and what HROs work so hard to avoid, are catastrophic failures, the big incidents where avoidable mistakes result in devastating consequences, including loss of life. They do this by learning from all the smaller mistakes that happen along the way. To avoid disastrous end-stage failure you must fail in a small way lots of times, and learn from each one. You learn from the small mistakes so that you get the big things right.

Risk-consequence

Risk-taking is a sign of strength. It toughens us up and it's a necessary path to our resilience.

Every time you take a risk there is the chance that you will fail, and we take risks all the time. Some are big and some are small; many you may not even recognise as risks, but they are. Starting a conversation with a stranger is a risk, but possibly not as big a risk as the first time you tell someone you love them.

Big risks carry the promise of major rewards when they go right, and very painful consequences when they go wrong. Marriage is a big risk. If your marriage works well, your life will be enhanced beyond measure; if it doesn't, you may face heartbreak, financial loss, social disruption and other significant difficulties. Small risks offer smaller rewards but also smaller consequences if things go bad: the stranger you engage in conversation may prove to be unpleasant, but that's likely to be the extent of the consequence.

There's no such thing as a risk-free existence, even for people who would never describe themselves as risk-takers. If you're alive then you're taking risks, knowing they're not all going to pay off.

We must accept that experiencing failure – as a consequence of consciously deciding to take a risk – as being necessary in life. Stephen Hawking said, 'Intelligence is the ability to adapt to change.' If we don't change then we'll stagnate, which is the precursor to death.

Failing doesn't define you; it's just an opportunity to improve. You can never be a failure at life, no matter what anyone says. There's a name for failing and learning: it's 'experience', and you cannot be competent without experience. If you don't learn how to fail, recover and retry, then you can never grow to become resilient.

Neil Armstrong took failure in his stride. In preparation for the moon landing that he and Buzz Aldrin would attempt, NASA built a series of life-sized Lunar Landing Training Vehicles (LLTV), dubbed 'the flying bedstead' by the astronauts. They had to master the skills of the LLTV on Earth in order to learn how to manually fly the real lunar landing vehicle, the Eagle. Armstrong's description of the learning process encapsulates his attitude to failure as a stepping stone to success: 'We built four . . . We crashed three of them. But the LLTVs gave us confidence that would help us later.'

No-one is perfect. Ask any successful person how they got to be where they are and they will say they have failed along the way. This human condition will not change. Teams, however, can be perfect. Because perfection is a measurement of the result, not the method. Perfect teams pool their resources to detect, block, fix and mitigate errors before damage occurs. Perfect teams comprise humble people who put their egos aside, accept and forgive human frailty, then come together to raise concerns and fix mistakes.

Failing is education, pure and simple. But only if you 'fail well'.

Failing well

Failing well is the hallmark of resilience. Failing well means understanding what happened and learning from the experience, figuring out how to improve, making the necessary changes, and being unafraid to try again.

The three big things that stop people failing well are ego, fear and mistrust.

Unfortunately, from an early age most of us are taught that failing is always bad, and we should do everything we can to avoid it. It can be hard to shake this philosophy even though it is an unsustainable way to live. Feeling confident and capable is very healthy, but if your self-image is built on the illusion of measuring, comparing and being better than those around you, failing at anything will crack your brittle ego. People like this try to hold things together by denying to themselves and others that they have failed, ever. They think admitting their failures makes them vulnerable . . . and they're right. What they don't understand is that humility and vulnerability are signs of great strength.

Those who stand secure in themselves, own, respect and accept their failures. They recognise them as a necessary part of the learning trajectory that got them to where they wanted to be; as stepping stones to an ultimate success. They know that revealing their mistakes doesn't make them 'less than' anyone else, because everyone else has chinks in their armour too. Fear and mistrust also prevent learning from failure. People who make mistakes in toxic cultures hide their failures rather than give others ammunition to use against them. They fear the overconfident leaders who project the illusion of being perfect and in control. When things go wrong, these leaders blame others and create scapegoats rather than being self-critical and genuinely seeking answers.

Once you accept the inevitability of failing, the critical factor becomes how you will recover when it happens. You should aim to fail fast, learn quickly and move on. The great inventor Thomas Edison took exactly this approach. When a lab assistant expressed frustration that despite conducting 9000 experiments trying to develop a new battery, they still hadn't achieved the desired results, Edison replied, 'I have gotten a lot of results! I know several thousand things that won't work.'

Humility is not a weakness

The leader sets the culture, especially when it comes to care, quality and safety. Great leaders open up and expose their vulnerability, knowing it doesn't weaken their authority, but rather begins to build teams that trust, disclose, learn from and protect each other. When leaders open up and are genuinely humble about their own failings, they build the foundations for a supportive and resilient culture. Leading from the front, they metaphorically live out the truth of an observation by General Sir William Slim: 'Nothing is so good for the morale of the troops as occasionally to see a dead general.'

The leader must create a psychologically safe environment for people to self-report their errors. When others offer their mistakes, it's important the leader supports them. After all, the leader is always ultimately responsible. When you support people who expose their vulnerabilities you help them improve, reward them for revealing their faults, and make them more inclined to reveal their next errors in a continuous learning process.

If I've made a mistake and haven't realised it, I want to be told about it at the right time. I aim for excellence on every flight I conduct, knowing I will never achieve it. Even though I've been flying for more than 40 years, I still make many mistakes. When I do, I want to know, own and acknowledge them so I can improve. This also presents an opportunity for others to learn.

The value of debriefs

Military pilots are indoctrinated with the practice of debriefs. All air force pilots attend squadron-wide debriefs following major incidents to help them pinpoint what went well, the mistakes made and the lessons they can apply in future. In my experience, post-flight debriefs at fighter squadrons were testosterone-filled berating sessions where the aim was to emerge as the victor. Those held at the training, transport and helicopter squadrons were much more pleasant and effective. By the time I became an airline captain I knew how to conduct effective debriefs.

Debriefing should be a process of honest, supportive group reflection. It is an individual and team mentoring process to acknowledge successes and learn from mistakes – the aim being never to repeat them. It's often an easier task to diagnose what went wrong after a failure than to identify the key elements that led to a success.

I conduct debriefs at the end of every take-off and after every flight. I set the stage by being the first to volunteer my mistakes to the team. Even if there's nothing major, I find something to highlight that I might have done differently or better, such as a radio call, or leaving home earlier to avoid traffic jams. It's a joy to be part of a team in which highly trained professionals come together harmoniously in a no-blame environment to selflessly volunteer and share failures that become opportunities to learn, and to improve and reinforce teamwork.

Leaders need courage to be humble and admit their mistakes, but when they do it authentically the effect is powerful. Ideas flow in a trusting environment where no topic is off limits, no-one is above criticism and no-one tries to find excuses or scapegoats. Often, I get and learn more from others than I give.

In our small company business, Coral and I hold debriefs for all the staff after trade shows and advertising campaigns, to see what worked and what would need improving for the next time. Debriefing improves the quality of all teams – at work, in the family and in the community.

Effective debriefs also include what went well. Giving and getting positive feedback for wise decisions and good outcomes is important. It reinforces good practices, habits and intuition. At the end, if the team feels both invigorated with success and determined to improve, the debrief has been a success.

Two weeks after the QF32 incident, I convinced the powers-that-be to let me conduct a NASA-style debrief for the rest of the A380 pilots and management where the QF32 pilots sat side-by-side at a long table. It was an unqualified success, but that doesn't mean all five pilots who were in the cockpit during the incident perceived what happened the same way.

In fact, there were many differences in perceptions among us. One instance of this, was a request I had made to climb to 10,000 feet to enable an Armstrong Spiral approach. The Armstrong Spiral is not an airline standard procedure. At Airbus's request for novel solutions for its new A350 aircraft, I developed this spiral descent in 2008 based on NASA's Space Shuttles' approach. Originally designed in 1959 by Neil Armstrong and Gene Matranga, I converted the Shuttles' approach into positions, symbols, sounds and commands that would guide Airbus pilots to the ground in the unlikely event that all engines failed. I never imagined then that just two years later, this Armstrong Spiral would be our defence.

My perception of the need for an Armstrong Spiral and control checks were not shared by the others because they were not company procedures, and one of the captains who took my seat when we were on the ground and I went back to visit the cabin thought that the events were more dangerous on the ground than in the air. I don't share this perspective but that's okay. There is never one version after an accident or near miss because stress modulates our memories as well as our perceptions.

I saw this in action not so long ago when I met up with Stewart McAlister, who had been my commanding officer when I flew Caribou transports in the air force. He spoke of a night back in 1982 when we did the first medivac flight to Lord Howe Island, recalling the stressful combination of bad weather, difficult terrain, short runway and a medical emergency. He was amazed when I couldn't recall a thing about it, even though my log books confirmed I'd been right there beside him.

It also arose during the QF32 investigation when, two months after I had related my story to the Australian Transport Safety Bureau, one of the investigators told me that the data from the flight data recorders disagreed with my recollection of how I managed engine 2 after the explosion. I was shocked, but I trusted the data recorder's accuracy and apologised for my error. The investigator said, 'Don't worry; we see things like this all the time.'

There are three lessons here:

1. People's perspectives are real to them. Respect them, even if you don't share them.
2. You need multiple stories to build an accurate picture. Lawyers and investigators know every observer will have different memories and perspectives of the same event, which is why courts need multiple witnesses to get to the truth.
3. If you are involved in a public crisis, reject the uninformed criticism of those who weren't there (including internet trolls and armchair critics). Look at systems and procedures before considering the individuals involved.

Culture

Safety is paramount in aviation. It's a non-negotiable and overriding business principle from which values, culture, priorities and procedures are formed. The potential consequences are simply too great to let errors or dangerous practices slip through. And yet, we know mistakes will happen because systems fail and we're all human.

Resilience in aviation is not about preventing errors, because we can't. It's about accepting that errors will occur and building systems to recover and improve when things go wrong. But to improve you need to understand what went wrong, and when the stakes are so high, people don't want to admit to errors, even small ones.

The key to getting people to open up is to make them feel psychologically safe.

No-blame culture

The concept of a 'no-blame' culture took hold in the industry in the 1980s. This was after investigations into shocking aircraft accidents found that not one, but many factors contribute to aircraft accidents.

Each factor is a link in a chain of events that lead to a failure. If any one of these mistakes is recognised and dealt with, the chain is broken and the failure is averted.

About 90 per cent of unsafe acts are 'honest errors', the kinds of slips, lapses and mistakes that even the best people can make. Learning from these blameless failures becomes an opportunity to improve. The 'no-blame' culture aimed to address this by creating an environment in which people could freely volunteer their own errors without fear of repercussion.

But two big weaknesses in the 'no-blame' culture quickly became apparent. The first was that it didn't include a way of dealing with people who repeatedly made mistakes, including 'honest errors'. The second was it didn't make any distinction between culpable (for instance, working while drunk) and non-culpable errors (for instance, a weary nurse who accidentally gives ten times the dosage of a medicine during a triple-shift their manager insisted they do). To address these gaps, 'no-blame' culture evolved into Just Culture.

Just Culture – it's hard

My airline operates a Just Culture, a term coined by British psychology professor James Reason in the late 1990s. Dutch-born Australian-based Safety Science professor and former 737 pilot Sidney Dekker then developed the concept into what we have today, an approach which satisfies demands for accountability and contributes to improving care, quality and safety.

Just Culture is an environment of trust where honest human errors are decriminalised and people are encouraged to report their errors so improvements can be made.

Trust is everything. Regulators lay the foundations for trust. An organisation's board builds on this, extending it to every leader, manager and employee. Trust takes years to build, yet can be destroyed in an hour. It's tested after every accident or incident, when the organisation decides whether to operate on Just Culture principles or to sacrifice employees in an attempt to protect its image.

A survey of the US nuclear industry found that poor procedures contributed to 60 per cent of 'human performance problems'. Punishing people whose actions result from systemic or procedural errors does nothing to mitigate those problems.

Just Culture starts with the premise that there are always many factors that contribute and combine to cause an accident. It then looks beyond the easy target of front-line operators to all the systems, procedures and people involved, seeking the root cause, asking *what* is responsible, not who. This requires safety to be valued more highly than ego and retribution, but it also requires that every person understands the clear line between acceptable and unacceptable mistakes and behaviours, and, more crucially, to agree on who draws that line.

Just Culture separates human mistakes into one of three categories.

1. Human error – the honest mistakes we all make, for instance misreading 83 for 88.
2. Increased risk behaviour – a drift from safety procedures and agreed standards, for instance, 'I know I'm supposed to log this information right away, but sometimes I'm too busy'.
3. Intentional reckless behaviour or flagrant violations – knowingly engaging in dangerous actions, for instance a pilot conducting illegal low flying or a person driving while drunk.

If the mistake falls into the first two categories, acknowledging it and coaching to prevent it happening again are the appropriate responses. However, if someone repeatedly engages in increased risk behaviour it signals that there is a greater problem with the person and/or system which must be addressed. Incidentally, there are also procedures in place for people who might be in danger of slipping into the third category; for instance, if a pilot self-reports an addiction to drugs or alcohol, protocols exist to remove them from operations and guide them to help and recovery.

Reckless behaviour is different. It cannot be tolerated. Air forces sack student pilots who conduct illegal low flying, not because of the activity, but because of their disregard for clear rules. The Global Aviation Information Network estimates that about 10 per cent of actions that lead to bad events are culpable. Consequences include demotion, dismissal or criminal charges.

The valuable information revealed through Just Culture is spread widely. Airlines are fierce competitors when it comes to attracting passengers, but are a united front on safety. Knowledge derived from accidents or near misses is shared globally with other operators, manufacturers, regulators and investigators so that trends can be spotted and faults fixed before more lives are endangered.

There are two good indicators of a successful Just Culture.

The first is the number of reports of errors versus time. This is the line on the graph which often resembles a bell curve. The initial low report rate indicates not an absence of incidents, but a reluctance of people to report them. The report rate first increases as the Just Culture improves, creating a positive environment in which people report their errors. It then falls as the organisation improves its systems, people and procedures and reduces the number of near misses and accidents.

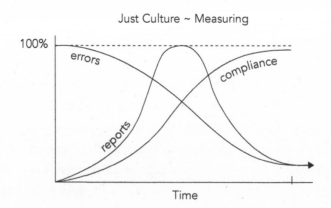

Just Culture ~ Measuring

The second is the line on the graph which shows the percentage of cases where management received voluntary reports of incidents prior to becoming aware of them. The target is 100 per cent compliance.

Consistency is key

Just Culture processes must be applied consistently in order to be effective. The aviation industry prides itself on its ability to review incidents without blame. And human errors normally occur in stressful situations after systems and procedures have failed. Yet not every airline can tame its ego, self-reflect and consider all contributing factors. During an interview in March 2016, one international airline CEO said (my emphasis), 'We will not accept *any kind* of lapses by pilots because they have hundreds of passengers whom they risked.'

Do these words reflect a Just Culture? Would you feel psychologically safe to report your errors or near misses in this organisation?

Expanding the Just Culture approach

Just Culture is used in other industries where safety is all-important, such as mining, exploration and nuclear industries, where lives are at stake and fear of reporting mistakes can and does lead to terrible consequences.

I am the Ambassador for Quality and Safety at St Vincent's Hospital in Sydney. The medical industry is struggling to implement a Just Culture. Clinicians do not go to work with the intention of committing a crime, but a culture of safety is destroyed when the system criminalises errors and puts front-line healthcare staff on trial. It's clear that working to adopt the Just Culture model across the medical industry globally will make health care better for the workers, safer for the patients and less expensive for the community. Safety *always* costs less than the consequences of its absence.

But the principles of Just Culture also belong in environments that are not about life-or-death situations, such as families and small business. The aim is to create an atmosphere of mutual respect where successes are celebrated and fear of failure is replaced by the desire to learn, adapt and improve.

Even in the smallest groups, lessons can be learned and systems improved when people have the confidence to report discrimination, harassment, health problems or even mistakes such as accidentally opening or sending inappropriate messages.

Just Culture in the family

Your children will fail often. (I hope! More on this in a moment.) So, show them how to fail well. Encourage them to reveal rather than hide their embarrassing mistakes. Proactively discuss addictions, anger, bullying, peer-group pressure, schooling, self-confidence issues, sex, social media and stress before it's too late.

The key is to stay calm and overcome your ego's need to get angry or demand reprisal. Together, identify the contributing factors that led to the honest mistakes, then guide your children to avoid, fix or recover. When you bring Just Culture into your home, every family member benefits and the family as a whole becomes more resilient.

A relationship Just Culture test

It's hard to build and maintain a Just Culture. Years of effort can be destroyed in minutes if trust and psychological safety is abused. Search for all contributing factors before attributing blame. Protect and forgive people who have made honest mistakes.

It takes courage to admit your mistakes, and when the stakes are high our vulnerability and forgiveness should rise to meet the challenge. On a personal level, the stakes are extremely high in your most intimate relationship – a marriage or long-term relationship.

If you're willing, this Just Culture test can be very revealing. However, since it involves imagined infidelity, I recommend only doing it if you feel you have a strong and stable relationship to begin with and if both parties are willing.

Sit down facing your partner, then work through this scenario. The aim is to maintain communication and respect despite the hurt ego, feelings and mistrust caused by what has (fictionally) happened:

Step 1: Your guilt-ridden partner surprises you by admitting to being unfaithful in their first honest lapse of judgement.

Step 2: You respond to this bad news.

Step 3: Now swap roles and repeat Steps 1 and 2.

How well did you and your partner go? Did you support each other and exercise Just Culture or was it one sided? This exercise can reveal a lot about the resilience of a relationship – read more on page 121.

Let your children fail, I dare you!

Children need opportunities to fail in order to recover and grow into the best versions of themselves. Instead of being shielded from risks and the consequences of their mistakes, they need to be allowed to make decisions, take risks and learn to fail well.

Ironically, many parents who were successfully raised this way themselves are reluctant to subject their children to the challenges they overcame that made them strong. They want to protect their children more than previous generations did, but these good intentions are often founded on misperceptions.

In his book *Enlightenment Now*, psychologist Steven Pinker argues that globally, deaths from birth, disasters, famine, ill health, homicide, hunger, poverty, terrorism and wars have all been declining while affluence, democracies, education and life expectancy have increased. He writes, 'The world has made spectacular progress in every singular measure of human well-being.' It might not feel like it, but most of the things that are bad today were worse in the past.

If the risks are decreasing why are parents over-protecting their children? Part of the reason is fear-based media coverage. We can reject this by reviewing facts from authoritative sources, rejecting bias and ignoring doomsayers.

If we deny children the opportunity to take risks and attempt things that are beyond them, we deny them the opportunity for the reflection, insight, learning and knowledge that is the gift from failing well. Sheltered and overly protected children grow up insulated from necessity, blind to risk, spoilt lazy by success and frightened of failure, inevitably setting them up for an unhappy adulthood. If you're raised in what amounts to a fail-safe environment, the first time you fail as an adult without the experience to deal with it will be a very nasty shock to the system.

Of course, parental judgement is still required as you teach your children to recognise, rate and live with risk, including knowing when to be afraid. There's a big difference between letting your seven-year-old build their own treehouse or enter an academic competition they won't win, versus letting them skateboard to school on a six-lane highway.

Letting your children fail isn't about throwing them to the lions, it's about mentoring them as they develop their all-important internal locus of control – a self-motivated ownership of their own actions, decisions and consequences – with the confidence and courage to persist when things get hard.

Kids given this latitude grow into confident and disciplined adults who fail well. Many of those who experience hardship and test their limits in childhood grow up to push the limits and occasionally break the rules. These are the weird, fearless, exciting, energetic and persistent Elon Musk types we like to be near, who challenge the status quo and change the world.

The mistakes you learn from don't have to be your own

Our lives are too short for us to experience all the things we need to become resilient in our chosen field. So don't limit yourself to learning from your own mistakes – also learn from others whenever you can.

Pilots have access to reports for every significant aviation accident worldwide. Each report goes into incredible detail, not to assign blame but to identify the many contributing causes behind the event.

I study these reports and learn from other people's experiences so that I don't repeat them myself. For example, I studied every crash of Airbus's fly-by-wire aircraft before I converted to flying A330s in 2004. I also reviewed the accident report for my Uncle Humphrey's Cessna 310 aircraft that crashed killing four people in 1974.

As part of my desire to build my own knowledge, I interviewed David Princehorn and John Bartels, pilots in my airline who performed brilliantly when faced with significant adversities (smoke, chemical fires, engine failures and explosions) and the lessons I learned helped me during the QF32 event.

You can also learn from others. You don't need to be in an industry that produces reports the way aviation does. No matter what you want to learn about, there will be plentiful material available (on the internet) describing it in detail. Opening a new branch of your business in China? Check. Hiking across the Atacama Desert? Check. Parenting a set of triplets? Check. No matter what it is you are likely to face or need to know, you'll be able to find books, videos, blogs, reports, fact sheets, theses and official advisories about it.

Supplement your knowledge by seeking out and communicating directly with experts. They might be senior figures within your company or your industry, or they might be experts in their field whom you've never met but who are accessible through social media. You can gather a staggering amount of knowledge on offer from those who've walked the path before, when you take the effort to find it. People are normally happy to help you – you only need to ask.

The more you learn, the better you will be at dealing with failure, for two reasons. First, because you can anticipate specific likely failures before they happen, based on other people's experiences, and can avoid the threat or mitigate the risks. Second, because your research will reveal that everybody, including leaders in their field, only got to where they are by failing along the way. As basketball superstar Michael Jordan said, 'I have failed over and over in my life. And that is why I succeed.'

Steve Jobs and Elon Musk are excellent examples of people who grew from failure. Jobs' greatest success came after he was forced out of Apple and faced disappointing sales for his subsequent venture, NeXT computers. Elon Musk of PayPal, Tesla and SpaceX fame exemplifies a leader with true grit who is unafraid to take risks. In 2015, when his SpaceX rocket exploded while trying to carry supplies to the International Space Station, Musk tweeted 'Space is hard'. Like Musk, Microsoft's Bill Gates understands that success requires the tenacity to persist through failure.

Chronic unease

Resilient people exist in a state of mind called 'chronic unease'. They constantly expect the unexpected and anticipate failures. It's a mindful process of being alert, keeping situation awareness, thinking about the 'what ifs' and staying open to new ideas. People with chronic unease are realists, not pessimists. They are prepared for the worst but hope for the best.

Chronic unease means you are proactive rather than reactive; you never take things on face value or simply accept the status quo. It means you must welcome criticism of your plans even when that's uncomfortable, and you must look past the obvious to identify non-obvious risks.

In the state of chronic unease, you subject your plans to what is known as a 'pre-mortem' or 'prospective hindsight'. Instead of waiting for something to go wrong and then analysing how that happened, you assemble your expert team and imagine that you are in the midst of a catastrophic failure.

Pre-mortems help you detect and address issues before it's too late. A pre-mortem begins with your team being told only that your plans have failed; you don't know why. It is then the team's task to identify the most likely reasons for the failure. There are no right or wrong answers, because what you're doing is brainstorming, trying to spot weaknesses.

The reason for doing it this way, with the catastrophe already supposedly unfolding, is to avoid groupthink, optimism bias and overconfidence – the feeling of 'that could never happen here'. Starting your analysis from the side and perspective of failure enables you to ignore the biases and drill down into every detail.

Chronic unease at home

Pilots' minds are in a perpetual state of chronic unease. We are preoccupied with the possibility of failure. When we are in work mode we plan ahead as if every take-off will be aborted, engines and systems will fail, the weather will turn foul, and every landing will be rejected. Yet curiously, many pilots don't apply chronic unease to their home lives. Almost every pilot I know has suffered an injury falling from a ladder while working on their roof!

Chronic unease belongs in the home. Think carefully about the everyday risks. Assume every power lead is live, every wet floor is slippery and every knife will sever (that way you might avoid the kind of surgery Meryl Streep had to have in 2012 after becoming a victim of an 'avocado hand' slip of the blade).

Coral has a chronic unease for driving. She walks around the car before driving off to check the tyres and look for obstacles. She doesn't stand behind reversing cars, expects drivers to not follow their signals, looks both ways, and never drives if she is drinking alcohol. These precautions seem obvious to us and yet we know too many stories of people who have been devastated when these steps have not been taken. Your chronic unease might one day save a life.

The value of near misses

Near misses are goldmines of information. They outnumber accidents by a factor of at least 10 to one. Near misses give you the opportunity to detect threats before they escalate into disasters. When near misses are continually ignored, a failure almost inevitably follows.

It's dangerous to skip over near misses and analyse only things that have gone catastrophically wrong. As Nobel Prize-winning physicist Richard Feynman eloquently put it, '. . . when playing Russian roulette, the fact the first shot got off safely is little comfort for the next'.

Many people are reluctant to report near misses for reasons including personal ego, a reluctance to cause embarrassment or get someone else into trouble, or laziness. They will also give up if the corporate reporting systems are too onerous to complete, or fail to deliver effective improvements.

Back in the early 1990s, when Just Culture had yet to be accepted across the aviation industry, an older and very experienced B747 captain flew an unstable approach to Cairns airport in northern Queensland. He approached the runway too high and too fast, meaning the aircraft had too much energy to complete a safe approach and landing. The flaps only extended fully after the aircraft was slowing down heading to the very end of the runway and the brakes overheated. The crew must have been startled, yet no-one reported the incident.

The near miss would have passed unnoticed if not for the flight data recorder. But reckless behaviour is rarely a one-off. What might have happened the next time or the time after that if the first incident had been overlooked? There are far too many situations where the relatively small failures and mistakes that create a near miss are not dealt with until it's too late.

Failing well in business

According to online research group Statistic Brain, 71 per cent of businesses fail within the first 10 years. This kind of failure can sting badly, because the chances are that if you've been motivated enough to start a business you've poured your heart, soul and money into it. Even so, you can either fail early and well, learning valuable lessons and minimising the damage, or you can fail badly and be left suffering for years.

Don't put all your eggs into one basket. Having a low-risk back-up plan in one realm permits and mitigates taking higher risks in another. By all means, pursue a new business idea, or start your first company, but don't give up the security of your current income to do it. If you need to free up some hours, explore the possibility of going part-time in your current job, but don't just quit and hope for the best.

In his book *Originals: How Non-Conformists Change the World*, management professor Adam Grant examines the success rates of those who jump feet-first versus those who are more cautious. He reports on a 14-year-long study, tracking 5000 entrepreneurs. The report found that businesses of those who followed their dream without quitting their day job failed a third less often than those who risked it all.

If this sounds counter-intuitive, Grant would agree. He writes about the fact that he missed an incredible investment opportunity because he thought caution signalled lack of commitment. In the planning stage of launching an online company selling eyeglasses, a student at Grant's university called Neil Blumenthal approached him to pitch the idea.

Grant thought it was a bad sign that Blumenthal and his co-creators decided to persist with their studies while starting their business and then, when they graduated, take up full-time jobs while still running the company. Grant declined the offer to put money into the start-up because, he writes, Neil and his friends 'played it safe instead of betting the farm. But in fact, this is exactly why they succeeded.' Less than a decade later, the company, Warby Parker, is worth over $1 billion.

Failing early

Failing well includes failing early. Even if you have a back-up plan and do your research, your business might still fail. In this situation, it is vital to recognise the signs early and make the decision to pull the plug before too much damage is done.

Coral and I have started many IT business projects in our small business. Some thrived, others tanked. We've never regretted starting the ventures, but we did sometimes persist too long. We've now learned to identify failures early and get out in order to limit collateral damage. We were able to make the hard calls because we consciously avoided the dangers of becoming prisoners to loss-aversion bias.

Loss-aversion bias

Back in the 1970s, psychologists Amos Tversky and Daniel Kahneman started looking at how people make decisions when the outcome is unknown. They found that our decisions are biased by what's called loss aversion, an asymmetry where we value a large loss about two times more than we value a gain of the same size. The trauma of being sacked or dumped in a relationship outweighs the joy of being recruited into a new job or finding new love. (Loss aversion might be explained by our mind's propensity to reinforce stressful memories more than peaceful ones.)

Loss aversion affects our decision-making, motivating us to work harder to prevent losses than we work to achieve equivalent gains. This can have devastating consequences because people who fall prey to loss-aversion bias enter a spiral of bad decision-making.

Reframing the question is usually a big help. Let's say you put money into stocks that are underperforming or a business that isn't turning a profit. Instead of questioning whether to persist with the loss, invert the logic and ask yourself, 'If I won the lottery, would I invest more into these ventures today?' If the answer is no, it's probably time to get out and accept the loss.

Gamblers who chase their losses exhibit classic loss aversion. On a losing streak, they stay in the game in a hopeless attempt to recover their money, despite knowing the more they play the more they lose, because the game is rigged to the house's advantage.

Our aversion to loss also affects relationships. Many of us avoid taking the risk of reaching out to another person because we fear the failure of rejection more than we want the reward if they reach back. With people who are already in relationships, this bias permits unresolved conflict to persist.

In a business context, loss-aversion bias also leads us to bad (or avoided) decision-making. As well as leading investors to hold on to poor performing stocks long past the point when they should have quit, loss aversion causes managers to hire fast and fire slow.

Flogging a dead horse

Of course, it's very difficult when you're in the middle of a loss-aversion situation to recognise it. At some point we will all have to decide whether to continue with a failing project or relationship. Do we keep going and commit more resources and hope the situation will recover? Or is it time to accept a failure and move on?

Let's take the hypothetical example of Larry, who has a good idea for a cloud-based social media app and sets up a business around it. His product has the potential to fill a gap in the market. In fact, several major Silicon Valley companies are interested, saying they wish to review its performance (a precursor to possibly buying it out) after it has been live for 12 months. Larry is understandably thrilled at this and estimates a market potential of over $1 billion.

Larry has put in place basic benchmarks and realistic time frames. However, he doesn't have coding or design skills, so he is reliant on contractors to realise his vision in a fully functioning form.

Fired up about the potential of his idea, Larry quits his job so he can fully focus on bringing it to market. But progress stalls when the programmers succumb to 'product creep', introducing extra features to stay ahead of other new products springing up. Deadline after deadline passes. Each missed deadline is an opportunity to assess the progress (or lack thereof), identify the new problems, fix them (perhaps by changing programmers), and make a new plan.

Unfortunately, Larry, who is an eternal optimist, sticks with his plan in the hope that the difficulties will be resolved soon. Money continues to sink into the venture with no finished product to show for it.

Other products are released that meet many of the needs Larry was aiming to cater to. His idea on paper is better than any of them, but it's not a functional product. Still, he's not about to abandon it now, after sinking years of time and effort into it (this is what's known as sunk-cost bias). Needing an injection of funds to keep going, Larry takes out a second mortgage on the family home.

The story plays out slowly, predictably and sadly. Larry's inability to adapt when things didn't proceed to plan sowed the seeds for disaster. There were many, many red flags along the way – all those missed deadlines and rival product releases – but Larry's optimism, overconfidence, and loss-aversion and sunk-cost biases stopped him from recognising the true cost of pursuing his idea.

The toll is heavy: Larry loses his savings and the family home, his marriage breaks up under the strain and he has great difficulty getting back into the job market when he needs to.

Larry's story is a fictional case study, but there are many people who make the same mistakes, failing catastrophically because they missed many opportunities to fail well. The lessons are clear: don't be afraid to fail but set benchmarks and checkpoints to stop losses and learn to recognise when enough is enough so that you fail well and don't lose more than you can afford to.

Creative destruction

Economist Joseph Schumpeter coined the term 'creative destruction', which means demolishing old ideas to clear space for new and better ones. Creative destruction draws a line under something so that you can start again and learn from what came before, not repeat it.

Your brain uses creative destruction to replace older less relevant memories with newer and more important ones. Software companies use creative destruction as standard practice. Microsoft Windows is rewritten every couple of years.

History is littered with examples of other companies that started out as industry innovators, became leaders and then found themselves left behind when they failed to embrace creative destruction. Kodak, Nokia and Blockbuster all fall into this category.

Kodak's fall was precipitous. One of the world's best known and most successful brands, it focused on research and development, churning out patents and anticipating customer needs. Among those patents were designs for digital cameras. But instead of disrupting its own successful business, Kodak attempted to use its huge influence to delay digital technology and prolong its legacy film market. It was a terrible decision. In 2012, the company filed for bankruptcy and has continued to shrink.

Nokia fell similarly, from an untouchable market leader in the mobile telephone market to a has-been. It failed to draw a line under its old successful business model in order to transition to smartphones. In a 2013 speech announcing that the company's phone division was being acquired by Microsoft after a failed joint venture, Nokia CEO Stephen Elop showed that Nokia still didn't understand what had happened, saying, 'We didn't do anything wrong, but somehow we lost.'

Blockbuster, the operator of video rental stores (remember those?), turned down the chance to buy Netflix for just $50 million in 2000, declaring it 'a very small niche business'. Netflix is now worth more than $150 billion.

Your unhappiest customers teach you the most

You can only fail well if you learn from your mistakes. That means if you're in a service business, customer satisfaction should always be top of mind. As Bill Gates observed, your most unhappy customers are your greatest source of learning.

Need convincing?

It's estimated that for every customer who complains, there are another 26 who are just as unhappy but have remained silent, until they turn away from your business. The old rule used to be that the average dissatisfied customer would tell nine to 15 people about their experience, and very dissatisfied customers would tell more than 20 people. But social media has blown that out of the water, as United Airlines discovered the hard way.

When the company failed to satisfactorily address the fact that they had damaged Dave Carroll's guitar in transit in 2009, he wrote a song about it, called 'United Breaks Guitars'. The music video he uploaded for the song has had more than 18 million views and Carroll has released a book of the same name.

But Gates's observation doesn't just apply to those in the service industry. Every business has customers, from an oil explorer to the freelance web developer. No-one can get it right all the time – failing is inevitable, remember – but no matter what your size, you need to see failure as the path to deeper learning and success.

I was once taken aback in a Dubai café when, after paying the bill, I was approached by a waiter from another section who asked, 'Is there any way we could have served you better?' It's a simple enough question, but I'd never been asked it before in this way. It was clearly a genuine query – if there was anything at all I might have liked done differently they wanted to hear it – and it seemed to be policy that a waiter from a different section asked, in order to make the customer comfortable enough to criticise the service if appropriate.

Everything had been excellent so I had no suggestions for the waiter. But that exchange brought home to me the importance of actively seeking the chance to learn from those you do business with, rather than wait until there has been a failure significant enough for them to raise it. I now ask, 'How could I do better?' after every flight and every presentation – in other words, every time after I deliver service to a customer.

The Golden Circle

In discussions about successful sales transactions, the term 'the Golden Thread' is used to describe the 18 interactions and experiences that occur during a sales cycle. The Golden Thread connects all processes, from the first contact through to the post-sales service. A bad experience at any point can sever the thread. I like this metaphor, but I've taken the concept one step further to create what I call 'the Golden Circle'.

The Golden Circle creates customers for life. It is formed when the end of the thread that represents the last customer touchpoint is connected to the starting point as the beginning of another interaction. It turns existing customers into repeat customers and advocates. This matters because recruiting a new customer costs seven times as much as retaining an existing one.

The key to maintaining the Golden Circle is repairing the thread whenever a process fails. For this, every person in the process is responsible, no matter what our official role is. When we see something wrong, we must step up, offer no excuses, take 100 per cent responsibility, then fix it.

Drifting to failure

Unfortunately, even the hardest lessons learned from failure can fade with time. NASA suffered a tragic and shocking disaster with its Apollo 1 mission (described in full in Chapter 7) and it learned huge lessons from this. The new procedures and systems it introduced as a result worked extremely well for more than a decade. But by the 1980s, NASA had begun a drift to failure.

The Challenger Space Shuttle explosion of 1986 was a preventable disaster. In the lead-up to the Shuttle's launch, rocket engineers Bob Ebeling and Roger Boisjoly, employed by NASA contractor Morton-Thiokol, had repeatedly warned that the Shuttle's booster rockets were only safe to launch in ambient temperatures above 53 degrees Fahrenheit (12 degrees Celsius).

NASA ignored the warnings. Boisjoly said later, 'We all knew if the seals failed, the shuttle would blow up.' The evening before, with the forecast for the launch just 18 degrees Fahrenheit (−8 degrees Celsius), the pair plus colleagues including Arnold Thompson tried desperately to convince NASA to delay until the temperature rose. Initially they were supported by their management, but this decision was reversed and Morton-Thiokol finally recommended the launch take place as planned.

On the morning of the launch it was so unusually cold in Florida that water sprayed over the launch towers froze. Icicles hung from the platform. Hawaiian astronaut Ellison Onizuka commented, 'My nose is freezing.' Arnold Aldrich, NASA's mission management team leader, reviewed the concerns of the previous night, then decided to launch after a brief delay.

On hearing this decision, Bob Ebeling said, 'The Challenger's going to blow up. Everyone's going to die.' Thompson decided he couldn't watch. NASA lit Challenger's candles when the booster's O-rings had warmed to 31 degrees Fahrenheit (−1 degree Celsius), still more than 20 degrees Fahrenheit colder than for any previous shuttle launch.

Challenger exploded 73 seconds after take-off at an altitude of 46,000 feet. All seven astronauts died. Debris rained down for an hour. The NASA engineers cried. I was flying jets at the air force base in Williamtown, Australia, when I heard news of the disaster. When I saw the videos and heard President Reagan's speech I cried too, along with millions of people around the world.

Why didn't NASA listen? Why didn't leadership defer to the experts' warnings? Gene Kranz, who was director of mission operations but not directly involved in the launch, told me unhappily, 'It was a case of safety fatigue.'

Secondary victims

Where mistakes result in lives lost, the initial victims are obvious. But there are secondary victims too – those who made the mistake. A Just Culture cares for secondary victims.

This is needed because guilt and self-blame are common after accidents, with secondary victims taking full blame for everything, even wrong procedures and company flaws, sometimes with fatal consequences. Bob Ebeling was a secondary victim.

On the 30th anniversary of NASA's Challenger Space Shuttle explosion, still despondent and guilt-racked, Bob reluctantly gave an in-depth interview in which he said, 'I think that was one of the mistakes that God made . . . He shouldn't have picked me for the job. But next time I talk to him, I'm gonna ask him, "Why me? You picked a loser".'

In response, NASA issued a statement saying that the deaths of the seven Challenger astronauts served to remind it, 'to remain vigilant and to listen to those like Mr Ebeling who have the courage to speak up'.

In 2014 I visited the Ellison S. Onizuka Space Center at Kona airport on the 'Big Island' of Hawaii. On the wall was a plaque inscribed with the words of Onizuka's inspiring philosophy he wrote before the launch. It finishes with:

> . . . If I can impress on you only one idea . . . let it be that the people who make this world run, whose lives can be termed successful, whose names will go down in the history books, are not the cynics, the critics, or the armchair quarterbacks.
>
> They are the adventurists, the explorers, and doers of this world. When they see a wrong or problem, they do something about it. When they see a vacant space in our knowledge, they work to fill that void . . .
>
> Rather than leaning back and criticising how things are, they work to make things the way they should be. They are the aggressive, the self-starters, the innovative and the imaginative of this world. Make your life count – and the world will be a better place – because you tried.

When is a failure not a failure?

While it's important to not deny or hide from failure, it's also important to consider the possibility that some things which are presented as failures might be opportunities when viewed from another perspective.

Many years ago when my son, Alexander, was aged 10, I was called in to see a psychologist who had been asked by Alex's school to assess him. His teachers felt he was failing their expectations because he sometimes had trouble concentrating and didn't always pay attention in class.

The psychologist, Paul, said he had confirmed that Alex had Attention Deficit Disorder. I interrupted, 'Alex appears to be normal at home. In fact, he takes part in many science- and engineering-based activities. What are his symptoms?'

Paul listed them, including, 'He can have trouble focusing on a topic, he can get restless and distracted . . .' I sank into my chair as he continued. Paul asked what the matter was. I said, 'Well you've just described my personality. If Alex has ADD it's my fault, he's inherited it from me!' 'Oh, don't worry about that,' Paul said. 'These symptoms are common; in fact we see them in most military leaders, company CEOs and police officers.' The solution Paul offered was a prescription for Ritalin.

There are children who benefit from medication of this kind. But in my view, there is a lot of over-diagnosis and over-medication too. Coral and I chose not to take up the offer. Instead, we focused on helping Alex build confidence, and cultivated his interests and passions in order to enable him to engage his natural drive, in keeping with the air force's motto *per ardua ad astra* – 'through struggle to the stars'.

This approach worked well. Alex applied himself strongly in the Science, Technology, Engineering and Maths (STEM) subjects. Leaving school, he was offered a place in the RAAF officer pilot course at the Australian Defence Force Academy and a place at university. He chose the latter and is now a successful mechatronics engineer.

The Just Culture relationship exercise – how did you do?

This exercise is a test of a couple's (and therefore two people's) personal resilience. How did you fare?

The principles of Just Culture are simple and immutable: forgive reported honest human frailty without reprisal and, for the person who made the error, learn and change.

Were you able to maintain a Just Culture with your 'cheating' partner, despite the intense feelings (which can include anger and betrayal on one side and guilt, weakness and embarrassment on the other)? Is your trust strong enough that you can discuss this situation without fearing consequences? Because of course trust is the key to the whole thing.

In your role-play, did you communicate and gather the facts while respectfully sharing each other's perspectives? Did you determine if the error was an example of human failure, increased risk or intentional reckless behaviour?

If it was an 'honest mistake', did you identify and analyse the many reasons for the lapse. Did you discuss how the environment, systems or procedures, and perhaps that both of you had contributed to cause the event? Just Culture protects the offender in exchange for their honesty, but improves the system and so protects the relationship. Or regardless of the fact that within the scenario it was the first instance of such a misstep, did you simply treat it as a reckless act with far-reaching consequences?

This is a very emotionally charged situation for most couples to imagine, yet working through it can explain a lot (and perhaps

---

prevent the infidelity happening in reality). Just Culture is really hard work, but it works.

It's not easy to forgive people who break and betray your trust at home or at work. Airline managers and leaders feel the same grief and anger after a preventable accident at work that you might feel at home. But Just Culture in both environments means losing your ego and asking questions, because when you ask the right questions you get the truth you deserve. Just Culture gives others permission to fail well so you discover, learn, adjust and recover to not just survive, but to grow from adversity.

Adopting Just Culture principles in your relationships will protect them and your personal resilience as effectively as Just Culture protects the flying public. (You can find more information on this at Fly-TheBook.com.)

Bottom line

We will all fail, many times in many ways. If we do not we will surely perish, because the only way not to fail is never to try anything new or take any risks, and it is not possible to live without change and risk. Learning to fail well means failing at the small things and using those experiences as stepping stones to success at the big things.

It also means recognising that you don't have to make mistakes yourself to learn from them. There is a wealth of information out there about other people's failures and near misses, as well as their successes. All you have to do is look for it and learn.

There are cognitive biases that can prevent us failing well if we are not careful, particularly loss-aversion bias and sunk-cost bias. These can trap sensible, capable people in ever-worsening loops. Reversing the questions you are asking yourself can be a useful tool in avoiding these biases. It's better to accept that things have not worked out well than be forced into that realisation when the situation has become catastrophic.

Failing well requires that we are genuinely humble about accepting weaknesses in ourselves and others and that we see the vulnerability that comes with admitting mistakes as a strength, not a weakness. It is vital that children be given the latitude to fail and the support and encouragement to learn to fail well, or they will become unhappy, dissatisfied adults.

Aviation is safe and resilient because of its Just Culture, which is built on the concept of failing well. Just Culture is a systematic approach which expects, accepts and forgives human frailty. It regards honest errors openly admitted as opportunities to learn and educate. But recklessness is not tolerated.

The Just Culture approach turns failures and near misses into opportunities to improve and thrive. It can be applied with great benefit in many different contexts, from corporate life to community organisations, families and marriages. But in hierarchical situations, it must start with the leader's genuine desire to improve. Just Culture is incompatible with false humility, finger-pointing and scapegoating.

Debriefs are an excellent Just Culture tool. Done correctly, they recognise a team's successes and motivate its members to learn from the mistakes and continually improve.

By adopting a mentality of chronic unease, we mitigate against the risks that accompany failures we can't prevent and we learn the lessons offered by past events so as not to repeat avoidable errors. Together, chronic unease and Just Culture are powerful armour for an unpredictable but exciting world.

Failure and Just Culture: Checklist

Failure cannot be prevented:
It is an unavoidable outcome of taking risks, and life is full of risk.

Failure should not be prevented:
If you don't fail, you're not learning.

The key is learning to fail well:
By truly accepting and owning your mistakes, you will build the foundation of successes to come.

Parents have a duty to let their children fail:
And a wonderful opportunity to teach them to fail well.

Just Culture allows teams to fail well together:
By recognising the inevitability of human error, it enables honest self-assessment and improvement in any group.

You can't fake Just Culture:
It is built on absolute trust, which must start from the top down. Blaming or shaming will kill it instantly.

Like any other culture, it needs to be nurtured:
Complacency will eventually allow even the strongest Just Culture to drift to failure.

CHAPTER 6

Making Good Decisions and Understanding Risk: Bias and Black Swans

To survive and thrive, to be resilient and perform at your best in any situation, you need to be able to make good decisions. To do that, you need to have the skills to recognise, rate and assess risks and potential gains. And to do *that*, you need to understand you're nowhere near as rational as you think you are.

No matter what time of the day you're reading this, you've already made hundreds, maybe thousands of decisions since you woke up – mostly small and inconsequential, but maybe some big ones too. About 95 per cent of the decisions we make every day are subconscious.

Few people are able to make good decisions during an unfolding crisis. When startled by fear, about 10 to 15 per cent remain calm, collect their thoughts and make decisions that will aid their survival. Seventy-five per cent are bewildered, stunned into thinking slowly, reasoning poorly and acting reflexively. The remaining group behave in a way that is counterproductive to their chances of survival. They scream, weep and freeze with confusion or fear, even when people are trying to help them. Fortunately, life-or-death crises are rare.

The golden rules

I made hundreds of decisions during Flight QF32. Some were fast, trivial and instinctive; others were slow, serious and challenging. I was comfortable making them, even in such a high-stakes situation, because I was prepared and had honed my skills and worked on techniques over many years to simplify the process.

Here are the golden rules of effective decision-making and risk assessment.

- There is a hierarchy of decision-making. It starts with subconscious instincts, habits and intuition. But biases and unreliable memories will impede you, and you will not always have all the information you need.
- Set your risk appetite. Manage threats. Accept, rate and live with intelligent risks and prioritise which decision to make first. Avoid gambles (unmitigated risks).
- There are many decision models. Select the decision model that helps you make the best decision in the time available for the circumstances.
- Don't seek perfection. Most of our decisions can be changed. When rushed and out of ideas, trust your gut feelings.

The good news is that effective decision-making is a learned skill, one that you can master. The first step is to learn what's happening 'under the bonnet' when you make a decision.

Hierarchy of decisions

The brain has a hierarchy of decision-making. Instincts (such as our fear response) and habits execute subconsciously, taking less than one-tenth of a second. Intuition is pre-learned decisions that executes faster than two seconds. Solutions that need conscious recognition and processing take at least eight seconds. Complex decision-making requires higher cognitive processes that take considerably longer. These three systems blend together so seamlessly that you perceive them as one.

Subconscious decisions

Most of us don't analyse what happens when we make trivial decisions, like which shirt to wear today or what sandwich to order for lunch. They're made 'on a whim'. The bigger the decision, the more rational we get about it, researching mileage and performance before choosing a new car, or comparing returns when considering whether to invest in a particular pension fund. But often that's a smokescreen.

Research shows we're consistently being driven by biases, illusions, intuition and patterns we don't consciously recognise. Richard Thaler won the 2017 Nobel Prize for Economics for his work in this area. The 'science' of economics was built on the idea that people act rationally, making carefully considered decisions in their own best interests. Furthering the work of Daniel Kahneman and Amos Tversky, Thaler has spent four decades showing this is not how things work in real life.

Instead of being the sensible, emotion-free creatures that economics textbooks describe, we tend to be overconfident, distracted, absent-minded procrastinators loaded with cognitive biases. And we find retrospective justifications for what we believe are careful choices, as Thaler explains in his bestseller *Nudge: Improving Decisions About Health, Wealth, and Happiness.*

Knowns, unknowns and the Dunning–Kruger Effect

What happens when we make decisions without knowing that we're missing key information? That's where Donald Rumsfeld and my stepmother, Mariea, come in.

Rumsfeld was US Secretary of Defense in 2002, when he was quizzed about the lack of evidence proving Iraq possessed weapons of mass destruction. His reply received world attention: 'As we know, there are known knowns; there are things we know we know. We also know there are known unknowns; that is to say we know there are some things we do not know. But there are also unknown unknowns; the ones we don't know we don't know.'

Back when I was a teenager, Mariea said it more elegantly, 'Knowledge is knowing what you don't know.' I've never forgotten these words because they taught me that recognising my ignorance made me miraculously more knowledgeable. For a few seconds she made me feel very smart. I could never have guessed how much her advice would benefit my life.

Rumsfeld's version brought him a lot of ridicule at the time. (The quote was so indelibly linked to him that he titled his 2011 memoir *Known and Unknown*.) But not everyone laughed. NASA was already using the phrase 'unknown unknowns', and Cornell University Professor of Social Psychology David Dunning listened to Rumsfeld with great interest, saying later, 'I thought, "That's the smartest and most modest thing I've heard in a year".'

Dunning was already delving into unknown unknowns and how they affect decision-making. Three years earlier, he and graduate student Justin Kruger had co-written a research paper called 'Unskilled and Unaware of It: How Difficulties of Recognizing One's Own Incompetence Lead to Inflated Self-assessments'. It was sparked by the case of a bank robber who had committed his crimes in full view of security cameras, then expressed amazement when he was arrested. He had rubbed lemon juice on his face before each robbery, believing it made him invisible.

The Dunning–Kruger Effect describes how incompetent people lack the competence to recognise their incompetence. It explains recursive incompetence and why a little bit of knowledge can sometimes be a dangerous thing. Overconfidence in a field in which someone has little knowledge leads them not just to reach stupid conclusions and choose unwisely, it also removes their ability to realise it.

'Knowledge is knowing what you don't know' really means: be humble, know your limits, avoid narcissism and defer to expertise. By doing so, you will protect yourself from the Dunning–Kruger Effect.

Many car drivers fall prey to the Dunning–Kruger Effect. They overrate their skills and underestimate the risk when they use a mobile phone while driving. Distractions divert our attention from monitoring our driving. What effect, expressed in numerical terms, do you think talking on the phone while driving – even using a hands-free device – has on the likelihood that you will be in a crash? Take a guess. Hint: think of distractions, the slow mind, free mental space, monitoring and situation awareness. The answer is at the end of this chapter.

So many biases!

Biases are subconscious processes that warp our perception and reasoning. Some people are biased in their perceptions about social, ethnic or religious groups, pre-judging individuals they've never met. But that's not the kind of bias Richard Thaler and other behavioural economists and psychologists are referring to when they identify the biases that affect our decision-making. They're describing cognitive biases – filters on *how* we think, not what we think.

Availability bias, champion bias, confirmation bias, experience bias, loss-aversion bias, status quo bias, sunflower bias and the sunk-cost fallacy are among the key biases that affect the way we make decisions.

Repetition strengthens **availability bias**. An untruth repeated often enough is eventually perceived as a truth. In effect, the more 'available' a mantra is – that is, the more it is heard and repeated – the more the brain becomes captive to it. Our perceptions are biased by ease of recall. This bias can be used in a positive manner, for instance with the repetition and frequent use of safety slogans. Availability bias can be fed internally (for instance, by chanting) or externally by advertising, propaganda and social media.

Confirmation bias means giving significance to information that confirms your beliefs and ignoring or discrediting information that challenges these beliefs. Confirmation bias turns what feels like a rational and objective process into an exercise in cherry-picking only the facts that suit your preferred and predetermined outcome, even though you may have no idea this is what's going on. Confirmation bias affects everything from our religious beliefs and political leanings to preference for a particular yoghurt brand. It underpins the feedback that generates extreme fears including agoraphobia and the fear of flying.

To see how confirmation bias works let's take the example of buying a car. You have a preference for car-maker X. You read a comparison report from a trusted motoring organisation that rates cars for performance, safety and other factors. Car-maker X's models rate well, but don't come out on top. Even though you've told yourself you are seeking independent data in order to choose the best car, confirmation bias means you will find reasons to downplay the fact that maker Y gets a better safety rating and maker Z has better re-sale value, and you will give more weight to the categories in which maker X does best.

What feels like a rational, objective process is actually an exercise in fitting the facts to your preferred outcome.

It's not easy to overcome confirmation bias. After all, everything we say and do is a reflection of what we believe. We don't like being told we're wrong or hearing things that challenge our beliefs. But revered football manager Sir Alex Ferguson said it can be done. For him, watching his football players in action was an exercise in stripping away expectation and bias: 'The key is not just having the ability to "see things", but the ability to "see things you don't expect to see".'

Status quo bias is a subconscious preference for sticking with the way things are rather than triggering change, even when that change would benefit you.

If it ain't broke, don't fix it.

Thaler has done a lot of work on how governments can nudge people into better financial and health choices by working with this bias instead of fighting against it. The British Government used Thaler's 'Nudge theory' with great success to address disturbingly low pension-saving rates. In 2012, it changed UK pension-saving schemes from opt-in to opt-out. They remained voluntary, but where previously doing nothing meant a person had no pension savings, now doing nothing means the savings build quietly in the background. By 2016, the number of accounts had more than tripled, with millions more people saving for retirement. Spain used the same opt-out approach to organ donation to make itself a world leader in transplant numbers.

Take advantage of the status quo bias. Set up an automatic transfer of a portion of your pay into a special savings account. After making the initial arrangements it will always be easier to leave the automatic transfers happening in the background than to make manual payments. You'll be surprised how quickly you can save for a special gift, treat or holiday.

Loss aversion and the sunk-cost fallacy is where we fear losses more than we enjoy gains. It's the reason we often throw good money after bad. This is something we touched on in Chapter 5 in the context of failing businesses. But it applies to all sorts of other situations too, affecting supposedly rational decision-making. We skew our decision-making to avoid the pain of loss, even when doing so isn't rational.

Studies show we value large losses twice as much as we value a gain of the same size. In other words, finding a $100 note will make you feel good for a short time, but losing a $100 note will make you feel twice as bad for a longer time.

The loss-aversion bias influences our perceptions and selection of options. People are more likely to select an option that is measured in units of success rather than failure. For instance, cancer patients deciding between surgery or chemotherapy choose very differently depending on whether the chance of success is presented as a survival rate or a mortality rate – even though the underlying risk is the same.

Which option would you select – the one that had a 95 per cent chance of survival, or the other that had a 5 per cent chance of death?

The related sunk-cost fallacy makes people persist in worsening situations. People stay too long in bad jobs, unhappy marriages and underperforming businesses.

Sunk-cost thinking is influenced by loss aversion. It's also known as 'the Concorde fallacy' because the development of the supersonic aircraft was a perfect example of sunk-cost thinking. Discussions on the project began in Britain in 1956, the French Government joined in 1962 and the first service was launched in 1976. During the intervening years, both governments poured money in, investing huge sums long past the point when it was obvious there was no economic case to do so. As former British Deputy Prime Minister Michael Heseltine put it, 'The cost of cancelling [Concorde] was always bigger than the cost of going on. Whether it actually was, of course, no-one ever knew because nobody could face either the financial cost or the ignominy of cancellation.'

Sunk-cost bias kills. 'Get-home-itis' is the name given to the state of mind of pilots who persist in flying into dangerous weather conditions because, 'we've come so far, we're almost home'. 'Summit fever' is the equivalent name for mountain climbers who ignore their plans and brush off warnings with, 'We're going for the summit, no matter what.'

Other signs of sunk-loss blindness include:

- 'It's a matter of principle', from people who persist with a costly legal action they are unlikely to win
- 'I've lost too much financially or emotionally', from leaders who stubbornly refuse to close a failing project
- poker players who say they are 'pot committed' as justification to stay in a hopeless game when the logical option is to fold and lose just the bet
- 'It's too late to turn back', from leaders of high-cost projects.

My friend Adrian Wischer resisted the sunk-cost bias. About 30 years ago, after discovering one of his executives had fraudulently sold company assets and pocketed the money, Adrian notified the police then moved on. When I asked him why he didn't dedicate more time to bringing his fraudulent employee to justice, Adrian said, 'That would be a distraction. I now have to focus on keeping the company solvent.'

Sunflower bias is the tendency of people in a hierarchy to make decisions based on what their leader thinks, or what they guess the leader would think, even when they think their leader is wrong. It's also referred to as **authority bias** or a **steep command gradient**. People operating under this bias ignore their own knowledge and experience and simply go along with what the boss says, even if it's a decision they would reject coming from someone else. Often this is a subconscious process where people dismiss their own opinions because they feel their leader 'must know better'.

Champion bias is about giving the benefit of the doubt to an idea because of the track record of the person suggesting it, regardless of whether that particular idea has merit or not. It is similar to sunflower bias in that rational assessment of an idea goes out the window.

See the Teamwork and Leadership chapters for practical ways to counter these biases.

Experience bias and the drift to failure

There's one more important bias to watch out for: **experience bias**. Left unchecked, this kills creativity and sets you on a drift to failure.

Experience builds habits and intuition – cumulative benefits for steady, mature or legacy domains. But habits and intuition also become a straitjacket for the mind. When you have a lot of experience in a particular area, it's easy to become overconfident. The problem with overconfidence is that it breeds ignorance, complacency and sometimes recklessness. It's a 'been there, done that' mentality that leaves you blind to new possibilities.

History is again littered with examples. For instance, Digital Equipment Corporation (DEC) founder Ken Olsen, described by Microsoft co-founder Bill Gates as 'one of the true pioneers of computing', said in 1977, 'There is no reason anyone would want a computer in their home.' Thirty years later, then Microsoft CEO Steve Ballmer laughed about Apple's newly released $500 iPhone, saying, 'That is the most expensive phone in the world! And it doesn't appeal to business customers because it doesn't have a keyboard, which makes it not a very good email machine.'

> 'I should have moved faster.' – Steve Ballmer, former CEO of Microsoft

Experience can be a curse. Familiarity does not only breed contempt, it breeds biases and, sometimes, complacency. Any increase in experience and expertise is normally associated with an increase in bias and a reduction in creativity. When bias builds, we become blinkered and prisoners of our own mind.

'I used to say "experience kills". In my business I would see people do unsafe things just because they had always done them that way . . . often shortcuts, and the way we found out about them was in an investigation after they died.' – Ann Pickard, Former Chair of Shell Australia

Experience bias makes us hold on to legacy beliefs, things we accept without proof. Without creativity and scientific scrutiny, beliefs persist forever.

Experience bias combines with confirmation bias to warp our values. Along our journey of acquiring experience, new values that are reinforced become confirmed and anchored as core values. When these values become strong enough, we reject new evidence that counters those core values.

To minimise this **drift to failure**:

- Maintain expertise as you age. Do not succumb to ego, complacency or the skills gap.
- Welcome change, don't fear it. Equilibrium is the precursor to death. Our competitors continue to evolve – so we must do the same. I like the Chinese proverb, 'When the winds of change blow, some people build walls. Others build windmills.'
- Commit to a lifetime of learning and experiencing. Adaptation and learning multiplies experience and improves our resilience.
- Embrace creative destruction. Information, just like computers and other tech gadgets, has a half-life that is continually getting shorter. Accept that you must get rid of laggard skills to make way for the new.

Goodbye creativity

Experience and creativity are mutually exclusive. Creativity exists in the young because they have little experience to contextualise their abundant facts into wisdom. As you age, maturity, experience and intuition are acquired at the expense of creativity and recklessness. And there's nothing that you can do to prevent it. We all become prisoners of our experience. For most of us, by the end of our life, even when we think we have it, there is almost no creativity left. Even those who had been keen-eyed proponents of innovation early on can fall into this trap.

Supporting graphs and findings at Fly-TheBook.com present the basic relationships between age, grey and white matter, experience, wisdom, creativity and recklessness, and the metamorphosis every person goes through as they age.

Experience bias test

This simple test demonstrates experience bias. Look at the two lines of text. The letters of the alphabet are placed, in order, with some on the top row and some on the bottom. Your challenge is to start a timer then determine whether 'Z' should be on the top or bottom row. If you can't figure it out, consult a teenager. If you're both stuck, ask a younger child to help.

A				E	F		H	I		K	L	M	N					T		V	W	X	Y	?
	B	C	D		G			J						O	P	Q	R	S		U				?

(The answer is on page 161)

Harness creativity and experience

Life offers you different qualities at different stages. Make the most of them.

- Recklessness and creativity are highest in our first 30 years. Enjoy being young, scared and reckless. Enjoy and be proud to be creative. Be weird, think outside the square and push boundaries, 'because the crazy people who think they can change the world, are the ones that do', as Steve Jobs said.

- Wisdom peaks in your fifties. Since we can't prevent experience bias, take advantage of it. Focus on your wisdom born of experience. Experimental innovation is the key to sustaining originality as we age. Adapt, experiment and innovate using your existing knowledge to attain eminence in your STEAM (Science, Technology, Engineering, Arts, Maths) field. Read, brainstorm and invert the logic.

The dangers of groupthink

Groupthink refers to the fact that most people behave differently in a group than they would on their own. In her book *The Unthinkable: Who Survives When Disaster Strikes – and Why*, Amanda Ripley describes groupthink as 'the adaptive strategy of prioritising group harmony'. People follow the group view to support each other and reduce conflict.

But in the process of 'drinking the Kool-Aid' to bolster the culture, they become passive, uncreative and tunnel-visioned. In a disaster, most people move in groups if they can. Many passengers die in aircraft emergencies because they follow the rest of the crowd rather than escape through closer exits.

To counter groupthink, everyone should gather their own data and make their own decisions independent of others, especially their superiors. My Ramp decision-making process (pages 223–5) helps with this.

Unreliable memory

Unreliable memories hamper your ability to make good decisions. Kahneman and Tversky described the way people try to figure out the likelihood of complicated things happening – we compare the available information to the closest mental model we have, creating scenarios. We do this for everything from 'Is my partner preparing to leave me?' and 'Is the company I've invested in failing?' to 'Is my country heading towards war?'

We create these scenarios based on our memories. We predict the future and change our behaviours based on the past. Unless we have 100 per cent accurate and unbiased recall, we create confabulated scenarios based on fabricated, flawed and incomplete data. And no-one has 100 per cent accurate recall.

When you ask a group of people to describe a shared experience, no two accounts will match perfectly. Each person will have noticed some things and not others, got some things right and misremembered others. The more time that passes, the more unreliable our memories become. Remind yourself of this next time you're making a decision based on little more than the scenarios you have dreamed up.

Coral has refused to eat oysters her entire adult life. She always told people it was because, when she was young, someone thrust an oyster into her mouth. That's what she remembered. Forty years later, when she mentioned this to her older sister, Neralie replied, 'No, you're wrong – that happened to me, not you. That's my story!' Coral remains incredulous to this day, still not sure whose memory is correct.

Making better decisions

With so many things affecting our decision-making, how can we learn to make consistently good decisions? Using strong decision-making models can help. Such frameworks don't tell you what to decide, but guide you through the process in a way designed to minimise the effects of unconscious bias and knowledge gaps.

Traditionally, the office of US President is about as high-pressure as it gets, with intensely important decisions needing to be made every day. Being able to prioritise competing demands is a must.

Each President has had their own preference for how to make fast decisions.

- Dwight D. Eisenhower used a four-point grid. 'Urgent' was on the left of the grid and 'Not Urgent' on the right. 'Important' on top and 'Not Important' below. Things he needed to consider were allocated one of four possible priorities: urgent and important; urgent and non-important; non-urgent and important; or non-urgent and non-important.

	Urgent	Not Urgent
Important	1	3
Not Important	2	4

- Barack Obama separated decisions by allocating the documents that reached his desk to one of three piles: Agree, Disagree, Let's Talk About It.

No decision-making model is perfect, but many are useful. Danish system safety and human factors expert Professor Jens Rasmussen developed a Step Ladder Model that provides the most concise sequence of tasks and required knowledge to detect errors then make decisions to solve problems. I've simplified the model to:

1. Detection: Recognise that a problem exists
2. Understanding: Define the problem, predict consequences and resulting limitations
3. Prioritisation: Prioritise the problem against other failures
4. Selection: Identify, decide and plan appropriate countermeasures
5. Execution: Execute the action plan

Organisations share many decision models that generally conform with Rasmussen's decision ladder.

- The military uses the OODA loop to make many rapid decisions faster than the enemy. OODA stands for Observe, Orient, Decide and Act.
- Boeing uses NMATE: Navigate, Manage, Alternatives, Take Action and Evaluate.
- The US Federal Aviation Authority uses DECIDE: Detect, Estimate, Choose, Identify, Do, Evaluate.

IGRADEE decision model

When I have time, I use the IGRADEE mnemonic when making complex decisions. IGRADEE stands for Identify, Gather, Review, Analyse, Decide, Execute and Evaluate.

Step 1: Identify the problem

Sounds simple, right? It's not. Many people (and computers) mis-identify the problem, confuse the issue and come up with a decision aimed to treat symptoms rather than the cause. In the worst cases, the cure is worse than the disease.

It's easy to misidentify errors. In 1993, I was First Officer, flying a Boeing 747 that had just taken off from Frankfurt heading to Bangkok when we had an emergency (more on this in the next chapter). Initially the aircraft warning computers displayed a warning message about low oil pressure in engine 2 and I started acting on this. Fifteen seconds later I realised that we had a much greater problem than just low oil pressure – the engine had failed! During the QF32 crisis, ECAM's synoptic displays indicated false information and checklists about the brakes, electrics, engine, fire, fuel, hydraulics and a couple of other systems. We had to rely on our own skills to get to the truth.

Most problems in life don't come with computer read-outs, making identifying the crux of the problem even trickier. The first rule is to slow down, sit on your hands, look around, and think.

It can help to write things down. Try to express the problem in one simple sentence. Then, separately, list the effects that problem is having on you. Be sceptical if there are no secondary effects – perhaps the warning is false. Now review the problem you've written to see if it is, instead, a symptom of a deeper fault.

Be aware of subconscious biases at play. Ask a trusted and impartial person for their thoughts. Before I action an emergency checklist, I ask my support pilot, 'What do you see?'

Step 2: Gather your information

Resist placing blind trust in computers and software. Even the best are still only programmed by humans to deal with known possibilities and their behaviour may become unpredictable in unusual or unexpected situations. Whenever software programmers say, 'pearls in, pearls out', the sceptic in me thinks, 'garbage in, garbage out'.

Be sceptical of your sources for information. There has never been a greater need to separate facts from beliefs, rumours, assumptions, fake news and subterfuge. Understand the difference between opinion, anecdote and verified fact. Beware of citogenesis (the circular process of creating reliable sources from false facts). Don't base any important decisions on blogs, Google searches or social media. Look at who is providing the information and why they are doing so.

Use as many reputable and reliable sources as possible. Get second opinions to harvest the knowledge of the creative and the experienced experts.

Step 3: Review your information

Review the facts. Do you have enough information to be able to identify all your options, or do you need to revisit Step 2?

Remember the Dunning–Kruger Effect, where our incompetence shields us from realising our incompetence. Reach out again to those you trust to give you a wise, considered perspective. What factors or options can they see that you have missed?

Dissenters, sceptics and iconoclasts acting in good faith should be welcomed in the decision-making process. Although it's confronting being challenged by someone who is in a position of chronic unease (pages 108–9), they identify threats and risks that others miss. These people bulletproof your decision-making process.

Step 4: Analyse your options

Analyse the information and identify your options. Only start this when you are sure that you have sufficient quality data and you are considering the issue from every angle.

'What are the options?' – Sophia de Crespigny

'What are the options?' For their entire lives, my children have heard me ask this question, from the simplest of decisions such as choosing dinner through to the most difficult facing our family. There is never a silly answer. When it's their turn to make a decision, I'm proud to hear them ask the same question.

What are the possible consequences for each option? Listing them as pros and cons is often a good tool in helping to weigh up different possible paths.

There is a useful way to decide the best of many options for one need, such as which car or laptop to buy. First, prioritise your desired features into essential and desirable criteria. Make a grid, listing the prioritised essential criteria followed by desirable criteria down the left axis. Then list your options across the top. Drop options that miss any essential criteria. The final choice is then the option that satisfies the most desirable criteria.

Step 5: Decide

Remove distractions. Clear some space in your diary; turn your phone off; arrange for someone else to take over carer responsibilities. Avoid getting jittery from too much caffeine.

Take the time you need. Don't rush. Put yourself in the best possible state. Wherever possible, sleep on big decisions. Dreams can be creative. You will make a better decision when you have a rested, clear and creative mind.

Get your body moving in the lead-up to important decisions. Habitual exercise such as running or swimming boosts alertness and memory and expands free mental space, improving creativity and problem-solving ability.

Consider the options you have identified, and the pros and cons of each. Then make a decision, confident that you have put everything in place to ensure it will be a successful one.

If you are finding it hard to select one solution from many equally acceptable options, then trust and follow your gut instincts (more about this at the end of the chapter).

It's important to know when to break the rules, because sometimes you will have to.

'Rules are for the guidance of wise men and the blind obedience of fools.' – Solon, Athenian Statesman, Lawmaker and Poet

There's no point following all the rules if you don't survive. Pilots face this dilemma occasionally. Our operations are governed by multiple tiers of regulations, but rules and Standard Operating Procedures can never cover every scenario, so we must be confident about breaking the rules when safety is at stake.

Be legal, but if you can't be legal, then be safe. Make decisions knowing that afterwards, if you were to stand in a court of law, you could justify your decisions because they were made to protect and save lives.

Step 6: Execute

With so much careful preparation and the support of an engaged team, you've given yourself an excellent chance of making the best decision. So, go ahead, act on it.

If it's appropriate, delegate tasks so that you can sit back, maximise your free mental space and monitor the actions and their outcomes. If you made the right decision, your situation awareness will extend comfortably ahead of the operation.

Remain alert for any signs of surprise or a response that is not what you expected. These are signs that you might have made the wrong decision and need to restart the IGRADEE loop.

Step 7: Evaluate

Every decision you make is a learning opportunity. Feedback on how well things turned out is extremely valuable information. Engineer, innovator and CEO of Tesla and SpaceX Elon Musk said, 'It's very important to have a feedback loop, where you're constantly thinking about what you've done and how you could be doing it better.' In fact, these loops are a critical part of decision-making processes.

Major General John Cantwell, former Commander for the Australian Forces in the Middle East and Afghanistan, has an excellent checklist for evaluating decisions:

- What were the intended results?
- What were the actual results?
- What caused our results?
- How can we do better next time?

Understanding risk

Making good decisions doesn't eliminate risk. And nor should it. We must take risks in life in order to progress, because there can be no reward without risk-taking.

First, set your risk appetite. Risk appetite is the level of risk you are willing to accept when pursuing your goals.

Your risk appetite will change with the stages of your life. Young single people can take greater risks such as skydiving, racing motorbikes or investing in speculative shares, because the consequences of failure affect only a few. Your risk appetite must decrease with the arrival of children who need a home, healthy parents and an education. Your risk appetite must reduce even more as you save and protect your assets for retirement. Only when you determine your current risk appetite can you then select your range of acceptable risks.

Good decisions are based on balancing calculated risks and security. In his book *Beyond Fear: Thinking Sensibly About Security in an Uncertain World*, privacy and digital security expert Bruce Schneier suggests we take 'street-smart' risks, moving beyond fearful headlines to get a feel for the real threats, risks and countermeasures. This knowledge lets us think sensibly about opportunities and trade-offs, improving the odds of us making sensible decisions and taking risks that pay back.

When you gain the ability to make such decisions, you are what British High Court Judge Sir Charles Haddon-Cave calls 'Risk Sensible'. Haddon-Cave describes the three other possible states as Risk Ignorant, Risk Cavalier and Risk Averse, all of which are potentially dangerous. We should all, he says, be Risk Sensible. This means 'embracing risk, unbundling it, analysing it and taking a measured and balanced view'.

But how much do you really know about risk and how to calculate it? In normal conversation, the words risk, threat and gamble are thrown around very loosely – they're often used as if they are interchangeable. But they are not.

A **threat** is the possibility of something bad happening. Untreatable cancer and a fatal meteorite strike pose the same level of threat: death in each case. The concepts of Threat and Error Management (TEM) require that all threats be prevented, fixed or mitigated.

A **risk** is the probability that something will occur multiplied by the consequence if it does. The risk of death by cancer is far greater than the risk of dying by meteorite strike because the former is much more likely to happen than the latter.

A **gamble** is an unmitigated risk. Rock-climbing with a safety harness is a risk. Alex Honnold's 2017 solo free climb (with no harness) of Yosemite National Park's 900-metre high El Capitan was a gamble.

Most of us are poor judges of risk. Why do people who fear flying not also fear driving or going to the hospital? According to the Chapman University's 2017 Survey of American Fears, nine per cent of Americans experience fear of flying, while fear of driving does not make the top 80. Does this make sense? In 2017, 40,100 people died in traffic-related incidents in the United States. Over the same period in the same country not a single person died in a commercial aviation incident. Worldwide the figures for the year were an estimated 1.25 million road deaths and just 44 in commercial aviation incidents. Fear of sharks is another example of an illogical fear. On average there are only six unprovoked fatal shark attacks each year worldwide. People who fear succumbing to sharks or fear flying should more logically be terrified of driving.

To make good decisions you need to understand risk, and to do that you need to know at least the basics of how probability works.

Understanding probability

Probability is the likelihood or chance of something happening. This stumps a lot of people, but it doesn't have to. If you're not maths-oriented you might feel you'll never grasp it, but stick with me here. Try the following two challenges.

Probability challenge 1
You are tossing a coin (a perfectly fair, evenly weighted coin). The coin has two sides, heads and tails, and each side has the same chance

of coming up as the other. In other words, when you first toss the coin into the air there is a 50 per cent chance it will land on heads and a 50 per cent chance it will land on tails. You toss the coin five times and it lands on heads every single time. What is the chance it will land on tails on the sixth toss?

Probability challenge 2

As you board a flight, the cabin attendant greets you and tells you you're being given the opportunity to upgrade to First Class. Nice!

In front of you are three seats. On each seat is a cushion turned face down. On the hidden side, two of the cushions are labelled 'Economy' while the remaining cushion is labelled 'First Class'. All you have to do is pick the First Class cushion.

You pick a cushion.

Instead of turning over your chosen cushion immediately, the cabin attendant pauses and turns over one of the remaining two cushions, revealing its label 'Economy'. He asks, 'Do you want to stay with your initial choice or would you like to change to the remaining cushion?'

What gives you the best chance of winning the upgrade?

a) Keep your original selection.
b) Select the other remaining cushion.
c) It does not matter which of the two is chosen, the chances are equal.

The answers are on pages 161–2.

The micromort – a tool for comparing risk

The micromort is an excellent measure of risk. Created by Stanford University Professor of Management Science and Engineering Ronald A. Howard, it is a unit that represents how likely any given situation or activity is to result in death. One micromort equals a one in a million chance of death. If something has a micromort of 10, on average 10 people in one million will die doing it.

How would you rate the relative risks of skydiving versus running a marathon? Skydiving has to be riskier, right? It is, but it might surprise you by how little. Each skydive has a risk of eight micromorts, slightly more than seven for running a marathon. Each ascent of Mount Everest has a risk of 40,000 micromorts.

You consume one micromort of risk every time you:

- complete 660 rollercoaster rides
- take a single horse ride
- fly 10,000 km in a commercial aircraft
- drive 400 km in a car
- ride 10 km on a motorbike
- fly nine km in a private aircraft
- run six km in a marathon.

The micromort is a good measure of industrial safety. For instance, researchers at Johns Hopkins University estimated there were 251,454 deaths from medical errors in 2013 from a base of 35,416,020 hospitalisations.

Medical error, at 9.5 per cent of all deaths, is the third cause of death in the United States. A better comparison is that each and every hospitalisation in the United States in 2013 had a risk of 7100 micromorts, the same risk as flying more than 70,000 one-hour commercial flights.

Is our fear of terrorism justified? The risk of an American dying from guns is 234 times higher than the risk of dying from terrorism. From 1995 to 2016, an American consumed one micromort from guns every three days, and one micromort from terrorism every 670 days.

Black Swans and accidents waiting to happen

A Black Swan event is something so improbable and unprecedented that 'no-one saw it coming', but which happens anyway and has severe consequences.

(The phrase was popularised by statistician turned hedge-fund manager turned academic Nassim Nicholas Taleb, now Distinguished Professor of Risk Engineering at NYU. It comes from the fact that in Roman times, 'black swan' was a metaphor for something theoretically possible but non-existent. European exploration of Australia, where the birds originate, proved otherwise.)

Real-world Black Swan events

Pilots are trained to recover from engine failures. Most engine failures are contained, meaning the cowlings prevent exploding engine parts escaping and damaging the rest of the aircraft structure. Uncontained engine failures are rare, but certainly not unknown.

But QF32 was different. QF32 was a Black Swan event. The ATSB report stated the failure of the IP turbine disc in QF32 was the first uncontained rotor failure involving a third-generation high-bypass turbofan engine. It was the first failure of this kind of engine in 40 years and 200 million engine hours. Not to mention that half of the aircraft's computer networks and around 650 wires were severed.

Most of the world would describe 9/11 as a Black Swan event. But as unlikely as it was, Rick Rescorla (whose story is told in Chapter 3) had envisioned just such a scenario. People thought his concerns were unwarranted, but he was proved right. Without his preparations the death toll from the attacks may have doubled. What other 'impossible' threats might he have foreseen?

Like the very few financial analysts who saw the Global Financial Crisis coming, Rescorla didn't let groupthink lull him into dangerous complacency. Neither should you when you are assessing and analysing risk as part of your own decision-making.

Deepwater Horizon – when is a Black Swan not a Black Swan?
As CEO of BP at the time of the Deepwater Horizon disaster, Tony Hayward was the polar opposite of Rick Rescorla. Far from imagining the unimaginable, Hayward oversaw a culture in which clear warning signs were repeatedly ignored while risks piled up. The 2010 explosion on the offshore drilling rig, which killed 11 crew and caused the largest oil spill in US history, was not a Black Swan event, it was an accident waiting to happen.

Just five years earlier in one of the worst industrial accidents in US history, an explosion at BP's Texas City refinery had killed 15 workers and injured 180. It happened, the company admitted, because safety procedures were ignored. The following year, after warning signs were again ignored, more than 760,000 litres (200,000 gallons) of crude oil leaked onto the Alaskan tundra in two separate events. BP had 760 safety citations over the three years prior to the spill. Workers felt unsafe but management would not listen.

Despite this, in 2007 after Hayward was given the top job of the financially struggling company he said BP had become over-cautious in its decision-making procedures: 'Assurance is killing us.' Over the next few years, those who raised concerns about problems at BP continued to be ignored, while many stayed silent for fear of reprisal. Hayward seemingly wasn't interested in hearing about the risks inherent in the decisions the company was pushing through, saying, 'Either get on the bus or get out; the bus is rolling.'

Unmitigated risks are naked gambles. Eventually, under Hayward's rule, BP rolled the dice one too many times. In addition to the lives lost and damaged and the huge environmental toll, the Deepwater catastrophe cost the company more than US$60 billion in fines and settlements.

'Only when the tide goes out do you discover who's been swimming naked.' – Warren Buffett, Investor par Excellence

The Deepwater Horizon disaster was a preventable accident which happened, according to UC Berkeley's Center for Catastrophic Risk Management, because BP and Transocean, which owned the rig, 'forgot to be afraid'. Other than a few brave outliers who paid the price for speaking up, capable people in both BP and Transocean fell prey to groupthink. Their attitude was, 'If everyone is going along with it, it must be okay.'

Risk assessments – doing it right

If Hayward had wanted to speed up risk assessment and analysis at BP properly, he should have consulted the Kiwis at Air New Zealand, since they provide an excellent example of how taking your time and doing it right can deliver a competitive advantage.

David Morgan, the Chief Operations Integrity & Standards Officer/Chief Pilot at Air New Zealand, tells a compelling story about the way being proactive in calculating risks paid off when Chile's Puyehue-Cordón Caulle volcano erupted. This was just 14 months after the Eyjafjallajökull volcano had erupted in Iceland in 2010, grounding millions of passengers as 102,000 flights were cancelled at a cost of US$200 million per day.

At the time of Eyjafjallajökull, no industry standards existed to specify the concentration of atmospheric ash at which it was safe to resume commercial passenger flights. That was still the case on 4 June 2011 when Puyehue-Cordón Caulle went up.

All flights in the southern hemisphere were grounded as a result of the Chilean eruption. However, one week later an Air New Zealand crew delivered the first aircraft into Sydney since the eruption, bringing a Boeing 777 from Auckland full of happy passengers, including pilots from other grounded airlines. Immediately after the aircraft parked at Sydney, officials from the Australian Civil Aviation Safety Authority entered the cockpit, demanding to know why Air New Zealand aircraft were operating when other airlines were grounded.

The Air New Zealand crew handed over their risk assessment for volcanic ash, a 100-page document that had been prepared well in advance of the latest problem. Yes, it no doubt focuses the mind when your country has active volcanoes of its own. But New Zealand is not the only country of which that's true. Yet the flag carrier for a country with a population under five million was the world's only airline to have prepared a proper risk assessment for flight in the vicinity of volcanic ash.

Neil Armstrong – assessing risk and making decisions under pressure

Few people have had to make critical decisions or assess risks under such intense pressure as astronauts Neil Armstrong and Buzz Aldrin. Neil's name will live on in history as the first person to set foot on the moon, but despite four years' effort by 400,000 NASA workers dedicated to achieving this feat, and four days' space travel to get there, it all came down to the last 10 minutes before the planned landing. Things might have ended very differently if Armstrong hadn't been so good at sifting through the facts and making right decisions under intense stress.

If you were lucky enough to spend time with this remarkable man, you didn't ask Neil what it was like to land on or walk on the moon. Understandably, he was sick to death of those questions, having been asked them countless times since the Apollo 11 mission in July 1969. When I had the pleasure of taking him for a cruise on Sydney Harbour in 2012, my dilemma wasn't avoiding those questions; it was choosing one of the hundred others I had about aerospace dynamics.

Ultimately, there was one thing I wanted to know most of all. I asked, 'Neil, when you were sitting atop the 363-feet-high Saturn Five rocket and they were about to light the candle to launch you into space, what probability did you give yourself of coming home alive?'

Neil said, 'I think we had just a 50 per cent chance of landing on the moon. If we had a problem approaching to land, we would have aborted the landing and rendezvoused with Mike Collins in the Command Module and returned home. We also had special procedures to mitigate many failure contingencies, including a "free return trajectory" up our sleeve in the event of failures on our way to the moon. So, we gave ourselves a 50 per cent chance of landing on the moon and a 90 per cent chance of coming home alive.'

Executive overload

In fact, there had been problems as the lunar lander made its approach – not just one problem, but a series of them. However, Armstrong and the team supporting him methodically worked their way through them, making a chain of rapid decisions that led to the successful outcome watched by 600 million people back on Earth. As a navy pilot and NASA test pilot, Neil had made many critical decisions over the years, but none as high-stakes as this.

He had memorised many speed–position–height check gates for the approach, and saw that readings were now indicating the Eagle was above the intended approach path. (The failure to decompress the docking tunnel during lunar orbit had given it an extra push.) Neil and Buzz were as far from home and safety as it was possible to get. For all the support back in Houston, ultimately, they were on their own.

As mentioned in Chapter 5, the Apollo 11 crew had practised in specially built training versions of the Lunar Landing Training Vehicle (LLTV) until they knew it inside out . . . or so they thought.

As Armstrong and Aldrin descended towards the moon's surface, an alarm number appeared that they had never seen before. Back at Ground Control, 384,000 km (239,000 miles) away, 26-year-old guidance officer Steve Bales frantically searched through his fat folder of error codes for number 1202.

Bales relayed to Neil the message, 'We're Go!' This meant he should continue as planned, ignoring the alarm, which indicated data was overloading the lander's computer. The state-of-the-art computers built especially for the mission, one in the Command Module and one in the Lunar Module, had only 74 kb of iron core memory between them. A single 32GB iPhone has seven million times more memory.

The 1202 error warned the computers were going into 'executive overload' and restarting themselves. 'If it doesn't reoccur, we'll be go,' said Bales. But the error did reoccur, many times.

The Eagle was descending at more than 15 metres (50 feet) per second, flying on autopilot, responding to directions from the navigation, management and performance computers to perform an automatic landing. All the while information was being relayed back and forth with a three-second delay across that enormous distance to Earth. The plans were that Neil would be looking outside at this point to view the landing site early, but that was not to be. Armstrong's mantra to 'expect the unexpected' was now being put to the ultimate test.

A yellow caution light, the 1202 error message and alarm bells actioned twice more over the next four minutes as the Eagle continued descending. Then, descending through 900 metres (3000 feet), new alarms sounded twice for 1201 errors. Neil and Buzz didn't know what either warning meant – they had practised this descent a hundred times in the simulator without ever seeing them.

As the alarm bells rang for the fifth time, the controllers called, 'Descent 2 fuel critical.' Instead of having eyes outside, the two astronauts were still eyes inside, clearing the alarms, keeping the Eagle flying and assuring themselves they had sufficient control to continue without aborting. Armstrong's heart rate rose from 130 to 150 beats per minute.

Finally, after descending to the point where there was only 600 metres (2000 feet) left to go, Neil had his first opportunity to look outside and identify the landing site. What he saw was not what he was expecting.

Continue or abort?

As a pilot in the Korean War, Neil had often returned to his aircraft carrier with just enough fuel, landing on the pitching deck of an aircraft carrier. But this approach was harder. Their approach path was aiming them down inside a crater dotted with boulders, and they would not be able to take off again if the Eagle settled at an angle on unstable ground.

Weighing up his options, with just seconds to go, he made his next decision. He disconnected the automatic landing system and took manual control of the Eagle in order to extend the approach and reach a safer landing spot. Experience in the LLTVs was about to pay dividends.

Back on Earth, Ground Control staff were increasingly worried about the probability of an abort. On top of the computer errors, the high approach path and the unsuitable landing site, there was the issue of fuel. Practice landings were normally achieved with two minutes' worth of fuel remaining, but the Eagle's tanks were reading all but empty.

Warning lights, unknown warning messages, warning bells, high flight path, autoland disconnected, imminent fuel exhaustion – he prioritised these risks, cut through the noise, didn't panic and didn't abort. Instead, he calmly steered the Eagle towards clear ground.

Seconds later, in a phrase that became world famous, Neil Armstrong reported to Houston, 'Eagle has landed.' There was 20 seconds worth of fuel remaining.

Neil Armstrong = Resilience

Many factors went into Armstrong's ability to weigh up the risks and make strong decisions with positive outcomes. One was Deliberate Practice. Along with the other crew members, he had trained for the mission so purposefully and intensely that he knew the limits of his craft and how far they could be pushed. Even though he had not seen the two computer alarm codes before, he had seen plenty of other error codes and could rule them out. He also recognised that the Eagle was still operating well.

The previous study Armstrong had put into every aspect of the approach and landing enabled him to detect the approach course errors. And the skills and experience he had built up over previous missions gave him the confidence to make the courageous call to switch from autopilot to manual flight, and to see that to a successful conclusion.

No-one at NASA knew at that time why the 1201 and 1202 errors occurred during that approach. There were so many questions and so many threats for Houston to track that in the last stages, they went quiet and just called the fuel levels. It didn't matter. Neil remained on top of it all, kept calm and followed his basic intuition: that you never abort for a single indication.

An Everest story – when turning back is the right call

Dr John Taske is another who made a fateful decision that had to take into account many factors, in his case in May 1996. Like Neil Armstrong, Taske was so close to achieving a huge, longstanding goal that he could almost taste it. But unlike Armstrong, Taske made the hard call to turn back.

Taske, an Australian anaesthetist who had served in various capacities in the Vietnam War, including as a Special Air Services commando, was in the Adventure Consultants team led by New Zealander Rob Hall as they attempted to climb Mount Everest. Four other teams were also on the mountain when a blizzard struck. With many of the climbers far from the safety of their camp due to earlier errors and problems, the conditions proved catastrophic.

John Taske survived because he kept to his plan and turned back. He did so despite having spent six years (and a great deal of money) working up to the climb and despite being just 198 metres short of Everest's 8848-metre peak.

Due to the chain of delays, Taske was three and a half hours behind schedule when he reached this point, and he realised he would not reach the summit until 3 pm. However, the group's carefully constructed plan required its members to turn back if they weren't there by 2 pm.

Taske knew that pushing on would have meant descending in darkness, and the time overrun had left him with a dangerously low oxygen supply. He also knew that more people died coming down the mountain than going up it.

Therefore, despite being so close to a lifelong dream, he resisted summit fever, turned back and was safely in camp when the blizzard hit. Eight people perished on Everest that night, including four from Taske's team who decided to continue. Many more suffered permanent injuries.

John Taske said later, 'At the time I felt very depressed and disappointed, but certain that the decision was correct.' He survived because he followed his own golden rule of decision-making: 'Never change a technical plan for emotional reasons.'

Remember, good decisions aren't always easy and easy decisions aren't always good.

Habits, instincts, intuition and gut feelings

Sometimes time is limited, and decisions must be made without all the facts at hand. We must resist the urge towards perfection, because we can never achieve it. This is the time to trust our gut feelings.

- Gut feelings are subconscious instincts, habits and intuition, operating below the reach of conscious analytical reasoning and language.
- Instincts are innate, subconscious responses acquired naturally without any training. The startle effect (fight, flight or freeze) is an instinct.
- Habits are subconscious responses acquired through learning and repetition. Tiger Woods' golf swing is an example.

- Intuition is subconscious recognition-wisdom. It's cognition that does not require rational thought and inference. Intuition is created by making repeated complex decisions that are reinforced by positive feedback.

'The unconscious system recognises patterns using context to antici-pate events. It fills the gaps, reconciling disconnected elements to stitch together plot lines and our gut feelings to maintain a complete personal narrative.' – Eliezer Sternberg, Neurologist

Instinctive fears

Our most basic fears originate in the part of the brain known as the amygdala. The amygdala monitors input from the senses and responds to what it perceives as threats in the only way possible – fight, flight or freeze/play dead. When our amygdala alerts us to fear, it's in a gut feeling. There are physical manifestations, including raised heart rate and increased respiration, but words aren't required.

Intuition

Intuition is our subconscious perception of a situation. Intuition is the sum of our knowledge, experience, senses and mental model, bound by our values and beliefs (our WHYS), hidden beneath analytic thought and reasoning. It is like a dashboard that gives us confidence when we are safe, or a master-warning and escape path when danger is ahead.

When we find ourselves in a storm of unknowns, with no solutions from our analytical mind, this is the true test of our intuition and our resilience. This is normal life for test pilots, military commandos and firefighters, who survive with only their skills and experience as a defence.

Firefighters have great intuition. They have to, to survive. They routinely make life-or-death decisions about whether or where to enter a burning building. They are able to dynamically assess complex situations and make correct decisions within seconds. If you ask them how they made their decisions they are likely to say, 'I don't know; it just seemed obvious.' In fact, it is the result of intuition acquired from studying, making and learning from many similar decisions in the past.

Eliezer Sternberg explains how intuition works when we have to make decisions without all the facts: 'Whenever our perceptions are incomplete or we don't have all the facts, the brain unconsciously draws on the background knowledge to help supply the rest of the story.'

If we have trained and acquired enough experience to build habits and intuitions, then these gut feelings will inhibit our instinctive reactions and give us a path to the best outcome.

My intuition has served me well many times in my professional career.

- In January 1994, I refused to accept a B747 Jumbo from the engineers in Bangkok. The aircraft had suffered multiple vibration fractures in both loops of a fire warning system. Despite the engineers' insistence that we must accept the aircraft, my gut instincts made me feel something was not right. We agreed to do a test of the engine while safely on the ground. Sure enough, when we revved it up to 20 per cent thrust the $10 million engine exploded.
- Sixteen years later I experienced the greatest gut feeling of my career, 12 minutes after engine 2 exploded during my QF32 flight. Many ECAM checklists were confusing and wrong, the stress was increasing and then both fuel computers failed. My mind became overloaded. I thought, 'If I can't guarantee fuel, then I can't guarantee flight.' I pressed the radio transmitter button and said, 'Singapore, we have to climb to a higher altitude of 10,000 and we need to remain within 30 miles of the airport': my intuitive requirements to set up for an Armstrong Spiral.

What I would call intuition and Captain Sully Sullenberger calls para-digms saved all 155 lives on board Flight 1549 in 2009. Six years later, giving evidence before a US Senate sub-committee, Sully said, 'I saw the birds just 100 seconds after take-off, about two seconds before we hit them. We were travelling at 316 feet per second, and there was not enough time or distance to manoeuvre a jet airliner away from them. When they struck and damaged both engines, we had just 208 seconds to do something we had never trained for, and get it right the first time. The fact that we landed a commercial airliner on the Hudson River with no engines and no fatalities was not a miracle, however. It was the result of teamwork, skill, in-depth knowledge, and the kind of judgment that comes only from experience.'

Be critical of your gut feelings:
- Don't fall prey to conceit and the Dunning–Kruger Effect (pages 127–9).
- Don't change prepared technical decisions for emotional reasons.
- If something doesn't make sense, then you are missing or blind to something.

Trust your gut feelings when you must make a decision but there's insufficient time and information to make a slow, conscious and informed decision, and when working in your area of experience.

Don't fully trust your gut feelings when you are outside the domain of your expertise. Even when something 'feels right', you might fall prey to instincts, habits and biases.

Answers to the tests and puzzles in this chapter

Mobile phone (page 129)
You are four times more likely to crash when you talk on the phone while driving. Talking on a mobile phone, even hands-free, while driving distracts your slow mind from its role of monitoring safety and staying alert for exceptions.

It's possible to drive a car using habits alone. But when you reduce your free mental space and narrow your situation awareness, you raise the risk of being like the bird that flies at full speed into a window because it fails to notice the house.

Experience bias (page 136)

'Z' belongs on the top line, where the letters are all made using straight lines. The letters in the bottom row have curved segments.

Our biases complicate the simple. We miss the obvious. Instead of seeing dots, lines or shapes, we recognise abstract characters, look for sequences and come up with more abstract associations. We can't see the wood for the trees. Welcome to experience bias.

Coin toss (pages 146–7)

The chance is still 50 per cent. Probability tells us what is likely to happen over time. If you toss a coin 1000 times, the most likely outcome is that you will get heads about half the time. But coins do not have memories. You can't 'even up the score' toss-by-toss, because each toss is an independent event. The only certainty is that the higher the number of coin tosses, the more the outcome will approach the mean (or average).

The First-Class upgrade (page 147)

This is a version of the 'Monty Hall' problem (named for the host of the TV game show *Let's Make a Deal*) and the correct answer is b), you should switch your selection, even though that feels counter-intuitive to most people.

Here's why . . .

When the selection begins, each cushion has a one-in-three chance of being the right one. You make an initial choice, leaving two cushions. The two cushions have a two-in-three chance of including the winner. But then the flight attendant shows you that one of them is a dud. That means the cushion you originally chose still has its original one-in-three chance of being a winner but the cushion that remains from the other pair now has a two-in-three chance. Switching won't guarantee that you win, but it will increase your odds.

If you'd like to get into a good long argument and kill all other conversation, pose this problem to the group at your next social gathering. (And if you're still baffled, you'll find further explanation at Fly-TheBook.com.)

Bottom line

To thrive, you need to be good at making decisions. That means more of your choices will work out well than badly. But even when we think we're being cool, calm and rational, subconscious cognitive biases are influencing our decision-making processes.

The main biases and unrecognised influences you might need to counter are: availability bias, champion bias, choice blindness, confirmation bias, the Dunning–Kruger Effect, experience bias, loss-aversion bias, the sunk-cost fallacy, status quo bias, sunflower bias and groupthink.

Ignorance is not bliss when it comes to decisions. By becoming aware of these biases, understanding how they work and countering them, you can greatly improve your own decision-making abilities.

Decision models such as IGRADEE provide frameworks that make decision-making easier. They offer a step-by-step process with built-in checks and balances to try to minimise these biases, challenge assumptions and, for teams, create clear communication that minimises bad choices and poor implementation.

Risks are important in life. In fact, if it weren't for risk, life as we know it would not exist. But those who survive and thrive are the ones who understand the difference between threats, risks and gambles. They grasp how probability works and weigh up potential consequences. Their decisions are based on eliminating or mitigating threats, taking calculated street-wise risks, and avoiding gambles.

In life, there are some events so unprecedented and unlikely that they are genuine Black Swan events. But often what is presented as a Black Swan event is actually the predictable consequence of a chain of neglect and bad decisions.

The Global Financial Crisis of 2008 was a situation where known and compounding risks were ignored. A culture of ignorance, complacency, arrogance and groupthink makes these situations possible. People who could have made better decisions ignored the signs of increasing risk because everyone else ignored them. The result was a disaster waiting to happen.

Urgent and critical decisions in life-or-death situations draw on all the skills, knowledge and intuition you have built up previously. The more work you have put in and the more Deliberate Practice you have done, the better your chances of being able to sift through complicated information, weigh up options and make the best decision in the circumstances.

Don't make the mistake of thinking that because you know a lot you know it all.

Decision-Making and Risk Assessment: Checklist

Think you're rational? Think again:
We're all subject to subconscious instincts, habits, biases and blind spots. By understanding our cognitive biases we can use strategies to counter them.

But good decision-making is a learned skill:
Learn the skills to make fast and critical decisions.

Good decisions aren't always easy:
And easy decisions aren't always good.

Decision-making models can help:
Following a step-by-step process with built-in checks and balances will help you make better choices in any situation.

We need to take risks:
Set your risk appetite. Risks drive progress and give us individual fulfilment.

But risks, gambles and threats are not the same thing:
To make good choices you need to understand the differences. Every threat must be blocked, fixed or mitigated. Learn to detect, rate and live with risk. Avoid gambles.

Black Swan events:
Don't let groupthink blind you to risk. 'Black Swans' are sometimes just accidents waiting to happen.

Decisions:
Create time, because time gives you options.

1. Avoid jumping straight into non-reversible decisions.
2. If you are in a crisis and don't know what to do, sit on your hands, gather more information and do nothing.
3. If you are not in a crisis then any decision is better than no decision. Don't fall victim to inertia. You may, however, decide to do nothing. That is not the same thing. Whatever you decide, most decisions can be changed.
4. If you must make a decision but don't have time or enough information, then trust your trained habits, intuition and gut feelings.
5. Never change a technical plan for emotional reasons.

CHAPTER 7

Leadership:
Lead, Follow or Get Out of the Way

There has never been a greater need for better leaders. Waves of change, disruption and uncertainty roll in increasingly fast and hard. In this environment, only bold and nimble leaders who can surf the edges of chaos will survive.

The good news is that leadership skills can be learned, and the best leaders lead resilient teams that survive and thrive.

A Black Swan event is a pressure test of leadership. QF32 was a success because each of the teams involved had good leaders. Alan Joyce led the airline. I led the flight, passengers and crew. Michael von Reth led the cabin. Roz Wheatley led the Crisis Management Centre. We all worked effectively, independently and concurrently, with no communications between key teams for long periods.

'Sit down, strap in, shut up and hold on' – the cost of bad leadership

Bad leaders are everywhere. They run families, communities, organisations and governments. They affect our psychological, security, social and aspirational health. Bad leaders are dangerous and reduce our potential.

Bad leadership destroys opportunities. The bad leaders at BP progressively weakened its safety management systems until Deepwater Horizon, the 'accident waiting to happen', took 11 lives, damaged the environment, sea life and bird life, and cost US$40 billion. Thousands of staff and investors lost their life's savings when corrupt leaders destroyed Enron.

Kodak, the company that dominated the print film industry, is now a shadow of its former self because its leaders failed to disrupt their film business and adapt to digital photography that they themselves invented. Bad leadership leaves behind bankruptcy, poverty, trauma and shattered lives. But it gets worse.

History teaches us that many people don't learn from history. Among them are many bad leaders who acquire weapons and start wars, even though, as Sun Tzu wrote in *The Art of War* 2500 years ago, 'there is no instance of a country having benefited from prolonged warfare'.

Good leaders employ politics, strength and deterrents to effect peace. Bad leaders would improve if they thought like the philosopher Lao-Tzu, who supposedly said, 'It is only when you see a mosquito landing on your testicles that you realise that there is always a way to solve problems without violence.'

Why are there so many bad leaders? Perhaps it's ego. Some bad leaders think they were born with natural leadership skills and so need no advice. Maybe it's the result of chance. If, as has been suggested, a person needs to make just eight correct 'big decisions' to become a leader, and tosses a coin to make these decisions, then we can expect one out of 256 people to make eight out of eight correct decisions and, with no additional skills, be promoted into leadership. Perhaps many bad leaders are narcissists or psychopaths who simply don't care.

Bad leadership can't be ignored – the fish rots from the head

A poor leader weakens all those around them. Poor leadership pollutes culture, weakens an organisation's pulse and destroys its resilience. It fragments teams, creating disengagement, helplessness and groupthink. Left unchecked, it destroys businesses, careers and, in extreme cases, even lives.

Where corporate governance and leadership have gone wrong, you'll often find an autocratic CEO or chairman reigning over a board of sycophants. Warning lights flash for me when I see a title such as 'Chairman and CEO'. This means the same person is responsible for the often-competing demands of strategy, governance and execution. There's probably no tolerance in this company for checks and balances, counter-views and debate. It is a petri dish that allows bullying and groupthink to flourish. In this high-risk situation, success and failure could rest on the actions of just one person. When things come crashing down, the dangerous flaws are belatedly revealed.

The 'Chair and CEO' title has been a longstanding practice in the US which is wisely frowned upon elsewhere. Australia's ASX Corporate Governance Principles includes the recommendation: *'The Chair of the Board of a listed entity should be an independent director and, in particular, should not be the same person as the CEO of the entity'.* I am also sceptical of the title 'Founder and CEO', because different skills are required to start and lead a company; few people do both well.

There are exceptions to every rule. Warren Buffett has proved to be an excellent Chairman and CEO of Berkshire Hathaway. Nevertheless, the company runs a risk being under one person's influence and could fail if Buffett's successor turns out to be like the former Chairman and CEO of Enron.

Leaders who present themselves as superhumans should also arouse suspicion. We hear CEOs claiming to rise at 4 am (after going to bed at midnight) to begin a 15-hour work day. It's presented as something to admire. But would you be comfortable on an aircraft with a tired pilot who has had only four of hours sleep, or having heart surgery done by a surgeon who was similarly 'rested'? How can four hours of sleep produce the energy, free mental space and refreshed outlook required from an effective leader? Likewise, a leader's 15-hour workday, rather than being an advantage, might indicate poor delegation skills.

My cousin Robert Champion de Crespigny AC is a successful entrepreneur who created a mining empire, served as a university chancellor, an advisor to governments and a member on many not-for-profit, industry and educational boards. He has seen many leaders in action. He says, 'Success sometimes breeds cancerous ego and greed. Even good leaders can eventually fall prey to believing their own bulldust. If you look at successful businesses led by very good chief executives, who clearly are great leaders, ego, hubris and conceit nearly always creep in before a fall. They increasingly forget to credit the teams that enabled their success. This is when the rot creeps in. A cook is only as good as his last meal. Generally, when the ego takes over that's when they drop the ball and fall.'

The most effective leaders are aware of the dangers of this kind of hubris. They are empathetic listeners who solicit input from others. They are self-assured, courageous, have a fierce will, and when required, are disagreeable. They are humble and never conceited or aggressive. They are tolerant but not passive or bureaucratic. They adapt to change but are not impetuous. Like trees, they are strong and flexible, not rigid and stiff.

It's easy to recognise the bad leaders. They fail to bring out the best in you and leave chaos in their wake. This is often a deliberate choice. As a regional manager for an international software firm put it to me once, explaining his approach to running his team, 'Conflict is good. Treat them mean, keep them keen. Keep them on their toes.' He couldn't have been more wrong.

Leading with hostility or intransigence is always counterproductive. In any team situation there will be competing ideas and needs, differing views and opinions. Conflict creates stress, kills trust, engagement, teamwork and productivity, and damages health. He didn't last long.

Classic signs identify poor leaders. They:

- are driven and dominated by ego, power and control, using abuse, threats, intimidation and coercion
- hoard information as a source of power
- talk before they listen and think
- close their doors (metaphorically and literally) and selectively filter feedback
- cannot settle on decisions
- lack empathy
- don't trust, so micro-manage others and undermine confidence
- don't support whistleblowers and people who step up
- never admit they have failed
- take the credit for wins and find excuses or blame others for errors and losses.

Bad leaders can teach you a lot, if you can endure them. During the 18 years leading up to achieving my own command, I worked under captains of all kinds, some who embodied good leadership, others who were living examples of what not to do. Among the latter, some were idle and unmotivated, others were angry bullies.

Aggression is camouflage for underconfidence. People use loud, rude, aggressive, sarcastic behaviour to mask paranoia, insecurity and weakness. This is my theory derived after comparing the best captains with the worst over more than 40 years of flying. Leaders like this are most angry when panic sets in and their situation awareness shrinks. (But, by definition, they are not aware of their behaviour because they have lost situation awareness.) In the process they kindle fear and aggression, creating a toxic cockpit culture. Calm, trust and psychological safety dissolve as stress levels rise. Mistakes are made when stress rises and people withdraw support or the confidence level drops, and that in turn angers the leader even more. The cockpit environment could become so toxic that pilots scheduled to fly with the worst captains would often call in sick.

Fortunately, those days are over. Captains in my airline are assessed five times every year for their 'human factors' skills. They will be failed if they inhibit a safe cockpit culture. The worst offenders have been sacked.

For others who must endure a bullying leader, I have a possible remedy. If you must work with these people, then try to put yourself into their shoes and understand their fears from their perspective. If you discover their fears, then try to work around them and manage the problem. If the leader becomes a liability, then you must either stand up and take stronger action or resign.

What is 'leadership' anyway?

What does true leadership really look like? Success is not possible without it, yet it's a word that's tossed around far too lightly. Many who hold leadership positions don't have a clue what it really means.

Leadership is the action of leading a group of people or an organisation. In times of change and uncertainty, leadership brings confidence, trust and certainty, often motivating people to do the uncomfortable things they don't want to do, things that are required to survive. So, my definition of a successful leader is one who brings resilience to their team or organisation. A bad leader is one who fails to adapt and evolve with change, so ultimately perishes.

Don't confuse authority with authenticity. Having a corner office or a stratospheric salary doesn't make you a leader, nor does barking out orders at subordinates. Being in charge in a given situation does not make you 'a leader' in the most important sense.

Leadership is not about authority, seniority or ego. It's true that you can't be a leader without someone following you, but leadership doesn't just happen because there is a strict hierarchy or an organisational chart in place.

Leaders of small companies take heart. Leadership is as important in small flat businesses as in large hierarchical corporations. The leadership skills you learn at the bottom end of town are portable to the top.

There are great rewards for being a good leader, but leadership has its price. A win is a team win and a loss is always the leader's fault. If you can't carry the weight of this responsibility, you're not ready to lead.

Do not confuse managing with leading. Managers manage, leaders lead. These are different skills, although there is some overlap, particularly in the areas of motivation and communication.

Managers are accountable for processes and the performance of those they manage. Managing is about following existing procedures to achieve a set goal. Managers must build trust and engagement. They must motivate and care for their teams. Unfortunately, too many organisations promote managers who lack sufficient leadership skills into leadership positions.

Great leaders create great teams. Leaders create the overall vision, the destination, then set the path and procedures to reach that destination. They define values, strategy, culture, vision and priorities. They communicate the WHYs so that everyone is on the same page, working towards the same goal. They are catalysts for change and innovation. They welcome risks, make sound decisions, build effective teams, motivate and inspire. They create environments in which people can safely fail. Today's leaders must do all of this without losing control.

But not all great teams have great leaders. A team that performs well isn't always an indication of great leadership. A brilliant team can influence and carry a mediocre leader a surprisingly long way. By the same token, it's not always obvious who the best potential leaders are. Sometimes those who would do it very well don't wish to, although they may accept the mantle if the situation demands it.

Great leaders are confident of their own abilities but never conceited. They are not giant ego balloons floating over the landscape. They understand that leadership is always about service and the team.

Styles of leadership – positive and destructive

Different styles of leadership meet different needs. In a business context, for instance, the leader who successfully steers a start-up through its first years may not be the best leader with the skills to take it through an IPO, expansion and change.

Leaders are made, not born. While the military trains its leaders, most people receive little or no leadership training, and rise from the ashes and opportunities created by adversity.

Fortunately, leadership is a skill that can be learned, given time, resources and effort. The secret to becoming a successful leader is to understand the different types of leadership, figure out which type you want to practise, and then acquire the experience and hone the skills to achieve it.

The following are examples of different leadership styles. How many do you recognise from personal experience?

Trait leadership

The military uses the Trait model. Many engineers become Trait leaders. The aim here is to recruit only individuals who possess the traits needed to become autonomous leaders once they have been correctly trained. When this training is complete they should have the ability to take over and solve problems in the event that their leader is incapacitated.

Trait leadership suits organisations that have considerable training resources. Military cadets must be conformers, happy to be 'disassembled', then 'reassembled' in the company mould.

Functional leadership

Functional leaders command in a controlled environment. This is the kind of leadership needed for, say, a production line situation where people have defined roles and tasks, and follow tried, tested and documented procedures.

When things are going well, pilots and most other aviation industry leaders are Functional leaders, governed during normal conditions by rules, Standard Operating Procedures and checklists.

Functional leadership is not designed for non-standard conditions. During Black Swan events the rule book is useless, and additional (that is, High Reliability Organisation – HRO) leadership skills including creative thinking are required.

Transformational leadership

Transformational leaders change the culture. Creative and inspirational, they are needed when time is limited and an organisation must evolve or risk collapsing into irrelevance. This type of leadership requires trust and respect.

Transformational leaders take people out of their comfort zone, often when they don't know why, how or where they are going. These 'renaissance' leaders must be able to connect and motivate those who don't want to move. The process of change works best when everyone agrees on the problems, solutions and targets.

Transformational leaders are needed in laggard enterprises that are running out of steam. These leaders often move on when the change is complete.

Apple's Steve Jobs was a Transformational leader. He was also petulant and impatient and acted as though society's rules didn't apply to him. His method was to stay hungry and challenge the status quo, allowing Apple to make an enormous impact, marketing itself as 'the people who are crazy enough to think they can change the world'.

Servant leadership

Servant leaders change the world. Some of the most effective leaders in history have been poor and powerless individuals armed with only their authentic values and a charismatic ability to influence others. Mahatma Gandhi, the Dalai Lama, Martin Luther King Jr and Nelson Mandela are examples of Servant leaders.

Servant leaders connect to people's innermost values, emotions and aspirations, inspiring them to rise from isolation and intolerable conditions, energised by a feeling of belonging and shared purpose. They focus on the WHY of change, not the HOW or WHAT. In his most famous speech Martin Luther King Jr said, 'I have a dream', not 'I have a 7-point plan'. He contrasted 'what is now' with 'what could be', working on the belief that once people were moved by the WHY to change, the HOWs and WHATs would naturally follow. Servant leaders must be prepared to suffer to reach their goal.

Narcissistic leadership

Narcissistic leaders see humility as the ultimate weakness. These leaders are autocratic, selfish, overconfident attention-seekers who crave public admiration and surround themselves with sycophants. They become aggressive when challenged, and crush dissent and competing ideas. They often take irrational risks because they over-estimate their own abilities and refuse advice from others.

Can you think of any prominent world leaders who demonstrate Narcissistic leadership? The list starts with Adolf Hitler . . .

Narcissists destroy teamwork, so will never be resilient. They create cultures that instil fear, failure, inadequacy, distrust, shame and humiliation. They demand 'followship' – blind, unquestioning allegiance – not fellowship. Those they lead become underconfident, disengaged, withdrawn, paranoid and defensive, focused on protecting their positions rather than taking personal risks to ensure the team's and mission's success.

Narcissistic leadership has no place in developed societies. If you find yourself working for a Narcissistic leader, then your only solutions are to keep your head down, become a sycophant or leave.

Charismatic leadership

The most influential leaders of all are Charismatic leaders. Charisma builds respect, trust and obedience. It inspires better engagement and higher performance in teams. It empowers people to listen, open their hearts, take risks and make sacrifices for the team. Charisma is a behaviour that can be learned.

Charismatic leaders exhibit some of the following characteristics:

- focus: a clear set of values, beliefs and attitudes
- vision: a clear purpose, mission and plan for execution
- communication: they are masters at communicating their ideas and listening to others
- authority: they are comfortable with their authority and have excellent relationships with those above and below them
- kindness: they lead with empathy, warmth and care
- speech: calm, lower pitched and varying in frequency and cadence.

As well as being a Servant leader, Martin Luther King Jr was a Charismatic one. In 1963, with 20 years of public speaking experience, he addressed 250,000 people at the March on Washington. In doing so he helped catalyse and change his nation. Richard Branson is another Charismatic leader, unafraid to be his authentic self.

Hybrid leadership

Leaders don't necessarily fall purely into one category. Richard Branson is also an example of someone who adopts a Hybrid model of leadership, adapting his style as needed. One of the world's most authentic leaders, he can steer his teams and organisations when things are proceeding normally, in contingency situations and through major transformation.

Hybrid leadership is a compromise, and so one of the hardest forms of leadership. Hybrid leaders need a network of strong leaders to support them.

Non-leader collaboration – Amorphous Consensus

The Amorphous Consensus is a leaderless collection where many non-dominant players contribute to one cause. A good analogy is a stand of aspen trees, which look separate above ground but spring from a shared root system. Aspen forests, like Amorphous leaderships, are extremely resilient – a tree that dies is replaced by another feeding from the same collective roots.

Some clubs and religions are run as Amorphous Consensus.

My style of leadership – High Reliability Organisation leadership

Although each of the leadership styles above can be very effective in the right setting, I aspire to something different, something that I think better fits my style and my industry: HRO leadership.

Examples of successful HRO leaders include Gene Kranz, the Flight Director for NASA's $104 billion Apollo program, and Ann Pickard, who has headed some of the Shell Oil Company's most difficult and contentious operations, including Arctic Ocean exploration.

HRO leaders are mindful people who are knowledgeable, well trained and experienced. They possess the fierce will to enforce safety. They resist the urge to apply simplistic solutions to complex situations. They understand their systems down to their core components, using these skills to implement novel and creative solutions. HRO leaders trust (but verify) and defer to expertise. They give single-minded advice to their teams – if you are not committed to the company's culture, values and standards, then leave.

Gene Kranz gave an insight into this mindset, describing the critical moment at which the decision had to be made to launch or abort: 'There was no room in the process for emotion, no place for fear or doubt, no time to stop and think things over . . . You had to be prepared for any contingency, and those contingencies had to be as fully anticipated as possible before you pushed the button.' He added that a vital feature of HRO leadership is that leaders unhesitatingly assign critical tasks to someone capable of handling them and then, crucially, trust that person's judgement rather than overriding it.

My recipe for HRO leadership includes responsibility, authority, risk, confidence, courage, initiative, care and communication. It requires the leader to tame their ego and recognise their own vulnerabilities. HRO leaders know there are never enough learning experiences for them to 'know it all'. Their humility to admit their own weaknesses is a vital step and strength in building a strong and resilient team where each member is capable, valued and respected.

HRO leadership is hard work and not for the faint-hearted. You must be tough, fierce willed, competent and courageous. You must also be humble. Communicate your values to your team and protect them, because these are the people that build resilience.

My own leadership journey and principles

I was determined that when I became captain I would be as different as possible from the bad leaders I had seen. I knew that teams, never autocratic leaders, built resilient organisations. History proves that leaders who ignore their teams eventually fail. Survival depends on amassing the knowledge, experience and skills from many people into an intelligent and responsive team that learns, creates and adapts.

It was clear to me that a leader does not just determine the culture, the leader IS the culture! The leader's behaviour sets the tone for every activity their team undertakes, not just those that need direction and management. I was determined to set the best culture for my crews and passengers on every flight. So I looked around me for role models and exemplary leaders and studied them closely.

The importance of role models was something I discovered in my late teens after I bought Wayne Dyer's book *Your Erroneous Zones*. I'd misread the key word in the title as 'Erogenous' and the realisation that the book contained self-help advice was initially a let-down! But I read on and my life was changed by a strategy it offered to improve confidence. Dyer recommended looking closely at the people you most respected and dissecting their personalities. It turned out the

My role model

In my quest to be ready for leadership as I progressed towards my own command, I chose Captain John Pickhaver to be my ultimate role model. As well as exhibiting the traits I respected, John was also knowledgeable, experienced, modest and calm – the definition of a quiet achiever. He taught me about navigation, weather, radio waves and many more specifics of the job, but most of all he taught me by example how to be a good leader.

Flights with John Pickhaver were always a pleasure, even when the unexpected happened. John was my captain during the incident I described in the previous chapter, when an engine failed as I was flying us from Frankfurt to Bangkok. Under an aggressive, fearful leader this would have been an extremely stressful experience. But with John in charge everyone stayed on track, the pilots worked as a team, and after dumping 100 tons of fuel we returned to Frankfurt safely. Strange as it is to say, thanks to his excellent leadership the cockpit atmosphere was so focused, structured and calm that the engine failure was almost a pleasant experience.

I aspired to lead as well as John Pickhaver, building a fresh resilient team before every flight, and establishing a trusting, friendly and ego-free zone where passionate and competent professionals could perform to the best of their ability. I ask everyone to pick up others' mistakes, especially mine. When they do highlight my errors, I thank them. If the unexpected happens, I am confident the team would engage and am confident in their ability to take calculated and courageous risks to achieve the best possible outcome – not for me and my ego, but for the safety of everyone on board.

traits shared by the people I respected (my parents, a teacher and my good friend Adrian Wischer) were friendliness, sociability, an interest in others, curiosity, confidence, saying what they thought and rejecting peer pressure. These people had spine. They harboured no regrets. I decided I wanted these attributes as well.

In 2004, I attained commercial airline captaincy and since then I continue to work hard to ensure that every interaction I have with my team is personal, supportive, empathetic and caring. As a result, I have 100 per cent trust and confidence in the crews I lead. I celebrate our successes and seek genuine feedback on my own performance.

Mistakes are highlighted only to create opportunities to learn, adjust and improve. These procedures work equally well at work and at home.

- If mistakes are made in the air, it's probably my fault for not setting the right mood, identifying potential threats or monitoring performance.
- I present to organisations and the media worldwide. Coral critiques every event to improve my performance.
- Coral and I are happy to discuss any subject with our children. Each of us has equal rights to question or criticise one another's behaviour. When finances were tight, we let our children prioritise family events. We help our children help themselves.

Your leadership journey – building your leadership skills

The first step for any aspiring leader is to identify the WHY that drives you. Boiled down to a single idea, what is the thing that gets you out of bed in the morning? Why do you go to work? Why do you do the things you do?

Know and tell people your WHYs, because these are the constants that will guide how you think, act and communicate. When you tell people the things you believe in, you will attract people who believe in the things you believe in.

Identify the leaders around you and analyse their styles. What are their strengths and weaknesses? What are their WHYs? Compare these to your own. What strengths can you build on? What weaknesses can you address?

Actively seek responsibility; don't sit back and hope it will come to you. But do it from a position of humility and service, not one of an ego that needs to be stroked. As a leader you should be transparent, honest and authentic, and you should also be those things as a team-member. There is an old saying that you should dress for the job you want, not the job you have now. The same goes for behaviour. Don't wait to be appointed a leader to take on the qualities of good leadership.

If you are already in a leadership position, ask yourself honestly if you are bringing everything you can and should to that privileged position. It's never too late to address flaws and lift your performance. Remember, it is your values, trust and belief in teamwork that sets the culture and lights the way, not just command, regulation and control.

Customer service is a direct result of an organisation's culture, which is a reflection of its leadership. The way staff deal with the customers and suppliers is an open window into the culture coming from the leader.

Every time I board an aircraft as a captain or a passenger, it takes me less than one minute to assess the culture in the cabin: Do the crew approach with a smile to say hello? Do they actively engage, are they interested? Are they providing service from a sense of duty or because they genuinely care? You don't need to be a genius to sense these attitudes; their body language reveals everything, if you care to observe.

Motivated and inspired teams don't just happen, they need to be created. Good leaders do this by delegating authority, trusting those they are leading and actively helping them to succeed. They make work easy and fun. They acknowledge good work because they understand people give more when they are rewarded and less when they are punished. Positive feedback increases engagement, professionalism and reduces churn. As revered long-time manager of England's Manchester United football team Sir Alex Ferguson put it, 'A little encouragement goes a long way. There is nothing better than hearing, "Well done". Those are the two best words ever invented.'

Good leaders face their staff and customers. This applies no matter the scale of the company. Royalty, presidents and prime ministers should know what it's like to stand in queues and catch public transport, to talk directly to their constituents and understand their lives, not just a filtered version of them. As Captain, once we're safely cruising on a long-haul flight, I make a point to walk the aisles of the aircraft observing, talking to, and supporting, the crew and passengers. I sometimes take up to two hours to tour both decks on the A380. The passengers and most crew enjoy the interaction. Employees who don't like the leader mixing with the customers expose signs of a weak culture or paranoia.

Empathy is a critical skill for good leaders. You can test your ability to detect others' feelings with neuropsychologist Simon Baron-Cohen's simple 'Reading the Mind in the Eyes Test', easily found via an online search. For those who are not naturally empathetic, the good news is that there are just 43 muscles in the face, so reading faces (and body language) is a finite skill that can be learned.

Continue to look for opportunities to test and extend your skills. Understand the importance of lifelong learning. Join professional groups, look for workshops and conferences that might add to your skills arsenal and seek a mentor who understands the path you wish to climb. Request honest feedback and learn from it.

Always clearly understand your responsibilities, accountability and authority. These elements directly influence your WHYs. For example, pilots are responsible for the safety of the aircraft, crew and passengers and are accountable to the company. Company directors are responsible for the company and accountable to its shareholders. You must have the authority to exercise your responsibilities.

Don't create or tolerate ambiguities in the hope they will resolve themselves. In leadership the standard you walk past is not just the standard you accept, but the standard you set. So be ready to step up, take 100 per cent responsibility, offer no excuses and fix a problem.

Be clear about roles

Like all Qantas international pilots, my licence is checked and recertified seven times every year. There's a medical check, emergencies check, four simulator tests and finally a 'route check'. If I fail any check my pay plummets and my licence is put on hold. On the day of the QF32 crisis, I was undergoing a route check on the flight.

Every aspect of the pilot's performance is assessed during a route check, from pre-flight planning and procedures through to post-flight documentation and debriefing. It is conducted by a check captain. But that day the check captain was actually a check captain-in-training, which meant his performance was being assessed, in turn, by Captain David Evans. So, instead of having three pilots in the cockpit – myself as pilot-in-command, first officer Matt Hicks and second officer Mark Johnson – there were five with the addition of the check captain-in-training and Dave.

As Dave said later, 'It would be hard to find a more A380-experienced crew on the planet.' Strange as this might sound, this could have been a recipe for disaster, as you'll discover in Chapter 8. An international aviation safety investigator told me that with so many pilots in the cockpit during the QF32 incident, it was remarkable we didn't crash. He subsequently sent me an analysis of aircraft emergencies where the crew was augmented by extra pilots. Far from an additional pilot making the situation safer, it made it more likely to end in disaster. This might seem counter-intuitive, but the explanation is simple.

For some flights with augmented crews, the cockpit turns into a committee. Blurring the chain of command allows for distraction, confusion, indecision, arguments and bad outcomes. The investigator was astonished that this hadn't happened to us. In turn, I was surprised that he did not identify a failure to define every team member's role as an explanation for his findings, followed by the conclusion that some pilots needed training to become better leaders.

In the case of QF32, I confirmed before the flight, then later enforced, the command structure of our augmented crew, thus preventing confusion when things went wrong.

During the trip to the airport I'd told my two support pilots that the other two captains, the check pilots, would be silent and we must ignore and not be distracted by them or their activities. On the flight deck prior to pushback, the crew's positions and responsibilities were further reinforced during a stage that teamwork experts call 'storming'. (You can find out more about 'storming' in the Teamwork chapter.)

Naturally, as Pilot-in-Command, I was sitting at the front left of the cockpit, with my First Officer, Matt, beside me. Usually my Second Officer, Mark, would sit in the seat centred behind us. However, on entering the cockpit, Mark found his seat had been taken by one of the check captains, who was there to check my performance. This action relegated Mark to the rear, behind my left shoulder.

I was not happy with this and asked him to move. He said he would be unable to check me if he did so.

I understood his concerns. But I also knew that my responsibilities to ensure a safe flight overrode their interests, so I wasn't about to back down. The check captain offered a compromise: if required, he would act as Second Officer. I was happy with this and we took off with all five pilots having a clear, and shared, view of their roles, tasks and responsibilities. This was to prove all-important when the engine exploded.

Lives are not at stake during most leadership tussles or misunderstandings. However, these situations can still be damaging. In highly effective teams, people are capable of taking on various roles; leaders in particular should be able to undertake any role required. But in every situation where leadership is required, there should be no doubt who the leader is. And leaders must clearly know to whom they are responsible and accountable.

Confidence comes with experience. Knowledge, training and guidance will help, but ultimately you learn by doing. As you take on leadership roles you will face events that you might not fully understand. You might be confused, aware you don't have all the information and don't know the answers. Don't panic. Stay confident in your abilities and those of your team. Confident people don't know it all, but they do have the ability to stay calm and muster team muscle and creative brain power to navigate their way through. Confidence is the foundation for courage.

Great leaders have courage, which is derived, paradoxically, from fierce determination and humility. Their attitude is, 'I know the risks but I'm capable. I don't know all the answers, but I trust my team and am confident they will help me make the right decisions. I accept responsibility no matter what the outcome.'

Great leaders create protective environments where workers give their best and the team cannot fail. The vision and risks are shared, but decisions and responsibility remain with the leader. They understand that care flows down the leadership chain. People who feel safe are more engaged, efficient and resilient when dealing with uncertainty. Confident team-members are more likely to be courageous, step up, and take well-judged risks.

Influential Leadership

There will be many people reading this who, despite having some of the necessary qualities, don't want to be leaders. Some people have limited leadership goals, others just can't see themselves as leaders.

Nevertheless, you can still influence teams. This has been dubbed Influential Leadership by distinguished former army leader Major General (Ret.) John Cantwell AO, DSC (about whom you can read more in Chapter 9).

Anyone can be an Influential Leader. It starts with small steps – expressing your values, setting the example by living to the highest standards every day. Show your team that you care about them as people and colleagues. Be courageous and honest in offering advice and feedback. Speak up on the important issues and refuse to condone or ignore unacceptable behaviour like intolerance, discrimination and bullying. Show you are engaged and willing to adapt, by offering suggestions to improve processes and systems. Be accountable for the results for yourself and your team.

Influential Leaders act in small ways. But when you repeat them with honesty and self-belief they will become more natural; others will notice and start listening, watching and perhaps even imitating you. When they start committing to the goals you set for yourself and the team, this is when you've become an Influential Leader.

Key takeaways – leadership lessons

Life offers many lessons in leadership . . .

Duty of care

'Duty of care' is my key WHY. It motivates me to be the best I can be, so that I can protect others. It has guided my thoughts successfully through many difficult situations.

I learned one important lesson back in 1984 when I was a 27-year-old Flight Lieutenant with the Royal Australian Air Force (RAAF). All the officers on the fighter base where I was stationed took turns to serve as Duty Officer, dealing with issues that might arise after office hours, from vetting urgent communications and assisting any police inquiries through to resolving trivial problems.

On this particular night I took a call from an airman called John who lived with his family in a RAAF house. He told me that the hotplate the family used to prepare meals had exploded. He said, 'Sir, I've called the military housing maintenance people but the office is closed, so I can't get the hotplate fixed and so I can't cook dinner for my family.' His house was a long distance from supermarkets or fast food outlets, so I asked him what he would like to do. He said, 'Could I please have permission for my family to get a dinner at the motel nearby?' I thought about it for a few seconds then replied, 'Of course.' I hung up and documented the conversation in the Duty Officer's log book.

Three days later I got a call from the Wing Commander in charge of the base's support services. He was not happy. 'Richard, you should not have authorised the serviceman and his family to have dinner. He could have had a cold dinner, and by the way, he had prawns! There is no way the air force will pay the $30 he is claiming.'

I was incensed. What the airman had ordered was irrelevant and I had not broken any rules. The air force had a responsibility to ensure the house it supplied for him was functional. If not, it had a responsibility to provide an alternative solution, and that's what I had done. I told the Wing Commander that I stood by my actions. In fact, I would pay the $30 out of my own pocket if the air force was going to renege its duty of care. We argued it out. He clearly thought I was bluffing, but I wasn't. Finally, after a long and heated discussion, he reversed his decision.

I took three lessons from that experience.

First, you cannot delegate responsibility without also delegating authority. It is unreasonable to expect people down the line to be accountable without giving them authority, the means to deliver. The Wing Commander was fully entitled to question my decision and ask me to explain it, but in this case he was absolutely wrong to overrule it.

Second, it reinforced my views about the leader's duty of care. Leaders must protect those who are depending upon them, if necessary at the leader's expense. Author Simon Sinek explains it best in his book *Leaders Eat Last*.

Third, leadership is a privilege not a right and it comes with strings attached. Leaders must genuinely empathise and care. I decided then and there that no matter what the circumstances, I would never allow my leadership responsibilities for my team to be jeopardised.

Tough and competent – a leader changing the culture

Gene Kranz is one of my role models. So I was thrilled when he accepted my request for an interview at his Houston home he shares with his wife Marta. I expected the interview to last two hours, but before we knew it, six hours had passed without us noticing or breaking for lunch. I've done hundreds of interviews in my life, as research for my books and self-improvement, but Gene's interview was one of the most exciting.

NASA had a remarkable structure during the 1960s, with specific commanders, astronauts and flight directors allocated to a specific Apollo mission. Each mission had set goals to achieve, incrementally paving the organisation's long path to put a man on the moon within the decade. Every one of the 400,000 people at NASA played a role. Gene told me, 'There was no politics or tension between the teams, simply because everyone was focused and incredibly busy planning and executing their own mission, and expecting and trusting others to do the same.'

NASA astronauts are resilient. All the early astronauts except Buzz Aldrin were ex-military test pilots. (Buzz was a USAF fighter pilot who earned respect for his Doctor of Science thesis on the topic of rendezvous in space.) Test pilots were picked for their ability to work outside the box, to evaluate, modify and retry their decisions in real time during traumatic and unexpected life-or-death situations. Astronauts needed these skills because the technologies being used were either undeveloped or in their infancy. Space was hard and full of risks, no-one had experience in these fields and no-one knew what they didn't know. The only solution was to put the most resilient pilots in control.

As well as being Chief of the Flight Control Division for NASA, Gene was also the Flight Director of the White 'Tiger' team which was designated as the lead for Apollo 13 (with three other teams in support). In 1970, eight months after Apollo 11's triumphant moon landing, the three-man Apollo 13 crew found themselves adrift in a cold, dark and powerless spacecraft.

What happened next is one of the great single acts of resilience in human history. Over a period of four days, the Apollo 13 crew and Mission Control worked through many seemingly insurmountable problems to bring the trio safely back to Earth. Later, when a reporter asked Gene Kranz if he had ever doubted that the Apollo 13 crew would make it back alive, Gene's response was a forcible, 'NO – NEVER!'

Gene's confidence and certainty were evidence of a fierce will that arose in response to a tragedy that had happened three years earlier. On Friday 27 January 1967, Command Pilot Virgil 'Gus' Grissom, Senior Pilot Edward White and Pilot Roger Chaffee, the crew of Apollo 1, perished in a fire during a launch rehearsal test. Their Command Module split at the seams 14 seconds after horrified ground crews heard Chaffee's first cries over the radio.

Space travel was always going to be difficult, but these astronauts didn't die far from Earth from something like a meteor impact. They died as the result of a sequence of electrical failures while the spacecraft was parked on the launch pad. In the lead-up to this terrible accident the Command Module had accumulated 20,000 logged failures and Gus Grissom was so frustrated with quality control that he placed a lemon on top of the Module after one inspection. Apollo Program Director Major General Sam Phillips had written a report critical of Mission Control, noting 'the software is not written and the computers are not working'.

NASA responded to the deadly fire by pulling down the shutters. Operations were frozen, outgoing calls were stopped and media communications were severed. Gene wrote later, 'Everyone drifted through a mindless fog of war. No-one knew what to do. There were many rumours, few facts. Senior leadership was absent. Someone had to take control.' He stepped up and proceeded to do just that.

Gene gathered the teams together on the following Monday and delivered what is now referred to as 'the Kranz Dictum':

Spaceflight will never tolerate carelessness, incapacity, and neglect. Somewhere, somehow, we screwed up. It could have been in design, build, or test. Whatever it was, we should have caught it. We were too gung-ho about the schedule and we locked out all of the problems we saw each day in our work. Every element of the program was in trouble and so were we. The simulators were not working, Mission Control was behind in virtually every area, and the flight and test procedures changed daily. Nothing we did had any shelf life.

Not one of us stood up and said, 'Dammit, STOP!'

I don't know what [the investigative] committee will find as the cause, but I know what I find. We are the cause! We were not ready! We did not do our job. We were rolling the dice, hoping that things would come together by launch day, when in our hearts, we knew it would take a miracle. We were pushing the schedule and betting that the Cape would slip before we did.

From this day forward, Flight Control will be known by two words: 'Tough and Competent'.

Tough means we are forever accountable for what we do or what we fail to do. We will never again compromise our responsibilities. Every time we walk into Mission Control we will know what we stand for.

Competent means we will never take anything for granted. We will never be found short in our knowledge and in our skills.

Mission Control will be perfect. When you leave this meeting today you will go to your office and the first thing you will do there is to write 'Tough and Competent' on your blackboards. It will never be erased. Each day when you enter the room these words will remind you of the price paid by Grissom, White, and Chaffee.

These words are the price of admission to the ranks of Mission Control.

Remember the ultimate truth of leadership: the leader does not set the culture, the leader IS the culture. Gene Kranz's Dictum created a new culture at NASA which enabled it to advance and excel. He instilled the need for discipline, competence, confidence, responsibility, toughness, teamwork and trust.

Gene did not eliminate failure, because that is impossible. But he led a resilient culture that recovered from failures and stopped them from becoming catastrophes. Unfortunately, NASA would have to relearn these lessons decades later, during the Space Shuttle program, but Gene Kranz's approach remains the gold standard of leadership and resilience.

(I must digress to thank Gene for his blessing for me to publish his story. Of all the people I interviewed for this book, no-one has lived and expressed the elements of resilient leadership better than Gene Kranz.)

It's always the leader's fault

I devote a lot of effort to my leadership skills and know there's always room for improvement, as I was recently reminded. We have a small family boat that goes by the name *US NAVY*. Bringing it into dock after a day out on the water with my wife and daughter, I was navigating a tricky approach. It was important that Coral and Sophia work together to quickly secure the bow (front) ropes to the pontoon so that I could apply reverse thrust against them and torque-swing the stern (back) against the dock.

We had accomplished this exact manoeuvre many times before, so I skipped the briefing. I thought the plan was obvious to all. I was wrong. My trusty crew, unable to read my mind, were slow attaching the ropes, allowing a crosswind to push our boat against another.

My initial reaction was anger at the team. But this evaporated when I realised the entire catastrophe was my fault. I had not told Coral and Sophia what I wanted them to do; I hadn't outlined their roles, tasks and responsibilities. They were willing helpers who had been left uninformed and in the dark.

The lesson was clear to me. Leadership is needed in all situations where group coordination is required. Even for trivial things like moving furniture, someone must take the lead and coordinate others. When a failure occurs in this kind of situation it's always the leader's fault, especially if they don't take the chance to debrief, learn and adjust to ensure the problem doesn't reoccur.

Leadership has a lifespan

Leadership is like everything else in life; it has a time-span – a beginning, middle and end. The type of leadership you adopt will change with the industry you choose, and your stage in life.

Politicians who rise to party leadership usually undertake a long singular upward trajectory, contending with the problems within the party, election cycles and public issues along the way. Mistakes are not always forgiven.

Aviation leadership is the opposite. Like the movie *Groundhog Day*, every day starts the same way, with an unchallenged leader who forms a new team to tackle life-threatening risks for a short, predetermined period. This is apprentice leadership because mistakes can be identified, fixed and lessons learned before the next attempt.

Business leadership is somewhere between the two extremes. Directors of S&P 500 companies sit on the board for an average of nine years, while the average lifespan of US publicly traded companies is just 10 years.

Knowing when to hand over the reins

One of the trickiest challenges faced by good leaders is knowing when it's time to go. That applies to everything from moving on from a small team to stepping down as ruler of a country.

John Howard had an incredibly successful political career, holding a seat in the Australian Federal Parliament for 33 years and serving a remarkable four terms as Prime Minister. First elected leader of his party in opposition in 1985, he was replaced four years later. Many assumed his time near the top was over, but he was returned as party leader in 1995 and swept into power the following year.

John told me during an interview that while there was no single roadmap for effective leadership that applied in every case, four factors stood out:

To start with, a good leader must have a strong set of beliefs. He or she must know where the group of people in their care, and followers, ought to be taken, and furthermore how they can be inspired. In the political arena, with which I am most familiar, examples abound of failure, or at best mediocre performances, because men or women elected to leadership roles haven't had a strong set of values or principles to guide the decisions of their governments.

The most important relationship that any leader has is with the people that person immediately leads. The captain of a team must have a strong relationship with all team-members. An airliner captain must have the total confidence and support of all members of the crew. That relationship is even more important than the captain's relationship with the passengers.

Good leaders accept from the outset that they will get some things wrong. The leader whose guiding principle is that he or she will never make a mistake is a leader who will disappoint. The key to successful leadership is to get the big things right. The outstanding leaders in world history have been those who have got all the crucial decisions right, notwithstanding having made errors of judgement and decision-making along the way.

Finally, there are occasions when any leader must trust his or her instinct. This is despite advice and some evidence to the contrary. In my own career on several important occasions I decided to trust my instinct in preference to the orthodox advice and counsel I had received. This is not an approach which should be followed frequently. It is a crucial test of judgement when to abide by your instincts rather than the course of action suggested by the routine patterns of advice coming to you.

These are wise insights from someone whose sustained political success earned him an important place in his nation's political history.

Unfortunately, John Howard's record of serving as the Australian Prime Minister for the second longest period in Australian history did not end with his going out on his own terms. In 2007, he stayed on for one more election in which his party lost government in a landslide, and he became only the second Prime Minister in Australian history to be voted out of his own seat.

The ending of political leadership is often sudden, often with no opportunity or requirement to plan for succession. But businesses should be run very differently. Here, continuity is vital.

Corporate succession

Resilient organisations have a succession plan in place. Just as the co-pilots in my airline are trained and capable of taking over command in the event the captain becomes incapacitated, organisations must be able to survive in the event the leader is absent or busy on another critical task.

Eventually, every business leader must be replaced, so plans must be made accordingly to ensure the business survives. In his book *Good to Great*, Jim Collins analysed great companies whose stock performance beat the market average over a 40-year period. He labelled those who held the reins of these organisations 'Level 5 Leaders', with attributes aligning with those I've described above.

Leadership is a gift from those who follow.

Bottom line

Lead, follow or get out of the way.

Leadership is not for everyone. Many of those in leadership positions are not true leaders. There is no title or corner office in existence that can bestow leadership skills. As then United States Air Force Chief of Staff General Mark Welsh III told one class of graduating cadets, 'Leadership is a gift. Be ready for it. It is given by those who follow. But you have to be worthy of it.'

Great leaders understand that leadership is not for the insecure. Leaders must be ready, willing and determined to lead. It comes with responsibility and authority. They share credit and don't shirk blame. They understand that success belongs to the team, failure to the leader.

Such leaders create a culture of resilience. They know it's impossible to prevent failure and so they don't fear it or deny it has happened. Instead they work with their team to solve the problem, learn the lessons it offers and prevent a repeat.

They know leadership is something that must be learned and that everyone has to start somewhere. As Welsh advised, 'Try your leadership skills. If you fail, persevere and try again. Work on it.'

These leaders tame their own egos and combine responsibility, authority, confidence, courage, caring, and strong communication skills in an unbeatable package. They enable frictionless environments in which the teams they build and nurture can learn, grow, take intelligent risks and thrive. They are visionary and inspirational in their goals and clear about the chain of command and about roles and expectations. They delegate and, having done so, they trust their team-members to use their own judgement.

They commit themselves to lifelong learning, actively seeking to improve their own performance in every sphere. They are adaptable, able to use different leadership styles as different situations demand. And they are empathetic – by choice if not by nature.

Great leaders lead great teams. I like the orchestra analogy: the conductor leads the orchestra, but it's the musicians that make the music.

Leadership: Checklist

Leadership is personal:
True leadership has nothing to do with job titles. Be authentic and start acting and thinking like the leader you want to be.

The leader doesn't set the culture:
The leader IS the culture. The team should know the leader's WHYs. When you follow your WHYs, the HOWs and WHATs will look after themselves.

Build resilience so your team can thrive:
Nurture your team, delegate with trust and don't micro-manage.

Share the credit:
As leader, your successes belong to the whole team.

Take the blame:
When there are failures the buck stops with you.

Look for the lessons:
Critique all of your performances; there's always room to improve.

Get the big things right:
Accept you will make mistakes along the way. You will be remembered for only the big things, so learn from, adjust and retry the little things so you get the big things right.

CHAPTER 8

Teamwork:
There's No Success Without It

WHY

I am alive today only because of teamwork. It saved me in a crisis situation, but in every aspect of life, I cannot overstate the importance of teamwork to you personally and professionally. A happy, fulfilled and meaningful life can only be achieved by creating or joining great teams.

Teamwork is an essential element of resilience.

Teamwork allows human beings to thrive against apex predators such as Saltwater Crocodiles and Great White Sharks. These predators survive alone by using their aggression and strength to separate then conquer weaker individuals from groups. We protect ourselves by keeping our groups together, pooling our strengths and mitigating our weaknesses. Proving the concept of synergy, the team is always greater than the sum of its parts.

Humans are programmed to form groups. Our hormones and chemicals reward the team behaviours that build the foundations for our social structures. In his book *Leaders Eat Last*, Simon Sinek calls these 'the Happiness Hormones'. They motivate us to work better together in order to survive.

Humanity would collapse without teams. Civilisation would crumble into a short and brutal fight for survival, a case of kill or be killed. Working together in teams enables us to build communities, cities, governments, defence, infrastructure and health care. Individually, we remain exposed and vulnerable, but together we're a force to be reckoned with.

HOW

Teamwork relies on mutual trust between all team-members, and the understanding that achieving success and reaching a common goal depends on the actions of all.

No enterprise understands and takes advantage of teamwork more than the military. They receive individuals from all walks of life, then convert them into team players. Training involves challenging and steadily stressing these individuals until they stand emotionally naked and vulnerable. Recruits discover their team is measured not by the performance of the strongest but by the weakest, the last person to cross the line. When they grasp this, when they genuinely realise that survival depends not on competition and ego, but on everyone coming together, helping each other and pooling their resources, they have become a unified and resilient team.

The process of owning up to your weaknesses and accepting weaknesses in others as part of forming a team, creates values and friendships that last. My colleagues in my Air Force Academy Course #28 will be my friends for life. I clearly remember during every monthly fitness test run, Jerry Carter pacing me at the start of the race just as I would pull him up at the end. We were a great team who always finished together.

WHAT

QF32 ended in success, not disaster, because of exceptional teamwork. Teams of experts in the air and on the ground sprang into action and pooled their knowledge, training and experience to protect the lives of 469 passengers and crew, and thousands of others who would have been affected by tragedy.

I am proud of each of these seven teams because they did not just do what they were trained to do, they often acted alone without communications and without all information at hand.

1. Pilots – More on that in a moment.
2. Cabin Crew – It didn't matter that the communication systems between the cockpit and cabin weren't working. We trusted Michael von Reth (the Customer Service Manager) and his cabin team to do what they were trained to do, when they had to do it. They did that with the utmost professionalism, ensuring safety and preventing panic, hour after long hour.
3. Singapore Air Traffic Control – Our only communication with the outside world, they followed my instructions, cleared the airspace and directed emergency services over the four-hour ordeal, with no confusion at any point.
4. Singapore Police and Fire Services – The emergency services took up their correct and expected positions. Despite six of our seven radios having failed, their response functioned like clockwork. They managed the risks of the fuel spills, hot brakes and the recalcitrant engine that refused to shut down. They were prepared and ready for a dangerous evacuation.
5. Qantas Airport Staff – They exemplified the way great teams step up, as explained later in this chapter.
6. Qantas Crisis Management Centre – Our two satellite phones failed, denying us the ability to communicate with crisis leaders and engineers in Sydney. But I had visited the Crisis Centre four weeks before QF32. I knew the conditions that would trigger the three tiers of the Crisis Centre to convene. I knew their functions. They did everything we expected and more.
7. The Passengers – The emergency brought them together and turned them into an effective team. The pilots and cabin crew kept them fully informed throughout the ordeal, communications that made them feel valued, focused, confident and in control.

After we had landed, with jet fuel pooling under the aircraft, Michael von Reth told the passengers to turn their mobile phones off, to prevent the risk of fire. Later, when a passenger's phone started ringing, the passengers in that section yelled, 'TURN THAT PHONE OFF!'

I am proud of the passengers. They acted calmly and rationally and followed our instructions in times of great stress. They also became devotees of my airline and protected our brand.

As the Pilot-in-Command of QF32, the ultimate responsibility for the passengers rested squarely with me. An airline crew is not a committee and my team in the cockpit knew exactly who was in charge. I would be responsible if people died.

But the A380 is not a fighter jet, and commercial pilots do not act alone. The safety of any flight rests not on me, but on the team of expert pilots who know their roles and tasks and who must be left alone to do their best work. In this regard I am a facilitator, tasked to set up an environment in which my team thrives.

This is why I put so much effort into building teams before every mission. I care for them and they support me in return. I delegate tasks at every opportunity so that I can better lead and fly the aircraft. We come together with just one motivation – to protect our passengers. This is why I must have absolute trust in my team.

The final decisions in QF32's high-stakes situation were mine. However, they were made having the right leadership culture and using the shared mental resources of five brains that merged to form one super-brain which had 71,000 flying hours and 140 years worth of experience. On an ordinary day our solid teamwork would have resulted in a happy and efficient flight. When potential catastrophe struck it was life-saving.

The need for teamwork

You don't need a Black Swan event to prove the value of teamwork. Teamwork is involved whenever we come together in groups with common culture, values and shared goals. This includes marriage, family, friends, religious groups and organisations.

Teamwork also binds sporting teams, the ones you play in and even more the ones you support. When Americans stop once every year to watch the Super Bowl, tribal camaraderie becomes a measure of national unity and pride.

As with strong leadership, effective teamwork is needed now more than ever before. The world we live in is too complicated for any single mind, no matter how impressive. Fighter pilots, for instance, are no longer sole actors: they fly in formations and need weapons-systems officers and warning and control systems in support. Every one of us will join and lead teams throughout our lives. Even as a parent trying to raise children, you are ultimately building a team.

Teams need a leader, structure, and willing participants who value the performance and safety in coming together for a common cause rather than risking acting alone. No matter who you are, your resilience depends upon your ability to form effective teams. Fortunately, we can all learn how to do this.

Survival on the Moon

Visionary individuals are often needed to set the path a team will follow. But an effective team that pools knowledge, experience, skills and creativity will always outperform individuals ... and NASA designed an experiment to prove it. It's called 'Survival on the Moon' (and is easy to find online). It sets up a scenario where you are a lunar explorer who needs to rendezvous with your mother-ship. Unfortunately, mechanical failure and other misadventures have left you 200 miles away in a badly damaged craft.

Your task is to consider the 15 intact, portable items available to you, ranging from food concentrate, rope and a solar-powered FM receiver-transmitter to two 100 lb oxygen tanks, a portable heating unit, matches, a magnetic compass and a first aid kit. Then you must rank each item from 1 to 15 in order of their importance in helping your crew trek to the mother-ship.

Spoiler alert for those who want to do the exercise themselves: key answers are in the next paragraph.

Without exception, teams score higher in this exercise than individuals. In a group, what might perplex one person can seem clear to another. Matches are useless without oxygen, oxygen and water are both vital and easy to carry with the moon's lower gravity, and so on. Teams plug knowledge gaps and offer different perspectives, meaning teams make better decisions in novel situations.

Team drugs

Coming together in well-functioning groups doesn't just keep us safer and make us perform better; it also makes us feel good. The reason is oxytocin, a biochemical made in the brain.

Oxytocin is sometimes referred to as the 'love hormone'. The reality is more complicated than that, but it's true that oxytocin plays an important role in human bonding, from mother–baby attachment to workplace teams. It helps boost trust and empathy, which in turn helps us form deeper connections with those around us. This has been dubbed the 'tend and befriend' response. It also plays a very important role in our own health and feelings of wellbeing, boosting the immune system and buffering us against the negative effects of stress.

There is a biological truth at the heart of the old saying, 'A problem shared is a problem halved.' The quality and quantity of your in-person social networks (as opposed to your online interactions) plays a major influence on your health, happiness and resilience. People in teams and partnerships fare better than those who are alone. Face-to-face eye contact and hand-shaking releases oxytocin, which increases trust and reduces the cortisol levels that mark stress. It also releases another feel-good chemical, dopamine, reducing pain and inducing pleasure. Julianne Holt-Lunstad, a psychology professor at Brigham Young University, did meta-analyses of studies covering more than 3.7 million people, and found that the evidence consistently showed that social isolation and loneliness increased the risk of early death. The American Psychological Association headlined its release of her findings, 'So Lonely I Could Die'.

But even though humans need teams and do better in teams, and even though each one of us has spent our whole lives as part of different kinds of teams at home, school, work and in our social lives, it doesn't mean we're automatically good at teamwork.

Over my four decades of flying I've seen every kind of team, from toxic to excellent. I've seen teams that came together under difficult conditions work together superbly and others that started out well only to fall apart later. I've learned the attributes common to good teams and the risk factors that destroy teamwork.

Whether you're in a boardroom, on a sporting field or sitting around the kitchen table, the same fundamentals apply. Just as leaders can develop and hone their skills, the techniques for building effective teams and maintaining great teamwork can be learned and practised. We can all become great team players.

Team players have empathy and respect for others. Their ego is controlled. They take pride in their own achievements and in the achievements of others in the team. Because they are confident and comfortable and secure about the value they bring to the team, they don't feel threatened by others' success. They clearly understand their own roles and responsibilities and their position in the hierarchy, but don't hesitate to take on other tasks if needed.

Five steps to successful team-building

US educational psychology professor Bruce Tuckman defined the sequential steps required to build and maintain successful teams, naming them Forming, Storming, Norming, Performing and Adjourning.

I absolutely agree with Tuckman's stages, especially Forming. When I get the Forming right, I find the remaining stages flow naturally. Conversely, when I sense trouble during the Forming stage, I am more vigilant for the remainder of the flight.

Forming

In this initial stage the group comes together and the beginnings of personal relationships are created as everyone measures each other up. A successful Forming stage lays the first building blocks of what's known as a shared mental model. This is a combined perspective within which each team-member is working to the same goal with a common understanding of roles, tasks, challenges and responsibilities along the way. Clear and friendly communications are vital during this process.

The first interactions set the tone. Once again there is an old saying that applies here: 'You only get one chance to make a first impression, so make it count.' Most of the information being transmitted is coming through tone and body language. Don't underestimate the importance of this opportunity.

Of the four other pilots on QF32, I knew two well, one slightly and one not at all. I'd flown with my First Officer Matt Hicks in the past, but had not met my Second Officer, Mark Johnson. As arranged, we gathered in the hotel lobby bright and early on the morning of the flight. We were joined by another captain, who was there to check my performance, and David Evans, who was training that captain to become a check captain. I had only flown once before with Dave, but I knew the trainee check captain well.

As team leader, I usually buy the other pilots a coffee before we commence flight planning. This is a simple gesture, but it signals my interest to form the team the best way I know how – in a calm, relaxed and friendly environment where we can work without distractions. If I have not flown with a person before, I always ask their background and flying hours on the A380, so that we can all understand each other's experience and help each other.

Our team Forming took place in the crew transport on the

20-minute drive to the airport. I remember telling Matt and Mark, 'Forget that this flight is my annual route check. That is my problem. Forget the two check captains, they have their own duties. Our priority is to fly our passengers safely to the destination.'

Once we arrived at the briefing office at the airport, the QF32 pilot team finalised the flight plan. This involved reading around 100 pages of pre-flight notices and plans between us, pooling information, discussing threats and route options to avoid volcanoes, and arriving at an agreed flight plan and fuel order. We had now built a shared mental model of the flight and its threats, and a clear understanding of how each person fitted into the team.

During this Forming stage, I am attentive to each person, observing their body language, inviting their input and resolving stresses that might degrade performance. For example, if someone is worried about time and feels rushed, I expose my bare wrist and explain why I don't wear a watch. Pilots are the last line of defence in aviation – it's important we do not succumb to time pressures. Small acts such as this help cement a clear and positive culture.

At the end of flight-planning I say these words to close the loop and join the pilots into a cohesive team, 'I don't know it all, and I will probably make mistakes. But I value your input and I expect you to be pedantic, call them out and speak up if you are not happy. Just prioritise when to tell me. This is a team effort. There are no egos. So let's all have fun and deliver our passengers safely home.' Invariably my co-pilots then say, 'Same for me.'

This offers humility and vulnerability. It gives respect to my team and authorises them to step up and call STOP! These are not glib statements; if you make them you must honour your agreement. You must involve the team-members in important and non-reversible decisions. Even if they raise a concern that turns out to be false, you must thank them for their effort.

I make an effort to visit and join in with the cabin crew's briefing either in the office or on the bus. I speak to each one personally, introducing myself to those I don't know and greeting those I have met previously. With a crew of 21 on an A380 it can take quite a long time to do this, but the effort pays dividends.

I inject myself into their world. I brief them on flight details, weather, turbulence, how this affects their service and at what stage we're likely to get good views outside.

I then invite them into my world. I offer them a seat in the flight deck to observe take-offs and landings and invite them to visit us on the flight deck during flight.

Finally, if the conditions are right, I also set the service bar to the highest level. I tell the cabin crew, 'I am going to tell the passengers that we want this flight to be the best they have ever had. This is a challenge for you in the cabin. It's also a challenge for the pilots. But we are here to help you. I will tour the cabin during the cruise so please let me know if there are any passengers with a fear of flight or if there is anything I can do to help. Let's aim for the best and make their day.'

I acknowledge these comments would be cheap and hollow if said by every captain on every flight by rote. But they are not, and I speak genuinely. Even though we cannot achieve the optimum result for everyone, it sets the team goal that we should not stop trying.

Even if you are not Forming a team with a large airline crew, the same rules apply. Neil Hardwick understands the importance of Forming. Neil owns a small building company and every morning he meets his trades crew at a local café, where he buys them a coffee and outlines the day's work. When his team arrive on-site at 7.00 am they are always fresh, happy and productive.

Show respect when you meet people. Stand straight, make eye contact, shake hands. Smile and speak clearly and confidently. Remember or note their names. Be social and attend work functions. Get a feeling for the culture and make a definite effort to meet everyone you can. When you talk to people make them feel they have your undivided attention. Take time to talk about their work, their families, children, their specialities, interests and concerns. Note something unique about every person – they all deserve to be treated with dignity and your respect.

Joining existing teams

There are many situations where you will join an existing team. You may be the new recruit in an existing workplace grouping where the team dynamics are well established. You may be welcomed into an expanding functional team, or be an unwelcome and temporary replacement for a liked person in a downsizing dysfunctional team. Whatever the situation, all curious eyes are on you. It's important in these situations to be confident but unthreatening and act as the respectful person you want others to see.

Don't be silent, but resist the Dunning–Kruger Effect (pages 127–9). You have two ears and one mouth – remember, often the person at the meeting who talks the least actually says the most.

Forming temporary teams

It's hard to join teams that change week to week or even with every shift. Communications are challenging and sometimes even the structure is not clear. My friend Frank discovered these problems as CEO of a major public hospital.

He found hierarchy and ownership to be a big problem. Not only was the answer to 'Who is responsible for the patient?' in doubt; when he asked clinicians who they were accountable to, 50 per cent did not know. Frank found most of the existing teams had not been set up to deliver a specific service; they had just grown over time. In many cases the only way to get clarity around clinical responsibility was to ask who would go to the coroner's court if the need arose.

If you are a member of a team that changes often it's very important to:

- know who you are responsible for
- know who you need to report to
- ensure you conduct thorough handover and takeover briefs

- ensure the other team-members know your proficiencies
- understand the company culture and your WHYs in the job. Without this you can't feel psychologically safe.

Storming

The second stage of team-building is known as Storming. This is where team-members start to express differences of opinion and perhaps react to differences in personal styles. People are making deeper judgements about others in the group and tensions can arise. If these can't be resolved in a way that makes everyone feel valued, one risk is that the group can splinter. Another is that members of the team will be so worried by tensions or disagreements they will go along with bad ideas in an attempt to restore peace, or quietly withdraw support. This too will ultimately cause major problems.

As described in the Leadership chapter, the make-or-break moment of the Storming stage for QF32 came before pushback, when

---

Simple solutions can make a huge difference

Dr Rob Hackett is an anaesthetist in Sydney. As with many surgical teams, those he works with change often. Doctors and nurses are no better than other people at remembering names after a single introduction (one study found we only recall about 30 per cent of them). But in the critical context of surgery where instructions need to be given and acted on immediately, it is vital that everyone present is immediately clear on names and roles.

Rob's very simple but extremely effective solution is to have all those present write their names and roles in large letters on the caps they wear – 'Dr Rob, Anaesthetist' or 'Dr Susan, Surgeon' or 'Matthew, Nurse'. This small step has gone a long way to improving communication, teamwork and ultimately patient outcomes.

---

the check captain and I disagreed over seating arrangements. Neither of us was prepared to back down over our duties, but we were happy to find an alternative path, a compromise. This can only work when all parties respect each other, accept the compromise then move on, as we did. Any lingering resentments that are left unresolved will hobble the team's performance when it matters most.

Toxic and dysfunctional teams

I have worked in many toxic and dysfunctional teams during my career. Invariably, the team was led by an autocratic leader who neither asked for nor ceded to suggestions.

Once, I considered withdrawing support from the team and leaving the cockpit before the flight, until I recognised that this decision would satisfy my ego, but damage the operation. So, I kept quiet, did my job, kept the operation safe, then rebuked the leader at the end of the flight. Interestingly, the infamous captain changed his behaviour thereafter and the problem never resurfaced.

Keep true to your values and your WHYs. In the short term, if safety is not affected, then you should absorb criticism and keep the operation on track. However, if the problem persists then you must report the incidents and if there is no solution, leave.

Not all problems can be resolved.

- If you do not share the values of the team or you are not the right person for the job, then step aside and find someone who is.
- If you find yourself in an autocratic team, with poor governance, without a voice, where your services are not valued, or you think the team is heading in the wrong direction, then leave.

Storming in family teams

Parenting is teamwork. If the family unit has two parents there are, in effect, two leaders and this can create confusion, but it doesn't have to. The key is to ensure that the parents act as one, and that the children see this.

Be clear that the parents (acting as one) make the decisions, exercise control, set clear values, lay the borders for unacceptable behaviour and agree on a plan for what will happen if those lines are crossed.

Storming is common in families. Rules and limits adapt as our children develop, so it's natural to have confusion and disagreements. The best strategy is for parents to have a clear understanding of their objectives and communicate these to their children, give them the facts and let them join in the decision-making process. I found it helpful when resolving disputes to first discuss how I feel, and why, before I detail the problem (what).

Love and care for your children, but don't lose sight of the fact that you are their guardians. You must position yourselves at the top of the hierarchy (above their friends, for instance). If you don't discipline your children, as Canadian psychologist Jordan Peterson writes, 'You're leaving the dirty work to someone else, who will be much dirtier doing it.'

Welcome confidence, fortitude, independence and diversity, but also understand the responsibilities parenting entails. Children represent the family, so give them clear rules and expectations that must be obeyed. The ultimate aim is to set your child up with the right values, behaviours, opportunities and self-confidence to be independent and socially successful.

Norming

Having passed through the Storming stage, the team reaches Norming. Here the bumps are smoothed out and people commit to the group identity. If adjustments are needed, they are made. Everyone comes together, committed and cooperative, ready for the next stage, with a shared mental model of how it will unfold.

Be a proactive team-member

It's important to be a proactive team-member even when you are not the leader.

- Don't be afraid to share your skills or thoughts if the leader did not bring them out earlier. You have been selected for the team because of your skills, so don't be shy.
- Also, don't be afraid to ask. If you aspire to a certain role or have a request, then don't be afraid to admit it and ask for mentoring or help. There should never be a stupid question. Whenever I thought I was asking a silly question, it always turned out others were wondering the same.
- Distributed leadership is a framework in which any team-members can influence team behaviour and leadership is based on tasks not roles. This philosophy insists that every member has a moral and personal responsibility to step up and influence the team activities, especially when lives are at stake.

Idiosyncrasies and normalised deviances

The safest crew in my airline is one where none of the pilots has flown with the others before. The five QF32 pilots had never all flown together before that day. Pilots in my airline share a mutual respect for each other because we appreciate the skills and effort needed to maintain our licences. We know there will be no confusion with personalities, idiosyncrasies and deviances if all of us simply and competently do the required tasks for our roles at the right time.

Familiarity breeds normalised deviances. When friends work together, they tend to accept each other's idiosyncrasies and errors rather than nit-pick and challenge the friendship or cause offence. For the same reason, friends tend to avoid debriefing in a work context. This is a problem.

If you find that friendship concerns are blurring work roles and communication, you need to sit down with all involved and address them before serious problems arise.

Performing

By this stage everyone in the team is supporting one another as they work towards their mutual goal. They are clear about procedures, they recognise strengths and weaknesses in themselves and other team-members, welcome support, provide help when needed and trust each other. No longer disparate individuals, they have become a resilient, effective team – the whole is now greater than the sum of its parts.

This was true for each of the seven teams that brought about a successful outcome for QF32. Even without intercom and satellite communication systems, the cabin crew, Qantas Crisis Management Centre and even staff in Singapore and at home all came together and did exactly what we expected them to do. In the cockpit, 120 different alarms blared out, instruments showed false data or no data at all, and sometimes the lists of ECAM failures appeared and updated themselves so quickly we couldn't keep up. It would have been very easy for any individual to have become overwhelmed in these circumstances, but each of the five pilots in the augmented crew knew and performed their role perfectly.

Matt ran the checklists, Dave ran the performance calculations, the trainee check captain monitored Matt and me, and Mark communicated with the cabin and monitored the four of us. I told Mark, 'If we are all looking up, you look down. If we all look down, then you look up.' We performed our separate roles and tasks and trusted and supported each other, functioning like a well-oiled machine.

Performing in crisis
Teams need to step up and do the hard things in periods of stress.

- In times of crisis, step up and offer your help.
- In times of recession, decisions must be made to let good people go to protect a company's survival. If you find yourself in this situation, protect their dignity and try to help them find alternative employment.

When Dr Bruce Tuckman first outlined his stages of team dynamics, Performing was the final stage. But a decade later, in collaboration with doctoral student Mary Ann Jensen, he proposed a fifth stage, one that would bring the team's work to a close. I regard this fifth stage as essential for team resilience.

Adjourning

This stage provides the opportunity for looking at what went right and acknowledging successes, as well as recognising what went wrong and identifying what could be improved next time. A debrief like this provides closure and the opportunity to learn, pay compliments, adjust and improve. Adjourning builds strong, resilient team players.

In the 24 hours after the QF32 event, I debriefed the cabin crew three times, the technical crew twice and the passengers once. The stress we all felt after the flight was progressively eased by these processes. I have been pleased to fly with people from all three groups in the years since QF32 and in every case the teamwork was excellent.

In the Adjourning stage team-members should collectively review objectives, actions and outcomes.

Well done!

Leaders and fellow team-members should acknowledge effort and reward success. While many captains simply pack up with a bit of general chit chat at the end of a flight, I make a point of shaking every pilot's hand in acknowledgement of their contribution to the team's success. Everyone deserves to be treated with dignity, to feel wanted and respected. Not only does this acknowledgement make people feel good (a dopamine high), it reinforces behaviours that will benefit future teams.

But it must be sincere. Lip service instead of genuine recognition breeds cynicism and ill-feeling. Leaders should demonstrate real appreciation of effort. If the situation allows, they should recommend exceptional people for formal awards and citations.

Welcome errors as opportunities to learn and gain experience. Each member of the team should be encouraged to identify and discuss failures in a blame-free atmosphere. We have to stop worrying about making mistakes, because this is the human condition. Often, the quietest, lowest ranked team-members and observers at the rear have the most insightful feedback.

If there are criticisms to be made, make them in a spirit of personal humility and team growth, then draw a line under them. As football's Sir Alex Ferguson put it, 'Do it after the game then move on. There is no point in criticising a player forever.'

I stand beside the cabin crew to farewell the passengers at the end of every flight. If I discover passengers who have any criticisms, I take them aside and offer my business card so that I can be their single point of contact later.

I still get a great sense of satisfaction when passengers say, 'Thank you – that was the best flight I have ever had.' I touch the shoulder of the crew member standing next to me and say, 'Did you hear that? Well done!'

Debriefs

Debriefs are when the best learning takes place. We don't learn from experience only. We learn from reflecting on experience.

Debriefs promote the dignity of all team-members, making them feel valued and respected. I brief and debrief every take-off and landing. The after take-off debrief is made during the climb, while good and bad memories are fresh and unaffected by biases. It's amazing what I have learned after requesting criticism in debriefs.

Ray Dalio, the founder of $160 billion investment company Bridgewater Associates, has made a corporate artform of debriefs. In his 2016 book *Originals: How Non-Conformists Move the World*, Wharton Business School professor Adam Grant writes about the culture that has enabled Bridgewater to make more money for its investors than any hedge fund in history. Dalio doesn't just ask for feedback from every employee, he demands it. His view is, 'No-one has the right to hold a critical opinion without speaking up about it.' After one meeting with a significant potential client where Dalio had been clearly under-prepared, a subordinate sent him an email which said in part, 'Ray, you deserve a D for your performance today.' Dalio didn't fire him, he thanked him.

As the Bridgewater website puts it, 'We want an idea meritocracy in which meaningful work and meaningful relationships are pursued through radical truth and radical transparency. We require people to be extremely open, air disagreements, test each other's logic, and view discovering mistakes and weaknesses as a good thing that leads to improvement and innovation ...' Open and honest feedback improves knowledge and prevents groupthink. Bridgewater was one of the few financial companies anywhere in the world that warned its clients about the 2008 Global Financial Crisis a full year before it hit.

Human Factors

Human Factors is the name given to non-technical skills that affect the way real people behave in real-world workplaces. It covers all our mental, social, personal and communication skills (or lack thereof) in situation awareness, problem-solving, teamwork, leadership and managing errors, fatigue and stress.

Crew Resource Management

Crew Resource Management (CRM) is a framework for building safe and effective teams. CRM brings together all aspects of human factors and risk to maximise air safety. Originally titled Cockpit Resource Management (and not to be confused with Customer Relationship Management), CRM was created in response to the world's worst aviation accident.

In 1977, two Boeing 747 Jumbo jets, one of them commanded by Captain Jacob van Zanten, KLM's chief flight instructor, collided on the fog-affected runway at Tenerife in the Canary Islands, killing 583 people. This was an avoidable accident. The world was aghast.

After the accident, NASA convened a panel to address aviation safety and undertook studies on the causes of previous accidents. It found that the problems were often failures in communication and team coordination, rather than a lack of technical proficiency. CRM was the result, and by the early 1980s the Federal Aviation Administration had made it a requirement for all US military and airline pilots to receive CRM training.

CRM starts with the premise that humans are vulnerable and make mistakes. It teaches participants about the human biases, limitations and weaknesses covered earlier in this chapter. But it also looks at strengths, and specifically recognises the importance of teamwork ahead of the individual, and the power of pooling resources to improve resilience.

The aim of CRM is to build better teamwork to improve safety and resilience in high-tech and high-risk environments such as HROs. These environments have humans overseeing computers and machines that perform repetitive 'known' things with precision. Two problems arise: first, that the hardware sometimes fails; and second, that no machine or procedure can be designed for unknown unknowns. Therefore, resilience requires creative and expert human teams that take over and recover the situations when the automation fails. True resilience can only be achieved when humans are taught to work together in one expert team that can make creative decisions to recover from the unknown unknowns.

When my airline started CRM training in the mid-1980s, the first challenge was to convince aggressive and autocratic captains to build and join in effective teams with their subordinates. I was a co-pilot at that time and I remember the captains who complained the loudest about CRM were the ones who needed CRM training the most. Aviation hardware and computers were advancing faster than the individuals, who were unable to keep up. Safety and resilience lay not with a life-or-death gamble in the hands of one domineering captain but with the combined skills of a unified and coordinated team who effectively worked with technology.

Today, CRM forms one part of the human factors study of how to build resilient teams for any situation. This covers: assertiveness, automation, bias, briefs, command gradient, communications, decision-making, delegation, dignity, distractions, ego, errors, fatigue, gender, honesty, humility, Just Culture, leadership, managing upwards, mental model, modesty, overload, personality, priorities, respect, roles, shared mental model, situation awareness, startle effect, stress, tasks, teamwork, threats, time and workflow. I think CRM should also cover post-traumatic stress.

In a team environment where decisions have major implications, the CRM model significantly increases the likelihood of a good outcome.

Diverse experience and viewpoints – a shared culture

The least resilient teams are the ones in which every member is similar and they think and act the same. This opens the way for the development of huge blind spots in decision-making, where a risk or problem that might be obvious to people outside the group is invisible to those within it. Even these teams will perform better than individuals, but they'll be left in the dust by teams that draw on diverse strengths and life experiences.

There is no one ideal personality type. We need leaders, followers, maintainers, auditors, scientists, artists and farmers. The best teams comprise the widest range of personality and cognitive diversity, each person bringing their own unique skills and interests to the table.

In business, the value of diversity is well established. The management consultancy firm McKinsey & Company has shown a serious performance advantage for companies whose executive layers have better gender balance and an ethnic and cultural-background mix that reflects the wider population.

Looking at 1000 companies in a dozen countries as part of ongoing measurement around the topic, McKinsey found that companies with the most diverse executives were significantly more profitable and did much better in value creation. Companies with the least diversity underperformed their industry peers in profitability by almost a third. The McKinsey analysts attributed these findings to the fact that more diverse companies were better able to attract top talent, to improve their customer orientation and their employee satisfaction levels, and to make more effective decisions.

Diverse skills and viewpoints are just as important in non-corporate teams too.

Don't try to push square pegs into round holes; instead, create a new template. When you create a psychologically safe environment for diverse people to contribute their ideas, there is a commensurate improvement in communications, creativity, wisdom, agility, engagement and morale.

We should welcome all types of people into our teams for the creativity, variation and opportunities they bring. For example, the addition of Arts to STEM, creating STEAM, acknowledges artists' ability to translate science. As well as writing the novel *Deliverance*, which became a hit film, James Dickey was a poet inspired by the modern world who wrote 'The Moon Ground' on the occasion of the 1969 Apollo 11 moon landing. Describing the need for these artistic skills, the 1997 movie *Contact* had Dr Ellie Arroway played by Jodie Foster say of her experience in space, 'No – no words. No words to describe it. Poetry! They should've sent a poet. So beautiful. So beautiful . . . I had no idea.'

But no matter how diverse its members are, the team itself can only succeed if everyone is operating under a shared set of values. Attitudes, expectations and behaviours all spring from these values: this is the overall culture the team is operating in. If there is no commitment to a clear, agreed culture, even the most talented teams won't be able to sustain success.

Adam Grant looked at the issue of culture fit in *Originals*, reporting on the research into the success of three different recruiting models used by Silicon Valley start-ups and their effect on growth and resilience. Under the three different approaches, people were hired for one of three different primary qualities: their specific current skills; their potential to become a star performer; or the way they fitted into the company culture.

Two hundred start-ups were studied. Once they had launched as public entities, companies that recruited people based on cultural fit grew 25 per cent slower than those that recruited based on skills, and 140 per cent slower than the ones that hired based on potential. So, doesn't that indicate cultural fit isn't important after all? No, because as Grant explains, companies that hired for cultural fit proved more resilient during the crucial start-up period: unlike those recruiting for skills and potential, not one failed.

But, Grant says, if culture remains stagnant the team loses its ability to adapt to the challenges being thrown up by the outside world. The result is groupthink. The answer for sustained success is to hire not on culture fit, but on culture contribution. This means that instead of seeking team-members who can slip seamlessly into the existing culture, you ask what is missing from the culture and look for people who can enrich and stretch it.

Roles can be swapped, but clarity is needed

In an effective team, members know how to do tasks performed by other members. They can step in, or step up, as needed. Pilots understand this well. In aviation, a captain could be assigned the role of pilot-in-command of a flight one day then as a co-pilot for the next.

When people have different roles it's important that you know and perform the tasks for your role, and leave other people alone to do theirs. In a cockpit, tasks include flying the aircraft, configuring computers, actioning checklists, making radio calls and maintaining the logs.

Every pilot knows how to do these tasks, but chaos and frustration grows when pilots action things outside their area of responsibility.

In crisis situations tasks should be actioned serially (the team-members involved giving full attention to one task at a time) rather than in parallel (team-members each doing their own tasks at the same time). During the QF32 emergency, Matt and I worked as serial, not parallel, team-members. When one of us actioned a critical task, the other stopped all other duties and monitored him.

But this technique can be applied to life in general for significant or non-reversible actions. Have someone cross-check critical thoughts and decisions before you commit to action. Always have important documents checked by another person before you send them. If this is not possible, sleep on a major decision before you make it.

Take action

Strong teams welcome humility and vulnerability

Every one of us feels vulnerable and underconfident about something at some point, but it takes courage to expose these vulnerabilities. Teams that share a strong sense of trust enable their members to open up, secure in the knowledge they will be supported, not attacked. In fact, when people are acting in good faith, nothing catalyses trust and teamwork more than a confident person expressing vulnerability.

Leaders should not be afraid to be humble and announce their weaknesses. When I expose one of my vulnerabilities, I nearly always find it shared by the rest of the team. In every case it encourages others to offer valuable solutions or increase their support. In all cases the team wins.

People may need a little extra prompting to express vulner-abilities if the issue is personal and they fear letting the team down. Don't intrude into others' privacy but do be empathetic and reach out to those who seem distracted or preoccupied. A few years ago, I noticed a pilot slip out of the room during the crew introductions to make a phone call. When I quietly asked if everything was all right, he revealed that his mother had been admitted to hospital the previous night with a very serious condition. Far from home and very concerned, he had been calling for an update. I contacted the Chief Pilot who immediately arranged for special leave and helped the pilot get back to where he needed to be, with his family.

Every contribution matters, so step up

There is an often-told story about US President John Kennedy visiting NASA's Space Center and stopping to talk to a janitor. In response to Kennedy's query about what he was doing, the man said, 'Well, Mr President, I'm helping to put a man on the moon.' The story may well be apocryphal, but it resonates because it contains a truth about teamwork: every contribution matters, and every person has an influence on the company's success or failure.

Effective teams understand this and have what's called a level command gradient. This means that even the most junior team-member believes their participation is vital to the outcome. They feel comfortable offering suggestions and raising concerns, and are treated with thoughtful gratitude, protection and respect when they do so.

In these teams, everyone has the confidence and motivation to 'step up'. Stepping up takes different forms depending on the circumstances, but at heart it comes down to taking responsibility and finding solutions. Facebook COO Sheryl Sandberg described it this way, 'Nothing at Facebook is someone else's problem. When you see something that's broken, go fix it.'

Team-members who step up don't waste time finding excuses or blaming others. They use whatever resources are available to fix a problem, then they include it in a debrief so it can be prevented from happening again. They live by the rule that the standard you ignore and walk past is the standard you accept, and the one by which your own performance will be judged.

Qantas airport staff was one of the teams that ensured a successful outcome for the QF32 crisis and they excelled at stepping up.

On hearing of the emergency, engineers, airport check-in and customer-care staff on rostered days off rushed in to work to offer help. They didn't need to be asked. They didn't know what they would face or be required to do. Their overwhelming response was, 'My team needs me. Time to step up.'

When stepping up is hard

In strong, effective teams, everyone including the leader recognises the value of stepping up and they support those who do it. But not all teams work so well. Sometimes stepping up feels easy and natural. But sometimes, when it involves delivering bad news or being the lone voice calling STOP! in a dangerous situation, it is confronting and takes great personal courage.

In its 2012 report, the Institute for Crisis Management reported that management and staff were responsible for half and one-third of crises, respectively. Many crises could have been prevented if people simply raised their concerns.

Why do people remain silent as a crisis unfolds rather than crying STOP!? Many people are held back by a simple reticence to risk embarrassment or censure if their concerns turn out to be unjustified or incorrect. Some fear challenging higher authority, even when their reasons for raising concern are shared by others. There are countless examples of people who have witnessed errors remaining quiet even though they knew the consequences would be fatal. Fortunately for passengers, pilots are not the silent type.

Pilots are taught the RAISE process. We are taught to recognise key words as signatures of the five escalating steps required to stop an action. I have used RAISE a few times in my career. Every time, the other pilot concerned recognised my intent early in the process and responded to resolve the problem.

Imagine you observe your boss making inappropriate advances to another person. Here's a step-by-step process to manage upwards. Stop the process when the person responds correctly:

R Relay information: *'John, I am aware that you are having meetings with women alone in your hotel room.'*

A Ask if they are aware, seek clarification – ask why: *'Are you aware they could feel uncomfortable? Why are you doing this? Is it against company policy?'*

I Indicate concern: *'I am concerned for these women and the implications this would have for you and the organisation.'*

S Offer a solution: *'Why don't you meet at the office, or include others in the meetings?'*

If the mindless or recalcitrant person has failed to respond, or if there is intentional recklessness or flagrant violations, then someone must call STOP!

E Emergency language: *'John, STOP!'* or *'John, you must listen!'*

Pilots are not always agreeable people. We will always tell you what we think, raise concerns and call STOP! if necessary. Status and respect derives from competence, not power. The rules of engagement authorise conflict when people must speak their mind to protect safety. This is one of the reasons why aviation is so safe.

Accept that people raising concerns or calling STOP! are doing it with the intent of protecting you and the team and preventing mistakes that could have far-reaching consequences. There is no place for ego in teams. When you ask your team to raise any concerns, you authorise them to monitor and become responsible for the consequences, empowering the whole team in the process.

Team decision-making – time to Ramp up

Even in great teams, where each person is confident about their role and feels free to speak up, decision-making can be tricky. That's especially the case when decisions need to be reached quickly in complex situations.

I created a technique I call the Ramp to work through this process. The Ramp produces rapid and excellent outcomes, provided it's done in good faith by a confident leader who values collaboration before ego . . . and learns to speak last.

The leader begins the Ramp process by outlining the issue that needs to be resolved and then inviting all team-members to contribute pertinent information. When all the contributions have been made, the leader then asks each person in turn to offer their decision and their reasons for making it.

This technique takes its name from the fact that in a situation with a clear hierarchy it is the lowest ranked person who is asked to respond first. One by one the leader moves up through the ranks until everyone has had their say. It travels in this direction so that those with less power feel free to express their genuine opinions with their reasons, without being pressured by groupthink, or sunflower, champion or experience bias (as described in Chapter 6).

The leader's role here is to facilitate input and keep the conversation focused and not to disclose their own views. If everyone else has spoken and all options have been covered but the leader thinks the team is missing something important or drawing some unsupported conclusions, they should prompt further discussion by injecting a modified question or an alternative option. This should be followed by another Ramp.

The leader conducts the orchestra rather than seizing the soloists' spotlights. If the Ramp has come to a decision the leader agrees with, they say nothing other than to agree with the team's views. Everyone in the team feels pride knowing the leader did not need to contribute to the decision, and the opportunity to participate and be heard has given them dignity. The leader always makes the final decision. But the Ramp process ensures they come to it from the most informed position, with the benefit they might even learn something new.

I use the Ramp when making fast and complex decisions. It was a critical part of QF32's success. It suits small sized teams where distractions can be controlled. It also works in situations where the hierarchy is less clear, say where a team leader and a group of people within a department all hold similar titles. In this case, ask the quietest and least confident people to speak first.

The Ramp also works for decision-making at home. Ask the youngest member of the family to speak first. Each input adds increasing wisdom and there's always unity at the end.

Why teams fail

The fault lines that develop in failing teams follow predictable paths. If your team is experiencing the following problems there's no point hoping the issue will somehow magically sort itself out. Unless there is some serious, focused intervention that changes the team dynamics, teamwork is doomed.

In his bestselling book *The Five Dysfunctions of a Team*, Patrick Lencioni laid out five critical reasons for team failure, to which I add one more.

Lencioni's model is arranged as a pyramid, where each stage isn't just a sign of dysfunction, it is the foundation for the following stage, topping out in performance issues that are obvious to everyone.

The first stage is **Absence of Trust**. If team-members don't trust those around them, they are unwilling to be vulnerable. But since we are all vulnerable in some areas, the only way to hide weaknesses and mistakes is to build walls to keep others out. Honest interactions become impossible.

The second is **Fear of Conflict**. With no trust that their team will support them, underconfident team-members guard their comments and become unwilling to challenge the norm. This stymies communication and leaves the team open to avoidable threats and errors.

The third stage is **Lack of Commitment**. In an increasingly toxic environment is it any wonder people no longer feel bound to the group and committed to its success? As things reach this point, people will no longer engage, communicate, take risks or accept responsibility for fixing problems. They won't report problems or step up. People may feign agreement during meetings, but there is rarely true buy-in or commitment to decisions.

Stage four is **Avoidance of Accountability**. The feeling here is 'This is a decision I didn't support in the first place, and I'm not surprised it's gone wrong.' But at the same time, no-one wants to put themselves in the difficult position of holding someone else accountable, so everyone just pulls into their own shells.

Lencioni's final stage, at the top of the pyramid, is **Inattention to Results**. Team success is built on effective monitoring, continual feedback and debriefing. If the group has become a fractured collection of individuals all looking out for themselves, success is simply impossible.

My sixth stage of team failure is **Lack of Recognition**. In a corrosive atmosphere where team spirit has been eaten away, the team leader often takes all the credit. This is a recipe for professional jealousy and disengagement: why make an effort if you feel your contribution is never going to be recognised? Teamwork is a distant memory.

Flipped on their head, Lencioni's reasons for failure offer the keys to team success that should be enshrined in the leader's and company's culture. Work fearlessly building foundations from the bottom up. Establish trust and psychological safety before you progress up to higher goals. If you are a team leader, you must protect your team.

Lessons in teamwork

There are great examples of teamwork all around us, offering inspiration and a chance to examine our own behaviour in teams. Here are a few:

'I have to trust everything she says'

I am very privileged to be Patron of the organisation Disabled Wintersport Australia (DWA). Through DWA I've seen many wonderful examples of individual resilience. I've also appreciated the way competitive events such as the Winter Paralympics offer some of the best examples of teamwork around.

One striking example features American vision-impaired ski-racer Lindsay Ball. Despite being almost completely blind since birth, she is fearless on the slopes, having raced in mogul events at the elite level for more than five years, hitting speeds that would terrify 99 per cent of skiers with full vision.

This is possible because of guide Diane Barras skiing ahead of her. In such a competition the guide has a loudspeaker strapped to their back, which amplifies the directions they call out at high speed, tearing through the gaps between marker flags. If the skier following them misses one of these 'gates' they are disqualified.

Lindsay and Diane and other vision-impaired skiers and their guides represent the ultimate in teamwork. They use constant communication and have an incredible amount of trust and commitment which leads to deep confidence. They also accept that there will be failures – as Lindsay said of Diane, 'I have to trust everything she says and we both know we're going to make mistakes' – but they know that the team will endure and persist.

The most important team

Many of us have the perfect example of two-person teamwork close at hand. It's marriage, and with so much at stake, it's surprising that many people don't put the same conscious effort into this team as they do into their weekend football team or their office team.

I began married life in 1987 as a type A personality, driven, impatient and competitive. But I have learned from my wife, Coral's emotional intelligence, building skills that I now apply in both my work and personal life: shared values, respect, trustworthiness, communication and care.

Coral has always had clear priorities. When our children were about 10 years old, a friend asked Coral what her priorities were in life. She said:

1. my husband
2. my children, then
3. myself
4. work.

She reasoned that if she looked after me, two relaxed parents would do a better job than one stressed parent of raising our children. She also joked that when the children grew up and flew the nest she'd be left at home with 'just her spouse'.

What are my own priorities? I've never forgotten Gene Kranz's wife, Marta's quote, 'Behind every great man is a woman, and behind her is a plumber, electrician, Maytag repairman and one or more sick kids. And the car needs to go into the shop.' So, my priorities are Coral, my children, myself then work.

What are your priorities?

Marriage is similar to a formation of two fighter aircraft. Where you take off from is never where you ultimately land. Along the way you face predators, threats, risks and adversity that will try to separate you. Change is not the problem; it's changing together that is the key. Above all, your strength and resilience depends upon you being flexible, changing course and adapting together, keeping a tight formation, never losing contact with each other, and communicating with and protecting each other.

Coral codified this approach into a list titled 'Suggestions for a long and happy marriage' that she sends to newly engaged friends.

Values

Put your relationship first. Find things to laugh about together. Share pleasurable experiences together – never make yourselves redundant to each other. Make time for just the two of you.

Put as much effort into your marriage as you put into your career. Help each other grow. Travel, holiday and make memories together.

Commit, be responsible and accountable for your marriage. Shed your ego and welcome feedback. Truly believe divorce is not an option. Remember why you got together in the first place. You're both in it for life.

Evolve and adapt. Be open, forgive and be flexible to change. Stay interesting. Stay educated, confident and up to date. Be optimistic.

When you maintain the same values, you will find you both independently and conveniently make the same decisions.

Respect
Respect each other equally. Be each other's best friend and biggest fan. Protect, support and acknowledge each other. You have to really like and respect each other to last.

Prevent contempt at all costs. A relationship is finished whenever one feels contempt for the other.

Trustworthiness
Trust, tolerate and be honest with each other. Don't distrust and control. Be prepared to leave your mobile phone on the table and share the unlock codes.

Communicate (Don't fall out of love)
Activate the oxytocin. Touch each other. Walk holding hands. Purposefully sit next to each other on the couch at night.

Prioritise intimacy and sex. Less sex and physical contact is the start to a slippery slide of broken communications and relationships. When both of you decide sex has become less important, find other things to do together.

No secrets. Fantasies are often subconscious desires. Communicate your failings, concerns and conflicts. Discuss openly and frankly any sexual uneasiness, desires or incompatibilities.

Praise or compliment each other daily.

Try to align your sleep schedules so you go to bed together each night and wake up together in the morning. Talk and cuddle.

Care

The more love you give, the more you get. Say 'I love you' every opportunity (but not so much that it's flippant or meaningless).

Say 'YES' more often. Be open-minded and do things (like an afternoon walk) that your partner wants to do, even when you don't.

Do something every day to make your partner happy.

Practising what I preach

As described in Chapter 5, 12 minutes into the QF32 emergency, I thought of the spiral gliding manoeuvre Neil Armstrong had developed and decided it would increase our chances of landing safely.

I sought permission from air traffic control to climb to 10,000 feet as needed for the spiral descent; however, just as permission was confirmed, the other four pilots said, 'No!' They were unfamiliar with the Armstrong Spiral and thought it was crazy to want to climb with such a damaged aircraft.

In that moment I was shocked at their response, but there was no time to discuss it. I followed the group's wishes and remained at the lower altitude. I decided to wait five minutes, then climb again if the fuel situation had not improved.

I have never felt embarrassed or angry that the four pilots said STOP! They had no knowledge of the Armstrong Spiral and there was insufficient time to explain it to them. They called STOP! because they didn't want to climb, and I respected their input.

When I fly, my passengers' safety is paramount, not my ego. Anything that increases safety must be respected and protected. I trust my crew and value their input. In fact, I value their thoughts even more when they run counter to mine because it probably signals I have not communicated enough. Have I missed something important or am I just plain wrong?

Bottom line

Teamwork is an essential element of resilience. I am alive today because of it. No matter how talented or capable or confident you are as an individual, you will always be stronger and perform better as part of an effective team.

We are all members of many teams throughout our lives, from the family unit to workplace teams to the wider community. We're biologically programmed to be team-players, with brain-chemical rewards for our interactions. But that doesn't mean we're inherently good at teamwork. Fortunately, like so many of the other elements of resilience, this skill can be learned and honed.

Mutual trust between each and every team-member is an essential part of teamwork. With this in place, team-members can and will expose their vulnerabilities knowing that their teammates are equally vulnerable and that everyone has their back. By being open and honest they enable themselves to work together and achieve great things.

Effective teams can be built and maintained following the stages described by Bruce Tuckman: Forming, Storming, Norming, Performing and Adjourning. Don't skip the last one – debriefs are an essential part of team excellence and morale, a chance to look at both what went right and what could be done better next time.

Every team-member, no matter where they are in the hierarchy, has the responsibility to step up and speak out about behaviour that could endanger the team or other people. This won't always be easy, but it must be done.

The strongest teams are the most diverse. Different life experiences and capabilities lift the team's performance in every way, as long as the team-members are operating on a shared set of values.

The most important team in your life is the one you form with a significant other. Work as hard to protect this relationship as you work to protect your job.

Tolstoy claimed all happy families are the same, while all unhappy families are unhappy in their own way. With teams, it's the opposite. All failing teams fail along the same lines, and each stage of failure leads to the next until the team is irreversibly broken. But knowing what can go wrong provides a blueprint for how to get things right.

Checklist: Teamwork

Our survival and progress depends on teamwork:
As a species and as individuals, we need effective teamwork to survive and thrive.

Without trust there is no teamwork:
Teams can only coalesce when every member trusts and supports every other member.

Teamwork proceeds in stages:
Each team that comes together goes through Forming, Storming, Norming and Performing.

Don't forget to debrief:
Make sure the stages above are followed by Adjourning, where the team draws even closer and finds opportunities for improvement.

Diversity is powerful:
Research proves that diverse teams perform best, as long as they have shared values.

Good teams give everyone a voice:
A process such as the Ramp ensures that everyone contributes and is heard.

It's never 'not my job':
Every team-member has a responsibility to step up and to call STOP! if something is wrong.

Ego is the enemy of teamwork:
Teams are built on empathy, respect, commitment and account-ability, not self-interest.

CHAPTER 9

Post-Traumatic Stress:
Dealing With Your Own and Helping Others

This chapter includes stories of incidents that caused post-traumatic stress (PTS) and post-traumatic stress disorder (PTSD). People coping with their own incidents, particularly ones that occurred while flying or driving, may wish to skip these stories and focus instead on the overall message of the chapter, including the most important thing I learned from my QF32 experience:

Just as success follows failure, there can be growth from trauma.

I am neither a psychiatrist nor a psychologist and this chapter is not intended to take the place of seeking professional help. However, I hope that by sharing the problems I experienced and the ways I found to address them I can offer encouragement to anyone who is suffering PTS and their loved ones who are trying to help.

Pieces of me I didn't have to give

Stress is a natural reaction to threats. We've already seen (in Chapter 3) that human beings need a minimum level of stress to focus and attain peak performance in critical situations. The brain responds to increasing stress by commanding the release of chemicals including cortisol to increase energy supply.

Cortisol levels ebb and flow with our circadian rhythms. In extreme fear and life-and-death situations the brain also commands the release of adrenaline, a turbocharger for every cell in your body and a key part of the fight, flight or freeze response. A prolonged overload of stress, of the kind a person endures when they suffer trauma, can confuse and exhaust and send the whole system into chaos.

I didn't know any of this when I stepped off QF32 onto the Singapore tarmac. But what happened that day affected me badly for many months. I was still turbocharged with cortisol when I left the aircraft and arrived at the terminal. Even after I debriefed each of the passenger groups and answered all their questions, I still felt in command and responsible for them all. I still feel responsible for QF32 passengers today.

I was prepared to use my influence and authority to guarantee continued passenger care. I initially refused when the airport staff asked me to leave the airport and take the other pilots and cabin crew to our hotel. I said the passengers needed continued support and I wanted to stay with them. Only when the staff pleaded with me, saying, 'Please leave! The buses are waiting for you, and you have to leave before the passengers can depart,' did I hand over the reins and go.

After arriving at the crew hotel, my focus swung to debriefing the cabin crew and pilots. This took place in the hotel bar. Qantas head office had given Cabin Services Manager Michael von Reth authority to spend $400 on drinks and I'd received a separate text message from Murray Crockett, Qantas's A380 Fleet Manager, who was on holiday at the time, thanking us all for our actions and asking me to 'buy a celebratory drink for everyone on me'.

I knew the severity of what we'd been through over the previous seven hours called for more than one drink. There were 25 crew members who would retire to their rooms after the debrief, watch the news and mull over those events. I had to ensure they were debriefed even more than the passengers.

I told Michael to put the $400 back in his pocket and organised for hotel security to close off the bar area and guard the entrances (to prevent the media eavesdropping). As a close collegial group who had experienced an incredibly harrowing time, we then spent the next six hours talking through what had happened, and sharing what we were each thinking and feeling. Together, we were slowly coming down from the 'cortisol high'.

We'd worked hard, and it was now our time to reconnect on safe ground in support of each other and in acknowledgement of what we had managed to achieve. It was a time to validate this wonderful crew for whom I remain grateful and of whom I'm so proud.

The QF32 cabin crew and pilots were all in good spirits when we boarded QF6 the next night bound for Sydney. It should have been a low-stress flight because we were 'passengering'; however, everything changed just after take-off when the Boeing 747 suffered an engine failure. The situation was exacerbated by one of the operating cabin crew who panicked and incorrectly called out, 'BRACE! BRACE!', effectively spreading panic. The flight was aborted. Back on the ground again, some QF32 crew members reacted to the second engine failure by becoming disconnected and unresponsive. Others were distressed and needed comforting.

Qantas sent word that we had been rescheduled onto another flight leaving the following morning. That was when Michael Von Reth said, 'STOP!' He could see that his crew were in no state to be going anywhere until they'd had professional help. He asked for a psychiatrist and psychologist to be sent to meet with them the following day; only after that happened would he clear them to depart. I too felt responsibility for the cabin crew and wanted to stay and help them. I asked head office to allow me to do this, but they refused, instructing me to return instead with the rest of the pilots. I complied, but I felt sad and hollow.

Arriving in Sydney, the other pilots and I were whisked out through the discreet terminal exit used for VIPs, avoiding the media massed in the Arrivals area. Coral and my children, Alex and Sophia, met me outside the airline's head office building. More media had been camped outside my home for the previous 48 hours, so we had agreed to go straight to the home of our great friends, Julie and Simon Ford, for a few nights, waiting for the pack to disperse. My beloved father, Peter, and stepmother, Mariea, were there too. We all had a calm and comforting low-key evening together and I felt that I was coping well with all that had happened.

But I woke early the following morning feeling much worse. Within minutes I was in the bathroom with a knotted stomach, retching. There was nothing to throw up because I hadn't been able to make myself eat. I was bottoming out. I had been on a cortisol-induced high-energy emotional rollercoaster ride over the previous three days, had barely eaten and felt distracted and tired to the bone. Safe at home, my body sank to a cortisol low, and I didn't appreciate just how fragile I had become.

I was fortunate. A journalist friend, John Connolly, came over and spent four hours recording my account of the flight. This was a masterstroke that would help me later, but I felt no better at the end of it. My phone was continuously sounding alerts: messages from media wanting interviews, friends checking on me and Qantas management offering help. I was cautious, perplexed, overloaded and exhausted. Everyone wanted pieces of me I didn't have to give.

The next day Qantas engineers sent us three typed pages listing the warnings and ECAM checklists that we had undertaken during the flight. Dad, who is a pilot, was curious, so I read the list, one line at a time, to him and Mariea. Their happy, interested faces slowly transitioned from curiosity to surprise then to doubt and then fear as I finished page one. I stopped partway through page two when they started crying.

In three weeks I was due to fly to France and take delivery of Qantas's next new A380 in Toulouse. This was a great privilege, a reward for my handling of a 24-hour delay on a flight in London earlier in the year and the resulting passenger plaudits. But I rang Murray Crockett, the A380 Fleet Manager, and said, 'I am not sure I am fit to fly that delivery flight. You need to allocate it to someone else.' He replied, 'Thank you, Richard – we had concerns, so thank you for approaching us first.'

I didn't fully appreciate my unpredictable emotional state until five days after the event. Investigators from the Australian Transport Safety Bureau (ATSB) were conducting an interview with me, planned to last for only one hour. The first question was, 'Tell us what happened after you arrived at the counter to check out of the hotel that Thursday.' My answer took four hours. My recollection was fine and controlled up until I began to describe the stage, 12 minutes after the engine failure, when I had wanted to climb to 10,000 feet to enable an Armstrong Spiral. At this point I broke into tears.

I was shocked. I didn't know why I was crying – but there I was, choked up, unable to speak. It was the first time I had lost my composure since my mother had died 37 years earlier, when I was 17.

The physiology of stress

Our amygdala and neocortex control stress. The amygdala is our high-speed 'smoke alarm' signalling emotions, uncertainty and fear. It has direct inputs to many senses via fast nerves and is trained to be the first to match critical patterns to identify in a fraction of a second novel events and threats, such as the sound of a gun or a threatening pair of eyes in the distant grass.

The amygdala outputs to the sympathetic nervous system to enable fast, pre-programmed and instinctive responses. Its output is almost binary: you are safe or you are not safe. The amygdala also biases processes in the hippocampus that create strong emotional memories that last. We remember things best when they are associated with negative emotions rather than positive emotions. We remember the school bully more than we remember the school captain.

Remembering the bad things improves our chances of survival, but the fear can spread and increase stress. If a dog attacks you as a child, you will probably remember and fear that type of dog forever. Your fear might even spread to be associated with all dogs.

Our emotions execute at many speeds. The neocortex is much slower than the amygdala, taking at least half a second to respond to stimuli. However, the neocortex adds cognitive value to decisions, as well as dampening and regulating the amygdala's output. When everything is normal, the neocortex pattern-matches information streaming from the five senses to predict outcomes and decide responses. For example, after identifying a flash of lightning the neocortex anticipates a thunderclap and so inhibits the amygdala's fear response to sound.

Problems arise when the neocortex overrates a risk, then incorrectly stimulates or fails to inhibit a startle response from the amygdala. When this happens, thoughts create panic or prevent panic from dissipating, causing stress hormones including cortisol to be released.

The amygdala's next-door neighbour, the hippocampus, plays a vital role in our everyday life by managing short-term and installing long-term memories. Both these things are crucial in, among other things, helping the neocortex integrate, rationalise and reduce fearful memories. These processes improve our abilities to recognise and process threats and reduce the likelihood of future false alarms.

If the levels of stress hormones, especially cortisol, get too high then the hippocampus becomes impaired, and that in turn impairs our more rational neocortex. The result is a range of potential symptoms that make up what is known as post-traumatic stress (PTS).

Post-traumatic stress and post-traumatic stress disorder

PTS is an evolved, natural and essential response to abnormal events. PTS builds persistent memories of dangerous places and situations well after the stress has passed. These memories are key to our learning, prediction and survival. PTS may initially cause us to sweat, shake, feel sick in the stomach and have bad dreams about what happened or dread the possibility of it reoccurring. But these symptoms should fade with time.

If the emotions don't fade you're left with post-traumatic stress disorder (PTSD). Sometimes it has a delayed onset, occurring after the person has seemingly recovered. PTSD wears you down physically, mentally and emotionally, damaging health, happiness and relationships. It can lock people into a state of overload and alarm. Instead of being able to assess and dismiss perceived threats, the limbic system (including the amygdala) creates a state known as hypervigilance, with fear, doubt and uncertainty at its core, with the slower prefrontal cortex unable to restore calm. This means the individual is perpetually on the verge of going to the finger-on-the-nuclear-button state the US military calls DEFCON 1.

The downward spiral continues. Sleep is vital physically as well as mentally, but too many stress hormones and poor sleep damages the body. A stressed person wakes still feeling tired, overloaded, distracted and possibly depressed.

Any small thing can trigger a PTS response. First, we need the mind to have made links, associating and connecting a particular image, sound, smell, taste or location with trauma that won't go away. Later, when a fragment of those patterns of senses re-present themselves to the mind, even if subconsciously in the most calm and safe surroundings, a person with PTSD can suddenly find themselves feeling they are back in that stressful and desperate survival situation without knowing how they got there.

Help at last

After the ATSB interview, I went straight to the Qantas Crisis Management Centre to meet and thank those who had assisted during the crisis. Describing some of the events to the 20 staff, I broke down again when I got to the point in the incident where I had wanted to climb. I had to leave. I soon discovered that every time I recalled this part of the flight I would choke up and cry. I found this very confusing. It seemed like such an unusual reaction and I couldn't figure out why it was happening to me.

My close friends were concerned for me and decided I needed a break. Simon and John took me to Byron Bay on the beautiful Australian east coast, where they tried to teach me to surf. I still couldn't surf when our four days were up, but the sun, surf, exercise, calm friendship and change of environment helped me level my thoughts. It was a valuable contribution towards my eventual recovery.

A week after the QF32 flight, the Welfare Officer at the pilots' union called to ask if I needed help. This made me feel paranoid . . . so I knew I did indeed need help. He referred me to Ronnie Zuessman, a psychologist who deals extensively with pilots. Coral accompanied me to Ronnie's office feeling rather nervous – she knew I would walk out if he asked lame questions and was hoping his reputation for understanding alpha-male pilots was deserved.

Ronnie was great and straight to the point. After we'd established the basics, he said, 'What's the problem?' I told him, 'When I recollect the flight, I'm fine until I get to a certain point and then I cry. I don't know why.' He understood just what was happening and said, 'When recollecting the flight, you sequence your thoughts to the position and time when your emotions became overwhelmed. At this point, these memories will trigger emotions that overwhelm your mind.'

He went on, 'Embrace the grief and stress. Accept you will cry when you revisit that place-time. Let it happen. Do not be embarrassed by or avoid the situation that triggers crying. Be comforted, knowing the crying is a natural reaction that will reduce with successive occurrences until it eventually disappears.'

Ronnie was right. Over the next month I found myself revisiting and reacting to the sensitive memories. My reactions did diminish.

However, as the first symptom receded, it exposed a second problem – one that was very concerning to Coral.

My mind was stuck in a four-hour continuous loop. The loop started with the engine explosions, went through two hours in the air and ended after two hours in the aircraft on the ground. I found myself reliving it again and again, when I was awake and in my dreams. My heart pounded with each memory of the 'SPEED SPEED' and 'STALL STALL' warnings on the landing approach. These were warnings that should not have triggered; warnings that suggested our performance data and flight instrument presentations were wrong.

I was worried news of these warnings might find its way into the media and cause additional concern in what was already a very delicate situation. Even without the ongoing demands on me from incident investigators and the media, I couldn't see how there were enough hours in the day to resolve all these concerns. So I just kept looping through the events, over and over. When I reached the end of the sequence, it started again from the beginning. These loops were incessant and exhausting.

One day a few weeks after the event, Coral and I drove from Sydney to the Hunter Valley and back, three hours each way. I was silent, but my mind was in a furious, intense replay of the four-hour loop the entire time. Coral tried without success to break through. During those six hours in the car together, I spoke to her only once, and then only briefly. She was frustrated and worried for me.

Coral and I returned to Ronnie. By now it was about a month after the incident. In his excellent to the point 'pilot-speak' manner he said, 'Rich, how's the choking-up problem?' I told him it was fixed. 'So, do you have any other problems?' 'Yes – I'm stuck in a continuous four-hour loop and Coral is going crazy.' Coral then described things from her perspective, saying I was almost impossible to live with because I was so preoccupied. My personality had flatlined – I was unresponsive to her and others.

Overshadowing

In his wisdom, Ronnie said, 'I'll give you the fix, but I question when you should start it. I can tell you how to stop the looping, but in doing so you will lose part of your memory for the events of QF32. Are you ready to lose those memories? If you must document the flight for the ATSB or for your own records, then you and Coral should make a pact that you spend one month documenting all your thoughts and only then should you start my procedure. Coral, will you accept Richard being non-responsive during this time, knowing you will get him back one month later?'

We agreed to the plan. I spent the next month documenting my memories and thoughts, then ran Ronnie's procedure to stop the four-hour loops. It was built upon a psychological concept known as 'overshadowing'. This is a powerful tool for disconnecting traumatic memories from the fear response. By doing so it helps to resolve PTS.

Overshadowing addresses the failure of the hippocampus in an over-stressed mind to prune or weaken and resolve fearful and traumatic memories. If the hippocampus can't do it automatically, then you do it manually and consciously.

Following Ronnie's instructions, I thought of the QF32 flight every time I tossed the ball to serve in a game of tennis. The idea was to create new connections linking QF32 to tennis, and in doing so weaken the existing strong connections from QF32 to memories that induced feelings of fear and anxiety.

Overshadowing relies on the fact that each neuron in our brain has a limited amount of neural growth factor, a substance required for neuron–synapse connections. This means that connecting a new synapse or strengthening an existing one comes at the expense of weakening other synapses to the same neuron. Overshadowing causes the brain to weaken and ideally prune connections to old memories, especially connections to our fear circuits.

It worked. Over the next few weeks, the act of thinking about QF32 during the serve and other events weakened then broke other synaptic chains. The looping ceased.

Overshadowing doesn't have to involve physical movement. It also works with any sensory input, such as particular sights, sounds, smells, touch or tastes, or with specific mindful thoughts.

PTS and you

Most people will suffer PTS at some time in their life. And each person will have their own triggers for PTS. I've been amazed at the number of people who have revealed their own PTS experiences in response to my story following the QF32 incident. Surprisingly, this group included about half my military friends. One of my QF32 crew members still finds it stressful filling her car with petrol. The smell of fuel takes her back to the two hours we spent inside our aircraft on the fuel-soaked runway. PTS is common in those having experienced family violence, sexual abuse, bushfires, floods etc.

If the signs are not identified and treated in a timely manner, some people with PTS will transition into the even more misunderstood PTSD, the consequences of which can be crippling. Experts are still trying to figure out why some people do transition and others don't.

But despite how widespread PTS is, many people don't understand or accept it. No-one teaches us about or prepares us for it. I didn't fully understand and appreciate it myself until it affected me.

Comments like 'Toughen up, princess', or 'Build a bridge and get over it!' do nothing to help a person who has experienced a traumatic event. Aside from being harsh and unsympathetic, these comments expose the speaker's ignorance of basic neuroscience.

Even well-meaning advice along the lines of 'Jump back on the horse as soon as possible', shows a lack of empathy and understanding about what's going on in a traumatised brain and body. Depending on the specific circumstances, 'getting back on the horse' might be an effective overshadowing tool for actions that you've done many times, which went wrong on a single occasion. But even so, this is best done under the guidance of a trusted professional.

What we know about PTS

- It's a natural response to stress and has nothing to do with weakness.
- It can result from either experiencing or witnessing many different kinds of traumatic events, particularly those involving death, the threat of death and serious injury. It's often worse in people who felt unable to control their situations or who thought they would die.
- The chances of PTS becoming PTSD are greater if the trauma was human-induced (for example, combat or sexual assault) rather than inflicted by nature.

Experts believe PTSD impairs many brain regions, including the processing of emotions and memory, one of the roles of the hippocampus. For example, during sleep, rather than deleting or archiving stressful memories to the prefrontal cortex, the damaged hippocampus retains these memories in full strength in active memory. So when it's time to go to bed, the same images replay, nightmare after nightmare, floods of terror drowning all other thoughts, with the same dreadful conclusions. Instead of offering respite, sleep becomes as terrifying as a Stephen King movie, with memories that are not just feared, but reinforced.

Long-lasting and repeated trauma such as family violence and childhood abuse greatly increases the risk of developing PTSD. Many people in the military, police and emergency services face extreme repeated trauma and can suffer PTSD that inhibits their return to normal life. One study found military veterans suffering from the condition had a hippocampus 10 per cent smaller than average, reducing the ability to process information and flush or reconcile traumatic memories.

Anyone, even army generals, can suffer PTSD. Major General (Ret.) John Cantwell AO, DSC is a distinguished former army leader who was involved in three military campaigns: with the British forces in the Gulf War in 1991; as Director of Strategic Operations for the coalition forces in Iraq in 2006; and as Commander for the Australian Forces in the Middle East and Afghanistan in 2010.

John documented his compelling story of PTS in his book *Exit Wounds*, describing how after each overseas campaign he returned home with increasingly severe symptoms, yet found himself always wanting to go back for more. He was one of two contenders for promotion to the Chief of Army position when his condition was finally diagnosed, and he committed himself to a psychiatric hospital.

He is now on a journey of recovery thanks to professional care and the ceaseless support of his wife, Jane, and family. In 2018 he told me, 'My own symptoms have not abated much but I generally manage okay, although nightmares remain a constant nuisance and I often become anxious for no apparent reason.'

One of John's PTS stories involves the so-called Highway of Death, the road Iraqi soldiers used when retreating north from Kuwait at the end of the first Gulf War. Their trucks were loaded with ransacked booty of all kinds including perfumes. Coalition air and ground forces blocked the highway then spent the next 10 hours strafing and cluster-bombing the traffic jam, annihilating thousands of vehicles and personnel. John told me, 'I was among the first ground forces to arrive and clean up the mess. My overwhelming memories include the stink of burning tanks, cars and human flesh. Among the stench was the smell of stolen Chanel No. 5 perfume. These memories have never diminished. Whenever I smell Chanel No. 5 I feel physically sick.'

Life for people with PTSD revolves around managing intense, persistent and distressing memories, emotions and endless spiralling pressure. Seemingly simple daily tasks may become difficult or impossible. The threat of suicide is increased. One in five Iraq and Afghanistan veterans is diagnosed with PTSD. In the US, military veterans make up 8.5 per cent of the adult population, but account for 18 per cent of suicide deaths – in other words, they are at more than twice the risk of suicide as those who haven't served.

In 2014, 7403 US veterans took their own lives, an average of 20 every day. That is more potentially preventable deaths every year than the total deaths suffered in conflict by US forces in the Gulf, Afghanistan and Iraq wars combined. This terrible situation is similar in other countries around the world.

It gets worse. A 2018 report by the American Association of Suicidology found that each death by suicide affects 135 people, and those close to the person who died were twice as likely to suffer depression, anxiety and suicide ideation as otherwise, and four times as likely to suffer PTSD.

Ask someone who's been through it before

Ronnie's professional insights did wonders for me, and so did John Connolly's wise counsel and support, along with that of other close friends and family. Coral was my bedrock through all of it. But something was missing. I had survived a high-profile event where no-one was injured. There was lots of publicity but I did not know what was in store for me privately, commercially and publicly. I needed to speak to someone who had been through what I'd been through. I knew who I had to call: Sully.

Our circumstances were different in many details, including the durations of our emergencies (Sully's is outlined in Chapter 2), but the fundamentals were the same – the weight of responsibility for the lives of all on board, life-or-death decisions made based on insufficient and imperfect information, and the intensity of being blinded in the world's spotlights with praise, but also with criticism.

Two months after QF32, still struggling to get back on track, I connected to Sully via his agent, hoping he might be able to help me. After we'd exchanged pleasantries I said, 'Sully, we have both survived high-profile unthinkable events where no-one was killed. I'm finding the media is unrelenting – everyone wants a piece of me. I am concerned about what lies ahead. Would you be able to give me a few clues?'

He said:

Richard, you will have to pace yourself. If you are short of time now this problem will only get worse in future. The media will ramp up the public's appetite for your story. You will be in great demand. Everyone will want you to present to them and there won't be enough time to do everything you are asked to do.

You need the support of your family because you will be on your own. No other families will be impacted as much as yours will be. Your family will also need psychological support. While everyone wants to know how you are feeling, few will ever ask your wife and children.

Many relationships will be strengthened. Your friends will always remain your friends regardless of any outcomes. They will contact you and want to help you. Talk to them, keep them close. You will gain the highest respect from your subordinates at work. They are proud of you and want to thank you.

Accept people's thanks with the same sincerity that it was given. It's not about you. It's about acknowledging their feelings and pride that you rose to meet a challenge and, in the process, protected their organisation and industry. It's like being called a hero or receiving a standing ovation in front of an audience. People don't remember what you say, they remember how you made them feel. So, respect their feelings, remain on stage and acknowledge their gesture rather than discounting their emotions and feelings and retreating in embarrassment.

I had speakerphone on and Dad was sitting next to me. What Sully said next shocked us both:

Your relationships with many peers and leaders will probably suffer. I tried to reorganise my job so that I could meet the external requirements that were being loaded upon me and to stay current at flying. I could not do both. I had to make a choice between my new responsibilities and my flying. I decided to retire from airline flying. I hope you can manage the stresses placed upon you from all directions. I hope you do not have to leave your airline.

At this, Dad started hyperventilating.

Sully's predictions and warnings were spot on.

My relationships with some above me changed. Many managers were not comfortable that I was receiving so much public attention, even though there was nothing I could do to stop it. Four months after the incident, the contacts and requests from media and the public were still so intense and growing that I signed with a professional management agency, the Fordham Company, to get some breathing space.

Sadly, Sully was also right about what I could only interpret as professional jealousy. Too many pilots approached me dismissively saying, 'What's the big deal? It was just an engine failure.' There was no way I could repeat the hours of explanations I had given to the ATSB. If I had to respond I could only say, 'Read the report,' or more simply, 'You weren't there.'

Other crew members were targeted. After one simulator session, an instructor said to one of my fellow QF32 pilots, 'I would have expected more from you after QF32.' At the one-year crew reunion I discovered that nearly every one of the 25 cabin crew had encountered similar reactions. In one case an attendant who was 'passengering' on a flight was approached by another cabin crew member who said, 'I should have been on QF32. And I would have done a better job!'

It was important for us all to remember that, as vocal as these people might be, they represented the minority. Nevertheless, their behaviour affected our recovery. Sully's advice definitely helped me pre-empt, avoid or cope with critics and to become stronger and wiser in my interactions. I anticipated problems before they occurred and either found a way to defuse the situation or braced myself until it was over.

No-one learns all these things in isolation. I gained from Sully's insights and experience just as he had gained from the insights of others before him. Soon after Sully's event he had received a call from Captain Alfred Haynes, whose United Airlines Flight 232 had crash-landed in Sioux City, Iowa, in 1989 after a turbine disc exploded. Al Haynes told Sully, 'I was never one to believe much in post-traumatic stress. I had heard a lot about it from World War II, Korean and Vietnam veterans and so knew it existed, but didn't believe it would happen to me. But I believe it now. And I'm asking you to believe it. It may never happen to you – or it may happen tomorrow.'

The topic of PTS comes up in almost all of my public presentations. I have become accustomed to being approached afterwards by women who tell me my comments about PTS are accurate and then ask me to sign my *QF32* book with a message to their husband. When I ask, 'Where is your husband?' they often answer, 'He's outside, crying.'

The great paradox of PTS is that despite its prevalence, so many people feel they are facing their struggles alone. After my conversation with Sully I realised I could gather my experience and use this information to help others facing PTS. Alongside professional counselling and learning about trauma and its impacts, talking with others who have had similar experiences helps the recovery process.

Even with all the help I received, I think it took me four months to fully recover. Coral says five. During that period, I lost 10 kilograms.

Signs of PTS

Possible signs of PTS include:
Emotional:
Low self-esteem, lack of confidence, unable to cope
Feeling numb, fearful, brittle, moody, resentful, detached, lack of intimacy
Pain, guilt and uncertainty about choices made and 'what ifs'

Mental:

Distracted, difficulty concentrating, apathy, amnesia

Sleep disturbance, insomnia

Recurring memories and nightmares

Anxiety

Depression

Anger, irritability, impatience

Survivor-guilt, blame, shame and responsibility for others' actions

Reliving past events in distracting continuous mental loops

Sensory degradation, loss of appetite and focus

Stress builds upon stress

Physical:

High blood pressure

Jerk and panic responses

Weight loss, sleeplessness, fatigue

Weakened immune system that leads to illness

Inflammation (increasing the risk of prolonged infection and cardio-vascular disease)

Upset stomach, indigestion, diarrhoea

Shaking, shivering, stuttering

Headaches, other aches and pains

Social:

Withdrawal, isolation, loss of interest in others

Behavioural:

Sighing, avoiding reminders, crying, appetite disturbance, resentment

Spiritual:

Emptiness, loss of meaning and purpose, apathy, cynicism, existential questioning

The PTS symptoms I experienced included feeling detached, numb, moody; involuntary crying; being plagued by torturous 'what ifs' about the choices I'd made; difficulty concentrating and remembering; nightmares; reliving the events in continuous loops; sleeplessness, anger, irritability and fatigue; shivering and anxiety.

My immune system was weakened. I had an upset digestive system and two months after QF32, I contracted a mild form of pneumonia.

It's the responsibility of the people around a person who has suffered a traumatic experience to recognise that support is needed and come to their aid, because that person will often be unable to see it for themselves – sometimes even when they have been trained to do so.

How NOT to deal with PTS

There are some strong lessons in how not to deal with PTS to be found by comparing my experiences after QF32 with those of Captain Peter Burkill. Peter was in command of British Airways Flight 38, a Boeing 777 flight from Beijing to London-Heathrow Airport in 2008. Thirty seconds before landing, both engines suddenly failed to respond to the pilot's command for more thrust. Everyone aboard survived the resulting crash, but 47 passengers were injured in the evacuation.

In his book *Thirty Seconds to Impact*, Peter describes what happened next. First, police immediately removed him from the accident scene, which meant he was not able to check on and reassure his passengers as I did. He was then put through a three-hour interview with accident investigators and others (my first interview was five days after the flight; an ATSB investigator told me they would never interview someone immediately after an incident). After this he was told to 'go out for a hot curry and get drunk'. Not only did I debrief with the crew at length in the hotel, I had a two-hour call with Coral when I got back to my room.

Peter was treated poorly by those who had a duty of care for him. Unlike me, Peter had to drive himself home (it is never a good idea to drive when you have been through a traumatic experience) and, although unprepared, he was required to appear at a stressful media conference the following day. Having been told by a senior manager that he needed to get back to a normal routine 'as soon as possible', Peter attempted to return to flying four weeks later only to find it was too much, too soon. He stopped flying again for what turned out to be many stressful months. Looking back, Peter wrote, 'Had I received the support and help I needed, I would not have had to endure months of distress.'

Many of my friends used these same words to describe how they were treated after their own traumatic events. In one case my friend Peter, who suffered a traumatic event (due to no error of his) wrote: 'After the accident I was diagnosed with depression and PTSD. I spent a couple of years taking anti-depressant drugs and eventually climbed out of that hole. Part of my problem was denial of PTSD as a legitimate response to my experience. This was not helpful at all of course, but I came to realise I'd always thought of PTSD as something that soldiers and first responders developed after long-term exposure to trauma; it was okay for General John Cantwell but not for me. I had no idea that a single event could cause this reaction and I felt like a fraud for being diagnosed with it, and ashamed for my lack of ability to just push through and cope with it. Regardless, I struggled with sleep and hypervigilance for years. I came close to giving up flying. In hindsight, I believe that the lack of effective support, unfortunate interviews with management, and my own denial of my circumstances led me to my lowest point.'

This could have been my story. If I had accepted the initial advice to 'take a week off' then I would not have recovered to be safe to fly. Instead I recognised that I was in no state to resume work and ended up taking four months off. I was relaxed and confident when I returned, which was fortunate because the Civil Aviation Safety Authority decided to put their A380 safety inspector pilot in the cockpit to monitor my first two flights.

But how are *you* feeling?

The tentacles of PTS spread like a virus. I expect most QF32 crew members suffered from PTS to some degree. And I suspect all 440 passengers were also directly affected by the QF32 incident – an incident in which no-one was killed or injured. But like the ripples from a stone thrown into a pond that go all the way to the edge, PTS can also spread to affect families, friends and colleagues. Stress, grief and trauma do not discriminate. These people may need help too.

Family can be overlooked in terms of secondary trauma. People may be affected by an incident merely by hearing about it. Family are often so worried caring about and for the 'primary' person who is stressed or traumatised that they overlook or place their own needs on hold.

At a party held four months after QF32 a colleague approached Coral and asked, 'Everyone is talking about the crew – but how are *you* feeling?' This was the first time someone had thought to ask that question. Coral broke down and sobbed. If you are close to someone experiencing PTS, recognise that you too are likely to be affected.

Paolo Pettinaroli – Linate Airport disaster '8 October 2001'

I met Paolo Pettinaroli after speaking to 600 safety leaders at the Flight Safety Foundation's 2012 conference in Singapore. He approached me, hugged me and wouldn't let go. Tears flowed down his face. He said, 'Richard, thank you for protecting so many people.' Then he told me his story.

Paolo's son Lorenzo was on board Scandinavian Flight 686 from Milan to Copenhagen on 8 October 2001. The aircraft collided with a business jet during the take-off in fog, killing a total of 118 people. Flight 686 is the deadliest air disaster in Italian aviation history.

Paolo Pettinaroli formed the 'Fondazione 8 Ottobre 2001' organisation to honour the dead and to improve flight safety. He said, 'Each year 8000 people amass in cathedrals to remember my son and the other 117 people that died. That's 69 people who come together grieving for every person that died. Richard, 469 passengers were on your flight. Thank you for saving over 30,000 people from trauma.'

Recovering from PTS

The key to recovering from stress is to develop a healthy mind and body.

A healthy mind will process even the most unpleasant memories, either causing them to fade or associating them with other memories that do not induce panic. Deep sleep and dreaming are very important parts of these processes, first pruning weak memories that are no longer needed then interlacing new memories with the old.

A terrible exam failure or the surprise at being dumped by a romantic partner creates deep wounds when they happen. But as the weeks and months pass and successes and other events dilute and bypass these failures, the sting lessens. The same thing can happen with PTS. You won't forget these memories, but you might look back and think, 'Yes, it was difficult and scary. But I understand stress and will no longer let these memories hold me back.'

Diet and exercise are important parts to maintaining a healthy body. Avoid foods that are unhealthy or trigger an intolerance in your system, instead focusing on what works for your individual constitution to help recovery. Avoid excessive food, alcohol or drugs to numb pain, because these actions, linked to stress, can build future addictions.

Growth from trauma

When it comes to recovery from PTS some people find the metaphor of a smashed vase useful – in fact, you may come across it referred to as the 'Shattered (or Broken) Vase Theory'. The idea is that if trauma shatters the sense of self you took for granted, you have two recovery options.

The first is to gather up all the shards and try to piece them back together just the way they were. But no matter how hard you try, you'll never be able to rebuild the perfect vase. To continue the metaphor, the best you'll achieve is a vessel held together by glue, vulnerable along each one of its fault lines.

The second option is to take the shattered pieces and use them to create something new – a mosaic is often used in the metaphor. This new creation holds your life's experiences in a frame that is stronger and more stable than the original vase.

I firmly believe this second outcome is possible. Just as in business where failure lays the foundation for learning, experience, growth and resilience, growth can follow trauma. After facing trauma, it's vital to look forward and navigate the threats in front of you rather than looking backwards, regretting the past, and walking into a wall.

There can be growth from trauma. Our target is not to go from −10 to zero, but from −10 to +10. Instead of just recovering after stress, we should aim to learn, adjust and grow. When we are willing to understand more about ourselves and the world around us, new qualities, attitudes and behaviours emerge that sow the seeds for growth.

Unchain my heart

It can be hard, there's no question. But if we can get the help we need we can unshackle ourselves from fear, accept the past and turn forward to the future. In doing so, we need to accept that while we have moved beyond PTS, many memories will remain. Coral knows this well.

One night in 1992 while I was flying a B747 from Hong Kong to Sydney, Coral was in the front passenger seat of a new SUV coming home after a visit to her parents' farm in country New South Wales. Our brother-in-law, Rick, was driving and four young children, his two and our two, were strapped into the child restraints in the back seats. Rick was doing the speed limit of 100 km/h (60 mph) climbing up a curving left-hand bend on the highway when, with no warning, a station wagon travelling in the other direction suddenly appeared in his headlights.

The driver was drunk and had been driving about 160 km/h (100 mph) when he lost control. To their horror, Coral and Rick saw the car skidding side-on straight towards them. By the time Rick hit the brakes, the other car was already upon them. In the milliseconds before the high-speed impact Coral thought, 'I won't see my children again.'

The SUV cut the station wagon in half then came to a stop in the middle of the highway. Coral's mind started to rebuild its senses and to understand what had happened. Unbelievably, everyone in the SUV had survived, although Coral and Rick both had all their ribs broken by the seatbelts that had saved their lives, and Rick's right foot had been crushed by the brake pedal.

As Coral emerged from her dazed state, one sense activated her terror: the smell of leaking petrol. Then she was overwhelmed by a symphony of deafening exhaust brakes and the high-pitched squeal of 28 skidding tyres. An interstate road train was desperately trying to stop behind them. Coral's relief at surviving the crash was instantly replaced with the fear of being incinerated and crushed. The truck stopped with less than a metre to spare, the light from its headlights blistering the SUV's interior.

Rick called emergency services. Coral pushed open her warped door then rushed to get the children out and away to safety. Rick called out, 'Coral, where are we? They want to know.' Coral said, 'We just passed the signpost for 18 kilometres from Maitland.' She has always maintained situation awareness – even on what should have been a quiet, sleepy trip home. Helicopters and rescue services arrived quickly but could not save the life of a passenger in the other vehicle. The six-week-old SUV was a write-off. Yet Coral, Rick and the four children had survived the unsurvivable.

Even now, more than 25 years later, whenever Coral hears the sound of exhaust brakes behind her, shivers run down her spine and tears fill her eyes.

Bottom line

Life is uncertain, unpredictable and uncontrollable. At some time, you or someone you care about will almost certainly experience a traumatic situation. Post-traumatic stress is likely to result; it is a natural response. But what happens next will determine whether there is a full recovery or PTS develops into crippling PTSD.

Ultimately, with help and support, I worked my way through PTS, as many other people have. Remember, even when things seem at their worst, there is a way through.

The first step to recovery is recognising what's going on and admitting it to yourself and others. As I discovered, it's not something you can ignore or hide from. If you are the one experiencing PTS, understand that you are not weak and failing. It's not about 'not coping'; it's about a natural response to an unnatural or unexpected event. Every trauma survivor experiences stress to some extent.

Processes are affecting your mind, brain and body that you might not understand, but they can be worked through. Help is available and there are effective techniques you can use to recover. Your colleagues, friends and family want to help you, although they may not be sure where to begin. It can be very cathartic to discuss your thoughts and feelings with someone you trust who is not judgemental and will bear witness to your story. Professional help is often necessary. Talking with your general practitioner is a good place to start.

Some people find it useful to write about their experiences immediately following or sometime after the event. I recorded a detailed account just three days after mine. I did this long before there was any thought of writing a book about QF32; it was intended purely for my own use and benefit. At a time when my concentration and memory were affected by PTS, the recording proved invaluable in keeping my recollection of the incident accurate, preventing me altering my mental picture of how it had unfolded.

Others find it too difficult to write and read about what occurred. We are all unique and individual. What helps one person will not necessarily help another. It's about finding your way – what you need to feel safe and supported at any given point during your recovery.

Sometimes people don't know what they want or need. Taking time and being patient with yourself is important.

Those experiencing PTS can be swamped by feelings and reactions that seem irrational: for instance, 'heroes' can feel guilt and shame. They can be trapped in mental loops replaying the event. They know what happened and how a split-second decision could have ended really badly. They can also be blindsided by unexpected reactions from those around them.

But the negative effects of a traumatic incident can be minimised. We can make life plans despite the continuing presence of unpleasant signs and symptoms. The key is a holistic response that reduces stigma; defuses the trauma; empowers the person to feel more self-compassion; and recognises that even after recovery there may be ongoing effects, with things such as the anniversary of a traumatic incident continuing to cause pain years later.

To support someone with PTS you must reach out across the 'empathy chasm' that separates you from them. The word compassion means 'to suffer with'. Help the person affected to express their emotions if they feel ready and able. Be careful that you don't become overwhelmed. You may need support also.

Finally, if someone tells you they are suffering PTS, then please believe and respect them. A young doctor approached me after my presentation at one conference and said, 'I think this whole PTS thing is overrated.' I replied, 'Then you haven't understood anything I've said.' It takes honesty, humility and vulnerability to admit the suffering of PTS. Be compassionate and caring, not judgemental. Those who have PTS need support, not ridicule, shame, guilt or rejection.

Post-Traumatic Stress: Checklist

Admit that something doesn't feel right:
There is nothing shameful about PTS. Denying what is going on will only make things worse.

Seek help:
Seek/recommend professional psychological help. You are not alone.

Take your time:
Don't resume your routine before you are ready. It can be difficult, but you need to resist the pressures and temptations to 'get over it' and 'jump back on the horse'.

Protect others if you are a leader:
If you are suffering PTS, remove yourself from leadership roles until you recover. Regardless of how you feel, your mind is not fit to make complex, rational and fearless decisions.

Protect others close to PTS:
PTS affects the families, colleagues and friends of those going through it. Ask them, 'Are you okay?' Acknowledge feelings of concern, stress and grief. Encourage them to seek professional help.

Don't give up:
Recovery from PTS and PTSD is absolutely possible. There can be growth from trauma. The keys are self-compassion, support and professional help.

CHAPTER 10

Lifelong Resilience:
You Have What It Takes to *Fly*!

It's an old truth that life would be very dull if we were all the same. Ours is a remarkable and wonderful world because every one of us contributes our strengths, interests, talents, ambitions and creativity to humanity. But there is one quality each and every person should individually develop – resilience.

We will all be buffeted by perfect storms and Black Swan events, some people more than others and often through no fault of their own. Being resilient won't stop this happening, but it will give you the best chance of making it out the other side.

Resilience is important outside times of crisis. When life is good and things are going well, it enables you to seek and make the most of opportunities, find creative solutions to problems and build your foundations for ongoing success.

Being resilient gives you the confidence and courage to take well-judged risks. It makes you feel 'bulletproof, not gun-shy'. It is the key to strong individuals, families, businesses and countries.

Resilience is something you develop, not something you are born with. It's like a muscle – hard effort builds it and laziness lets it fade away. It is something you must continually work on, because our world is constantly evolving and a complete understanding of the knowns and unknowns is always outside our grasp.

Resilience role models

My father, Peter de Crespigny, is my ultimate role model for resilience. He looks decades younger than his 92 years – so much so, that once when he boarded a Qantas flight the purser said, 'I've flown with your brother Richard many times.'

Dad swims a kilometre three times a week, still powder skis every January at 11,000 feet, is a passionate aviator who holds a pilot's licence (for which he breezed through a treadmill stress-test), still flies his own Piper Turbo Arrow and recently flew a Spitfire in the UK.

In June 2017, Dad sent an email:

Hi Family, this is an important message for all, to be taken most seriously. M and I depart for Salt Lake – Deer Valley to go skiing in 199 days. If you are not yet tied up to a serious 'Get fit' commitment, then I suggest you get cracking. Love, Dad

During his long life, my father has tried, succeeded, failed, learned, adapted and succeeded, both personally and professionally. He is an inspiration to everyone who knows him. When I told Neil Armstrong about Dad's dogged perseverance coming up to his pilot's licence renewal he replied, 'Give Peter my congratulations. He's my inspiration!'

Neil Armstrong, Warren Buffett, Gene Kranz and Sully Sullenberger are also resilience role models for me. They each started with sound values, then committed to a lifetime of learning and built up eminent skills. The result is fulfilling and meaningful lives that made a difference. But there's more to this – all these people worked in teams; Armstrong, Aldrin and Kranz worked in a NASA team of 400,000 people, Buffett worked with his lifetime friend Charlie Munger, Sully with co-pilot Jeff Skiles.

On 26 August 2012, once again in Singapore for work, I was woken by a text message letting me know Neil Armstrong had died following post-cardiac surgery complications. Tears filled my eyes. A year earlier I'd had the pleasure of taking Neil out cruising on Sydney Harbour along with my family. We had become friends and had conversed via email and phone about many aerospace issues including the sensitive and controversial topic of pilot-induced oscillations in fly-by-wire aircraft. On his admission to hospital I had sent flowers to Neil's wife Carol, expecting them to greet him when he returned home.

At the time of Neil's Apollo 11 mission, Richard Nixon, then US President, had a speech on hand in the event the mission failed, '. . . *Fate has ordained that the men who went to the moon to explore in peace will stay on the moon to rest in peace . . .*' But of course this speech was not needed. Thanks to their extraordinary skills, true grit and resilience, the pioneering astronauts landed safely on the moon and returned home successfully.

That August evening I was flying an A380 back to Sydney on, yes, the QF32 route. Before we departed I made a special announcement:

Ladies and gentlemen, on behalf of everyone in the world's aerospace industry, I dedicate this flight to the memory of Neil Armstrong. Neil, who represented all that is great in aerospace, died yesterday aged just 82 years. Most will remember Neil as having the Right Stuff, and the first person who landed on the moon. Some know him as a Navy Pilot (Korean War), Test Pilot, Astronaut or University Lecturer. Most of us are not aware of his contributions to aerodynamics, hypersonic flight, supercritical wings and fly-by-wire. I knew Neil as a modest warm friend and mentor with an acute mind through to his last day.

We'll be cruising at 40,000 feet tonight, three-quarters into space. This was Neil's playground, where he felt at home. We were fortunate to host him in our A380 simulator in Sydney last year.

Neil represented all that was great in aerospace and how flight has advanced to what it is today. During the cruise tonight look to your neighbour and make a toast to Neil – one of the greatest aviators of all time. We will all miss Neil Armstrong and give our best wishes to his wife Carol and family.

I believe there's a bit of Neil's resilience in all of us.

It all starts with your WHY

In order to become truly resilient, you must identify your personal core values and the differences you want to make, your own WHYs. Warren Buffett said, 'Find your passion. Without passion, you don't have energy. Without energy, you have nothing.'

Our values, our WHYs, are our central motivations that determine HOW we do things and WHAT happens as a result. You must pinpoint your WHYs to live authentically; it's the fuel for the learning you undertake, the hard work you put in and the risks you take.

I have many WHYs:

- My personal WHY is to be an innovator at the leading edge of STEM (Science, Technology, Engineering and Mathematics). This involves having one foot safely in the present while the other steps forward into the high-risk but exciting future.
- I have two family WHYs. I want to go to sleep and wake up next to Coral every day for the rest of my life. I want to instil confidence and courage in my children and to give them the best education possible.
- My professional WHY is my duty of care to my passengers. In the good times I am responsible to get my passengers safely to our destination. In times of crisis I will get my passengers home to their loved ones, wherever that is. I take the highest responsibility and assume unlimited authority in times of crisis. Success is in the customers' eyes, not mine. So, my WHY results in me turning up with the right attitude, facing the customer and making their day.

The fire of our WHY is stoked by the sense of joy in achieving a target we've set ourselves. When we're motivated, we build the confidence to attempt tasks that we might fail. True happiness can only be achieved by pushing yourself to achieve new goals, which means learning how to experience and grow from adversity. No-one wants to fail, but if you do, the goal is to fail well. When you fall down, get up again, stronger, wiser and more confident to try again.

'Knowing the "Why" and not just the "What" and "How" requires a deeper understanding.' – Sully Sullenberger

What are your WHYs? Everyone has different WHYs, so I cannot gift them to you. Pare down your ambitions and hopes in order to identify your core WHY. When you identify and tell people your WHYs, you will attract others who believe in the things you believe in.

If you're having trouble identifying your WHYs, reverse the logic. *What* do you want to achieve in life? *How* will you achieve these *WHATs*? Now ask yourself *WHY* do you do these things? The WHYs are always simpler than the *HOWs* and *WHATs*, which they explain.

When you know and follow your WHYs, the HOWs and WHATs will follow automatically.

Now add true grit

Your passion, your WHY, is a catalyst and a motivator but not an outcome. Passion by itself does not guarantee success, particularly in the presence of unrealistic expectations. To succeed in life and to become resilient, your passion must be accompanied by execution and discipline.

Passion is free, but execution is priceless. In people who lack the courage to commit and the stamina and determination to succeed, passion curdles into false hopes and disappointment.

True grit is persistence in execution. Never give up, never surrender. Winston Churchill lived these values. This is the drive to persist and push through pain and anguish to achieve our goals. True grit requires interest, practice, purpose and determination – attributes that develop with age in that order.

- 'Interest' is the seed of passion, something you genuinely love and find meaningful. Interest means having the will to seek challenges and improve yourself on a daily basis.
- 'Practice' means committing to hard and deliberate practice.
- 'Purpose' is feeling that your work matters to you and the community.
- 'Determination' is the ability to keep going even when the going gets tough.

Determination is good. But there is an important difference between persistence and stubbornness:

- Persistence empowers a plan. It means formidably pushing ahead against threats, intelligently managing risks and learning from your mistakes.
- Stubbornness is persistence in the face of increasing risk. Stubbornness is continuing despite the absence of feedback and the ability to anticipate or correct problems.

Be persistent, but never stubborn. Recognise when it's time to get out of personal and professional problems.

To develop this insight, you need to understand the limitations of thought processes, knowledge and experience described earlier in the book, and work to overcome the biases and limitations.

By doing this you can aim to achieve things beyond your reach, knowing that each time you try, you get closer to the target. You know that if you never fail you are not challenging yourself enough. But wisdom helps you experiment with and adjust your approach so that persistence is a good choice, not a blind or emotional one.

You learn to be comfortable when others are uncomfortable. You can see beyond the chaos you are surfing to the larger calm cycle of the tides. You gain courage, which is another name for believing you can guide your own destiny, secure in the knowledge that you are strong enough to eventually prevail despite setbacks and despite your fears and doubts.

Resilience is what a confident pelican has after having bulked up its strength and weight so it can comfortably fly across stormy oceans. It knows it has a high enough cruising speed to beat any ocean headwind home, while the lighter, slower storm petrels remain grounded on shore.

We can all get there if we try. It's wrong to think that some personality types are unsuited to developing resilience. Personality is made up of a whole lot of behaviours, but it is not hard to change your behaviour if you set your mind to it.

With conviction and practice you can become better at all sorts of behaviours, from becoming bolder about offering up ideas in group situations to resisting the urge to act selfishly or lash out in anger. Trusted friends, colleagues and mentors will help you if you ask.

Look to whom you admire. Identify the elements of what you admire in them, and what makes them resilient. Then bring these attributes into your own character.

Intention to change is a necessary first step, but it's not enough on its own. You must practise. Repeating your chosen behaviour converts conscious actions into subconscious habits and intuition. These in turn reinforce further positive behaviours and prune the old destructive ones.

Never give up – Captain Sully Sullenberger

Someone who knows all about the importance of true grit and persistence is resilience role model Sully Sullenberger. I asked him to share his thoughts on it with you . . .

> *Never giving up is a key part of resilience. And, as I write in my own books, 'realistic optimism' fuels never giving up.*
>
> *'Realistic optimism' is hope that you have prepared yourself to have, and – unlike mere wishful thinking – is thus warranted. It requires holding two very different thoughts in one's mind simultaneously:*
>
> - *The unshakeable confidence that you have accrued the requisite knowledge and skills to enable you to ultimately find a way to solve each problem in turn until you have either solved them all – or enough of them – to pull through; and,*
> - *To have the situation awareness to confront the immediate and very difficult reality, with a full and accurate appreciation of the risks, thereby making the decisions and taking the actions that directly lead to your survival.*

Adapt and evolve or perish

Individuals, corporations, governments and every other entity you can think of must adapt, embrace the future and surf the edge of chaos, otherwise they will perish.

The aviation industry is full of stories of resilience in an environment of continual change. The Boeing 747 Jumbo has been, and still is, a magnificent aircraft. But the technologies in its wings, aerodynamics, metals, engines and automation are no match for the disruptive technologies found in the newer B777, A380, B787 and A350 aircraft.

Jumbo aircraft that are still maintained in as new condition are being retired to 'boneyard' storage at Victorville, United States. As these aircraft slowly perish, they take with them many secondary victims: designers, engineers and pilots who are unwilling or unable to learn or adapt to the newer technologies. My career would similarly have been in jeopardy had I not committed to adapting to the newer and higher technologies. These changes never end.

I love and have the highest respect for the A380. When it was certified in 2006, it was the largest, smoothest, most advanced and quietest aircraft in the sky. The A380 is a pilots' and passengers' delight. Passengers often add an extra sector into their travels just to travel by A380. The aircraft was ahead of its time, an attempt to meet growing needs as the industry doubles in size every 15 years, producing gridlocked airspace and airports.

But that is not enough. From Airbus's side, being innovative and solving an existing problem isn't always going to be enough to guarantee success. Changed circumstances can see something that was innovative and in demand a very short time earlier become outmoded. The A380 is a case in point.

Despite its technological advances, the excitement which greeted the A380's initial release and the hopes pinned on its huge passenger capacity, it has struggled mightily. New orders have dried up as airlines select newer, smaller, more fuel-efficient airliners. So I, along with other A380 pilots and engineers, who have invested years of effort to master the machine, will have to eventually transition to other types.

At the age of 61, I remain committed to a lifetime of change and adaptation. I am required to finish international flying when I turn 65 years of age. But 'oldies' like me are not the only ones who have to adapt.

Younger pilots, who worked extremely hard to become junior pilots on the A380, also risk being left behind. Their careers, which started with piston engines, will transition through jets, rockets, composites, new fuels, unstable designs and hypersonic and space travel. Within 50 years they will have to accommodate the introduction of pilotless commercial passenger aircraft. Those who resist change will end up in a Victorville of their own making.

When the winds of ill blow, don't build walls, build imagination, creativity and windmills.

Embracing chronic unease – surfing the edge of chaos

We can't stop or control the disruption that is coming at us faster all the time, so we must stay ahead of it: we must become comfortable surfing the edge of chaos. As US business studies professor Leon C. Megginson wrote, 'it is not the most intellectual of the species that survives; it is not the strongest that survives', instead it is 'the one that is able best to adapt and adjust to the changing environment in which it finds itself'.

The mindset needed is chronic unease. As we saw in Chapter 5, this is the opposite of complacency: instead of a mindless hope that everything will be okay, it's a mindful scepticism, acknowledging that despite our best efforts, people, processes, equipment and systems will fail. It is the combination of Neil Armstrong's 'expect the unexpected' with Murphy's Law, 'anything that can go wrong, will go wrong'.

Committing to lifelong learning

Resilience is all about adaptability, which means continuing to learn and grow. One of the hallmarks of resilient people is that they commit to lifelong learning. The pace of social and economic change and the ever-shortening technology life cycles require us to continue learning, adapting and reinventing ourselves throughout our lives. What got you here will not get you there. When you leave school or university, your practical life and resilience training begins.

Yes, lifelong learning is challenging, but it's also rewarding. As wise Warren Buffett noted, 'Generally speaking, investing in yourself is the best thing you can do. Anything that improves your own talents, nobody can tax it or take it away from you.'

Even though I built a career of more than four decades around one central skill – flying an aircraft – there has been a great deal of learning and change along the way, and I have added many other strings to my professional bow, including entrepreneur, IT computer geek, author and speaker. As noted above, I must leave international aviation at age 65, but that doesn't mean I'll be giving up or slowing down. I plan to retire and play golf the day after I die. Following the lead of achievers such as Kentucky Fried Chicken's Colonel Harland Sanders, who started his iconic company at age 69, I will turn my focus to mechatronic engineering and building sentient robots that you can play with or have for company. I, too, must work to remain current and relevant.

To maximise the effectiveness of your lifelong learning, commit to Stress-Free Deliberate Practice. Continually challenge yourself. Step outside your comfort zone. Try the hard and learn from the little things so you get the big things right. Start with the simple, then ramp up to the complex; practise increasingly difficult things until you can deliver expertise on demand with minimal stress.

STEM literacy

I firmly believe everyone must have scientific literacy. I'm not talking about learning to code in HTML or discovering a cure for cancer, but the ability to ask the right questions, make observations of your own and weigh up information to arrive at the best answer. It's having a curiosity about how the world works, from common, everyday experiences to the rare and arcane. Scientific literacy is the key to everyone's future.

STEM literacy is a personal, corporate and civic responsibility. It's vital that citizens, corporates and governments make informed decisions on topics such as climate, security, privacy, data, guns, automation and sentient robots. It is our responsibility to be confident when we form opinions on these issues, not hindered by bullying, misinformation or groupthink. Remember: build windmills.

Roger Corbett is a successful and resilient business leader of industries that have suffered decades of disruption. A board member of the Reserve Bank of Australia and former CEO of the Woolworths Group, he keeps a slide-rule on his desk as a reminder of how many of the things he learned at school have changed.

But Roger is not concerned he can't write code. He follows the same decision-making process on IT projects as he does for any other business project. He tracks a project through four categories: Idea, Feasibility, Live and Harvest. The Feasibility stage is the most critical, since this is where features, costs and benefits are defined. Projects are regularly reviewed and feedback on them is then used to revise plans and benchmarks, or to terminate the program. Roger doesn't suffer sunk-cost thinking.

Creativity matters too

It would be a mistake to think that our digitally disrupted world only needs scientists, technicians, engineers and mathematicians. Our future relies just as much on musicians, writers, filmmakers, poets, painters and dancers. As Einstein said, 'Imagination is more important than knowledge.'

Creativity is something we should all try to protect because the more we learn, the more experience bias corrals our mind. We assess new information only in reference to how it fits within the patterns we already know, rather than seeing it as it really is.

But there are defences to protect us as we age and lose our creativity. Answers that seem elusive can often be revealed when we step out of the locked confines of habits, bias and expectation and free up our minds to brainstorm and invert the logic.

STEM vs STEAM

Way back in 1918, the Carnegie Institute of Technology declared that only 15 per cent of financial success is due to technical knowledge, while the remaining 85 per cent depends on 'soft skills' – the ability to communicate, negotiate and lead. The artist's role is to translate complex and abstract ideas, including those from science, and communicate them in a way that can be widely understood. As I mentioned earlier, when we add Arts to STEM we get STEAM. But there should be a qualification. The artists in STEAM are translators who integrate STEM for the masses.

Wisdom is the final piece of the puzzle

Knowledge and creativity are both important, but they're not enough to produce resilience on their own. They must be accompanied by something for which there are no shortcuts: wisdom.

Neither intelligence nor knowledge is the same as wisdom. The smartest people in the world are capable of making terrible choices if they don't have wisdom. Knowledge is having the right answer to a question, but wisdom is knowing when to give it.

Wisdom is gained by learning from experience. There is no fast-forward button and the path for each person is different. Every one of your successes, near misses and failures will make you wiser if you consciously take time to reflect on them and learn from the lessons they offer. Wisdom is the name we give to applying knowledge, context and experience of what has been to develop an understanding of what is likely to come. Wisdom turns hindsight into foresight.

Taking care of yourself – tips and tricks for resilience

Healthy brain, healthy body
To achieve and maintain lifelong resilience you need to make a point of taking care of yourself, both physically and mentally.

The human brain can do incredible things, but only if you take care of it. Like high-level machinery it needs to be taken off-line for periodic maintenance and repairs. For the brain, this needs to happen seven times a week. We call it sleep.

Your alertness, attention to detail, memory and executive functions will deteriorate quickly and substantially if you are getting insufficient or irregular sleep. Deep non-dreaming sleep is essential for memory processing, archiving and restoring the brain's homeostasis. Dreaming sleep is important for interlacing new memories in context with the old, incrementing your search capability and wisdom.

You can't remain resilient if you're not sleeping well. To sequence these processes, decrease your cortisol energy levels and to protect your mental health, it's important to keep regular hours for waking and sleeping. Cat-naps (or 'power-naps', if you prefer) are good, but if you have ongoing sleep problems seek professional help to get back on track.

Well-balanced nutrition is needed by both the body and the brain, and so is regular exercise, which promotes healthy and new neurons, memory growth and creativity.

Control your reaction to stress

When you feel your stress levels rising, make a point of using techniques described earlier in the book, including slowing your breathing and pumping your senses (see Chapter 2). If you can prevent your stress rising, you will give yourself a chance to remain mindful, giving you time to think and react in a better, more effective manner.

Don't just wait for stress to hit. During quiet periods, engage in purposeful and deliberate practice to hone this ability to control your body's reactions. That way when you need it most, you'll be ready.

Public speaking comes up in survey after survey as one of the things people around the world fear most. If you're one of the many who feels this way, it can seriously inhibit your ability to perform at your best, especially in leadership situations. But you can take charge and move beyond these fears.

Even though I have given countless public presentations and media interviews, I still feel my stress levels rise before each one, so I still engage in a deliberate process to reduce my stress response and prime my senses. My technique involves biofeedback and visualisation. Biofeedback uses the mind to change the body's responses. Part of the process is measuring those responses to see how well you are doing it. If you wear a fitness tracker that monitors your heart rate you can do this very effectively.

First, check your resting heart rate. Then think of something you find very stressful, whether it's public speaking, a one-on-one conversation you are dreading or a report you're not sure your boss will like. Feel your body respond as your stomach knots and your breathing changes. Now, take charge by sitting back or lying down, consciously slowing and deepening your breathing. Drop your shoulders and unclench your hands. Breathe slowly. Think of something you find peaceful and calming such as a waterfall, a green prairie or a rainforest. Look at your heart rate and feel the difference inside. It's a proven technique that becomes more effective the more you practise.

It's helpful to develop a visualisation that you can use every time you do this process. The specifics will be different for each person. My visualisation incorporates pleasant sights, sounds, feelings, smells and tastes and turns what could be negative stress into a positive, motivating anticipation. I close my eyes and picture myself standing at the rear of a large Bedouin tent in the Sinai Desert. A cool, gentle breeze blows through, caressing the hanging white drapes. Bedouins sit inside on Persian rugs laid upon the sand. I smell Arab perfumes and taste apple pie. Everyone is smiling and welcoming. By the time I step on stage or into the room where I am to be interviewed, I am alert yet relaxed and ready to perform at my best. Whatever works for you, think it, 'pump' it, then feel it.

Sometimes, of course, stress is ongoing and persistent, caused by issues that you feel unable to resolve yourself, even when you reframe the situation or invert the logic. In that case it's important to remember that seeking help from others is not a sign of weakness; in fact, just the opposite. It is something all resilient people have had to do at some time. Reach out to those around you or seek professional help.

Make your bed. No, really.

Use what we know about the effect of dopamine on the brain to your advantage. Harness its power to help you feel motivated, follow your passions and stay inspired. Do this by setting sequential, achievable benchmarks that trigger the release of this feel-good chemical every time you achieve one of them.

Keep active to-do lists and make sure you work your way through them – a list that just grows longer and longer with uncompleted jobs will sap your motivation in no time. The key to completing any task, no matter how large or difficult, is to go one step at a time. Whether you want to lose five kilograms, learn a new language or create a new business, if you approach it as a path where one element leads on to the next, you will maintain your enthusiasm, confidence and energy through to completion.

So instead of thinking of a big and complex project as a single to-do item, break it down into its component parts. Start simple and tick them off as you go. (Computer programmers start with a 'Hello world' program.) Look back over the list and focus on everything you have achieved so far. Give yourself positive feedback and celebrate successes, even the small ones.

> 'When eating an elephant, take one bite at a time.' – General Creighton Abrams

You can even apply this approach to something as straightforward as doing your daily exercise stint on the treadmill. Choose a timer that counts down from your goal, rather than counting up. It's more motivating to see the numbers counting down to zero than rising, and you will get a bigger dopamine reward.

Get your day off to the right start by making your bed. It sounds a bit simple, I know. But it is a small, easy, quick task that demonstrates a disciplined mind. It should take you three minutes at the absolute maximum, and doing it becomes your first achievement of the day.

Then at worst, even if you go on to have a lousy day, at least you can enjoy ending it in a comfortable, welcoming bed.

The Yes Man Plan

I've referred a few times in this book to Richard Branson, who is an inspiring leader and someone with great personal and business resilience. Among my favourite quotes of his is: 'The brave may not live forever, but the cautious never live at all.' (My wife, Coral's favourite quote comes from Richard Branson's wife, who said, 'The harder Richard works, the luckier I get.')

Being brave doesn't require you to tackle world extreme-adventure records, as Branson likes to do. But it does mean pushing yourself beyond your comfort zone and opening yourself up to new experiences in a spirit of building resilience. Not everything you try will be great, but resilient people know they will gain much more from new experiences than they will lose.

My family lives this philosophy we call the Yes Man Plan. This is a name my son, Alexander, coined for conscious openness and discovery at every opportunity. Coral and I enthusiastically embrace the Yes Man Plan and over the years it has resulted in us making new long-lasting friendships and travelling to places that we would have never imagined.

It's true that my work brings me into contact with many more people and takes me to many more places than an office job would. But the Yes Man Plan can be applied just as easily on a suburban commute or at a neighbourhood barbecue as it can on any international flight.

The plan couldn't be simpler – you reach out and engage with people around you wherever possible. Say 'Yes!' when you're asked to participate, and accept invitations to experience something new. Coral and I accept our friends' invitations rather than find a reason to decline them. I begin conversations with passengers or fellow travellers during my flights. When people we meet ask if they can post a book to me to sign, Coral replies, 'Why don't you come over and have a cup of coffee while Rich signs it for you in person?'

On one memorable occasion, Coral and I were on a Bangkok Airways flight preparing to go to the island of Koh Samui. I was settling in when my seat-neighbour arrived, put his bags in the overhead locker and sat down. I waited until he had sorted out his things and relaxed, then extended my hand and said, 'Hi, my name is Richard.' He replied, 'Hi, Richard, my name is John.'

The stiff atmosphere that prevails when strangers have to share a space had been broken. John then said, 'I'm disappointed, you beat me to it! I always say hello to the person sitting next to me in an aircraft or train, and I always enjoy the conversations that follow.'

Everyone has a unique and wonderful story if you choose to listen.

John turned out to be a fellow Aussie who managed the newest and best five-star hotel on the island. We spent the 90-minute flight discovering our common interests and by the time we landed we had become friends. Coral and I were booked to stay at a hotel at the other end of the island for a week, but John insisted that we come to visit his hotel and join him for dinner in the coming days, which, following the Yes Man Plan, we happily did, cementing the friendship.

I was also a passenger rather than pilot in 2012 when I noticed a fellow traveller playing with a mind-mapping tool on his iPad. I asked if it was a good app, he replied that it was, and we began a conversation. I hadn't recognised him when we first spoke, but many people would have, since my companion turned out to be Jimmy Buffett, the musician, author and entrepreneur.

Jimmy is one of the most resilient people I know, as well as one of the most enterprising, genuine and fun people in the world. He has a great family. He pilots his own jet aircraft, flying his Coral Reefers band to his concerts, which delight his devoted fans ('Parrotheads').

Now in his seventies, he's still an avid surfer who signs off his emails, 'Fins up'. He has two restaurant chains, an over-50s property development venture and has topped the *New York Times* bestseller lists in both fiction and non-fiction. In so many different fields, Jimmy has thought outside the box, tackled something new, worked hard and excelled. The friendship that sprang from that one initial exchange has continued to strengthen and grow: further proof of the power of the Yes Man Plan.

Seize the day

Every new day is a gift, so treat it that way. There are no dress rehearsals for life. Live each day as though it were your last, because once it's over it can't be replayed. Step up. Take responsibility for your actions instead of offering excuses. And harbour no regrets. Identify, then take your place in the world. And if you've done something you're not proud of, make amends and change your behaviour so you don't repeat it. Learn, adjust then repeat.

Let there be no confusion or doubt: there's never been a better time than today to be alive. In his book *Enlightenment Now*, Steven Pinker writes, 'If you had to choose a moment in history to be born, you'd choose now.' The book includes 65 graphs that show the world has made spectacular progress in almost every singular measure of human wellbeing. (One example is the fact that poor countries are getting richer faster than the rich countries are getting richer.) Yet almost no-one knows this or acknowledges it.

The late Hans Rosling's book *Factfulness: Ten Reasons We're Wrong About the World – and Why Things Are Better Than You Think* details the same positive outlook for humanity. *Factfulness* offers empirical facts and rational argument to unpower our stress that has been created by continuous and irrational political and media alarmism. Rosling gives us optimism for the improving state of our wonderful world.

The world I experience is so much better than the one presented in the news.

Seize the day. Centenarians live for 36,525 days. At 40 years of age you only have about 22,000 days remaining. Don't waste them. Read, talk, exercise and socialise.

Since the risks are decreasing, and the opportunities are increasing, now is the time to be intrepid and challenge yourself. Disruptive opportunities abound in big data, energy, storage, automation, sentient robots, gene manipulation, new materials and 3D printing. Some people regard these as threats. I think they are opportunities. Remember: don't build walls, build windmills. Disrupt yourself and keep control rather than letting others disrupt you and losing it.

Bottom line

No matter who we are or what we want to do in life, we all need to become resilient.

Resilience helps us make the most of the opportunities that come our way in the good times and it helps us to survive the challenges that are hurled at us in the bad times. It is the key to a fulfilling, contented life as an individual, a family member, and a member of the wider community.

My resilience role models include my father, Neil Armstrong, Gene Kranz and Sully Sullenberger. Who are yours? What separates them from other people you know? For me, it's their determination to try, their unquenchable curiosity to learn more, their commitment to continuous improvement, their ability to fail well, their perseverance, their contribution to the world around them, their confidence in themselves and their teams, their generosity in helping others succeed and their ability to enjoy their own success.

But even these role models weren't born resilient. No-one is. It's something we develop as we move through life. It requires work, but it is a quality every one of us can develop. For alpha personality types like me, it also helps to have a calm partner.

It all starts with figuring out what drives you as you live each day: your central motivation, your WHY. To that you need to add the true grit (execution and discipline) that makes you determined to bounce back when life knocks you down. (Just don't confuse persistence with stubbornness. Persistence will see you find a way through a seemingly impenetrable dead end; stubbornness will see you stuck there, banging your head against a wall.)

To become truly resilient, you must embrace lifelong learning. You must push yourself, attempting things that are beyond your abilities. Committing to purposeful and Deliberate Practice will bring your ambitions within your reach. Doing so will build your confidence and enable you to push ahead in a state of discomfort, knowing that by doing so you are strengthening the foundations of your future successes.

Scientific literacy and creativity are both necessary for resilience, but they must be complemented by wisdom. Without it, knowledge will not get you far.

To maintain your resilience, take care of your brain and your body; they are irreplaceable assets. Develop the ability to control your reactions to stressful situations so you can perform at your best no matter what. Use what neuroscience has taught us about the brain's 'happiness drugs' to keep yourself motivated and socially active. Break down large, intimidatingly complex tasks into small manageable chunks, and recognise your own achievements as you master them.

Great things happen when preparation meets opportunity, and all resilient people have greatness within them.

Lifelong Resilience: Checklist

Standing still is not an option:
Change is coming fast whether we like it or not. To survive we must surf the edge of chaos.

Resilience is a must:
You can't prevent life knocking you down, but resilience will get you back on your feet again.

Resilience is within reach for everyone:
It's not something you're born with; it's developed. You need to develop it personally and corporately.

Resilience is for the good times too:
People are not lucky – you make your own luck. Resilient people can make the most of opportunities, as well as recovering from setbacks.

Resilience is the key to great teams, including families:
Resilience is the predictor for success in every team, from a couple to a corporation.

This is not a dress rehearsal:
You get one life and you're partway through already. Make the most of every day.

Great things happen when preparation meets opportunity:
Working hard, using chronic unease to your advantage and being ready to say Yes is an unbeatable combination.

So, what are you waiting for?
Passion, execution and discipline are the keys to success. Don't build walls – build windmills. There's never been a better time to be alive than right now.

Epilogue

The Elements of Resilience:

Knowledge:
Understand the brain, the fast and the slow mind. Optimise memory and performance.

Training:
Commit to a lifetime of learning to build and maintain expertise.
Fail well. Fail in the little things so you get the big things right.
Stress-Proof Deliberate Practice: do the hard and stressful things until you stop yourself being surprised.

Experience:
Build habits, intuition and wisdom.
When you lose your creativity, experiment and develop from your experiences.

Teamwork:
Build, nourish and care for the teams that protect you. Commit to marriage as much as you commit to work.

Leadership:
Leadership is doing the hard things others don't want to do.
Create a Just Culture with trust and psychological safety to bring out the best in people.

Crisis management:
Be prepared. Trust and defer to expertise.
Be present, communicate, give full and open disclosure and your personal guarantee.

Decision-making:
Know your WHYs.
Understand biases and the hierarchy of decision-making.
If in doubt, follow your gut feelings.

Risk:
Set your risk appetite. Prevent or mitigate threats. Avoid gambles.
The world is getting safer and better – take more risks.
Identify, rate and live with street-wise risks.

'Clear to Take Off'

Some people look backwards to find answers to the meaning of our existence. For me, the only important question is how we navigate ahead and lead meaningful lives that matter. One of the key rules of crisis management is accept your reality. The same goes for life. You have only one round, so make it count.

Dare yourself to be great. To succeed you must be passionate, a doer, and disciplined. To survive you must be resilient. Rather than building walls to repel the winds of change, build windmills to harness them. Be unafraid to fail in the little things so you get the big things right. Good spectators become great leaders when they step into the arena and shoulder humanity through adversity and change.

Don't delay. Live every day like it is your last. Be endlessly curious and creative. Reject the status quo. Own your destiny and be authentic, tough and competent when following your WHYs – your reasons for being. Love unconditionally, give back and never stop working to leave the planet a better place than you found it.

Be these differences and you'll be fulfilled to the end of your days.

So, what are you waiting for? You've done the hard work, the fuel tanks are full, checklists completed and there's blue sky to the horizon.

Now it's your turn to *Fly*!

Glossary

Brain: The hardware – the soft nervous tissue contained in the skull of vertebrates.

Culture: What people do when no-one is watching.

ECAM: The Airbus Electronic Centralised Aircraft Monitoring system that monitors aircraft systems and displays information, warnings and checklists.

High Reliability Organisations (HROs): Organisations that are required to operate safely in complex environments where there are extreme risks for disasters and loss of life (such as nuclear, mining and aviation).

Just Culture: A culture that decriminalises honest human mistakes, and in the process encourages people to voluntarily self-report their errors. Just Culture does not tolerate intentional reckless behaviour or flagrant violations. For organisations, it provides the opportunity to gather information to improve and protect systems.

Mind: The brain in action – the processes behind our thoughts, awareness, consciousness and predictions.

Psychological safety: The confidence to stand up and offer ideas, suggestions, concerns or admit mistakes without fear of repercussion.

Resilience: The capability to keep control despite failures, degrade effectively when required, then rebound.

Shared Mental Model: Shared team understanding of a situation, and the causes, threats, decisions and plans surrounding it.

Situation Awareness: The perception of what has happened, what is happening and what is about to happen.

Subconscious: The part of the mind that we have no awareness of, which recognises and responds to patterns and anticipates within the bounds of known contexts. It has been described as the 'home for gut feelings, habits, intuition, bias, confabulation'.

Acknowledgements

Fly! has been a four-year journey for me, my family, friends, colleagues and Penguin Random House publishers.

To all the people listed below, thank you for your time, interviews, encouragement and advice.

Special thanks to Hazel Flynn, for your extraordinary skills to condense my 180,000 word draft. Thanks also to Andrew Willoughby for helping (mostly at the 11th hour) with clinical analysis of voice, premise and structure.

At Penguin Random House, thank you Sophie Ambrose for your multifarious skills and support. Thank you also Jessica Malpass for your masterful publicity campaign, and Ben Ball for having confidence in me.

To every cabin attendant, director, engineer, leader, manager, pilot and worker at Qantas and other airlines, I thank you for your professionalism to share knowledge and for working together to be tough, competent, and above all else, safe. You should be proud because you are the hallmark of, and exhibit, the elements of resilience. We accept we will fail in the little things so that we get the big things right. The travelling public deserve nothing less.

Finally, to Coral and my children Alexander and Sophia, I thank and owe you greatly for your patience and support. Coral's words

'I'm not sure this wife has another book in her' expresses the cost and commitment she, family and friends made to support and tolerate this author every day.

Success belongs to the team. *Fly!* would not have been possible without your support. To all of you, I owe my deepest love, thanks, respect and gratitude.

Airbus: Pascal Andreix, Fabrice Brégier, Richard Carcaillet, Tom Enders

Arts: Gulhan Gulsun and Coplu, Jaak De Koninck, Konstantin Shamray

Aviation: Eric Auxier, Chris Bart, Johan Bergström, Stewart and Phil (dec.) Brentnall, Peter Burkill, Martin Dolan, Philippe Domogala, Niall Downey, Andy Green, Noel Jackling, David Learmount, Kerryn Macauley, Roxley McLennan, Najmedin Meshkati, Eric Moody, Valeriya Mordvinova, David Morgan, Phil O'Dell, Frank Ogilvie, Christopher Orlebar (dec.), Steve Padgett, Paolo Pettinaroli (dec.), Thurai Ruhulan, Charles Schlumberger, Jeff Skiles, Dick Smith, Sully Sullenberger, André Turcat, Bill Voss, Roz Wheatley, Chuck Yeager, Bernard Ziegler

Boeing: Terry Lutz, Bill Roberson

Business: Rodney Bowry, Jimmy Buffett, Gareth Byatt, John Connolly, Charles Curran, Charles Duhigg, Mike Farmery, Jane Ferguson, Sarah Ferguson, Simon Hackett, Neil Hardwick, Tony Hughes, Harry Konterud, Ian Mayer, Daniel Petrie, Ann Pickard, Thomas Netter, Fiona Shand, Giles Tabuteau, Andrew Willoughby, Ron Young

Family: Peter, Mariea, Alexander, Sophia, Michael, Simon, Christopher, Philip (dec.) and Karen, Robert, Lachlan, Lynne Thomas

Ford: Betty, Roy, Neralie, Noel and Michelle, Kerrie and Rick Michael, Lyn and Ian Pine

Friends: Jimmy Buffett, Jan Chesterfield-Evans, Geof Fethers, Peter Ford, Simon and Julie Ford, Sally Loane, Ben Sternberg, Adrian Wischer

Media: Steve Creedy, Fred George, Margo Marchbank, Paul Marks, Christine Negroni, Tim Robinson, Ben Sandilands, Geoffrey Thomas

Medicine: Paul Barach, Leo Davies, David Dossetor, Linda Espie, Robert Hackett, Bill Kricker, Joe Lynch, Shanthini Naidoo, Kenneth Nunn, Les Posen, Paul Saddler, Anthony Schembri

Military: John Cantwell, Jerry Carter, David Cassebohm, Derek Knights (dec.), Brian Lugg, Stewart McAlister, Alan Rowlandson

Passengers: Carolyn, Derwyn and Nia Jones, Chris and Irma Sullivan

Penguin Random House: Sophie Ambrose, Ben Ball, Nikki Christer, Alysha Farry, Hazel Flynn, Foong Ling Kong, Jessica Malpass, Nerrilee Weir

Politics: John Howard

Qantas: John Bartels, David Evans, Ian Flett, Andrew Foxton, John Fysh, Mike Hawke, Matt Hicks, Mark Johnson, Alan Joyce, Peter Lipsett, Andrew McGinnes, Stephen Moynihan, John Pickhaver, David Princehorn, Mike Sterling, Kevin Sullivan, Dick Tobiano, Carl Vandersyde, Michael von Reth, Olivia Wirth, Steve Wright, Harry Wubben, the directors of Rort Air

Space: Buzz Aldrin, Neil Armstrong (dec.), James Hansen, Christina Korp, Eugene and Marta Kranz, James Lovell, Randall Mumaw, Cody Onizuka

The Fordham Company: John and Veronica Fordham, Nick Fordham, Hamish Birt, Stacey Paton, Emma Polglase.

Index